IMAGES
of America

LENAWEE COUNTY

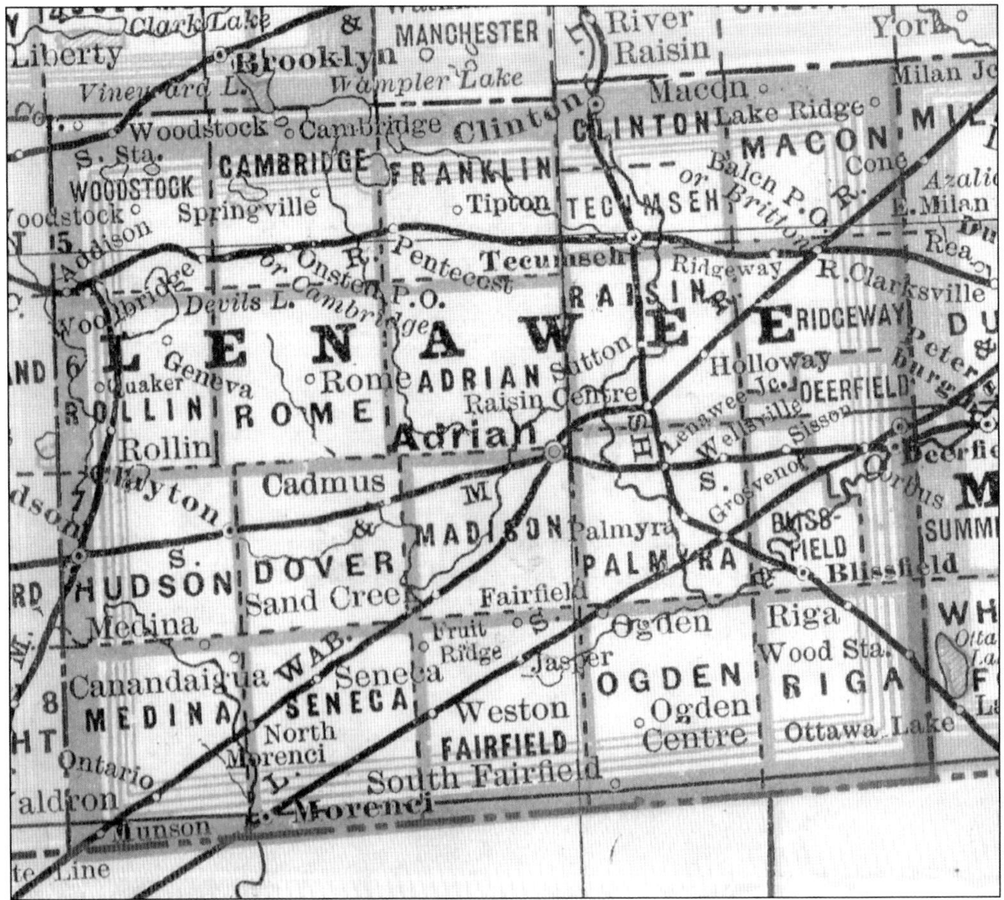

Lenawee County in 1892. This detail from an 1892 state map of Michigan illustrates the development of Lenawee County, including platted townships, named communities, railroad lines, and depots at the time. The southern border of the county is also the southern border of the state of Michigan. The state line runs at a southwest angle and is a result of the settlement of the Toledo War, which revolved around a boundary dispute over a narrow strip of land about eight miles long. The result of an error when surveying the Great Lakes frontier, this dispute lasted 30 years. This area included the harbor of the Maumee River at Toledo, which was of most concern for the state of Ohio in regard to trade. In compromise for this small strip of land, Michigan received all of the land known as the Upper Peninsula from the state of Ohio in 1836. (Courtesy of the Adrian Public Library.)

On the Cover: Barn raising was often an opportunity for a large gathering and a picnic. It is clear that this was a community event for the McClenathan family in Ogden Township on Horton Road. With the tugging, hammering, and lifting required to build the perfect barn, pride was to be expected and is well illustrated by the two waving American flags in this c. 1910 photograph. (Courtesy of the Winzeler family.)

IMAGES
of America

LENAWEE COUNTY

Brenda L. Burkett

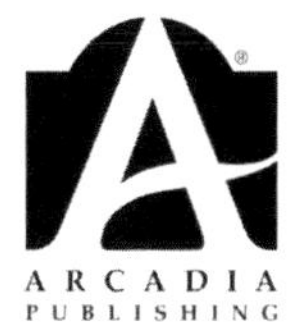

ISBN 978-1-4671-2403-4

Published by Arcadia Publishing
Charleston, South Carolina

Printed in the United States of America

Library of Congress Control Number: 2016936503

For all general information, please contact Arcadia Publishing:
Telephone 843-853-2070
Fax 843-853-0044
E-mail sales@arcadiapublishing.com
For customer service and orders:
Toll-Free 1-888-313-2665

Visit us on the Internet at www.arcadiapublishing.com

To the memory of the pioneers,
to those who documented history,
and to those who continue to preserve our history.

Contents

ACKNOWLEDGMENTS

Special thanks to the Lenawee District Library, Lenawee Area Historical Society, Tecumseh Area Historical Museum, Hudson Museum, Adrian Library, Hidden Lakes Gardens, and all of those who shared their memories of Lenawee County.

Unless otherwise noted, all images appear courtesy of the Lenawee Area Historical Society.

INTRODUCTION

A vast, unknown wilderness was on the edge of the horizon for the early settlers in the Northwest Territory. Although the Native American tribes had dwelled in this area for centuries, it was still an undeveloped, uncivilized region. Some came to the area with a plan to create a settlement similar to what they knew in the New England states, while many others came seeking a fresh start, with their belongings in a cart and pouches of seeds in their pockets. Not having a clue as to what they might find as they trudged through the mud of the lowlands and fought off the insects, their determination and dedication to convert the wilderness to a fertile farmland for not just themselves, but generations to come, helped them through. Most of the settlers journeyed from New York, many of Quaker descent. The decision to leave an established region was often influenced by the opportunity to be a landowner instead of a tenant, as many pioneers had been in New England and Europe. Others entered into the southern tier of Michigan from Ohio and Indiana seeking more fertile farmland or perhaps merely a fresh start in a land barely touched by the human hand. Entering an undeveloped territory required great courage and the knowledge of how to live off the land. Through this migration and transition to the ways of the Michigan Territory, these pioneers became American farmers.

For land to become available to the settlers of the new Territory of Michigan, it first had to be surveyed by the federal government. After the end of the War of 1812, when settlements on lands were reached with the Indians, surveying was able to begin in the autumn of 1815. With the cold and wet season, the surveyors ended their project abruptly within a few months, reporting that Michigan was a vast swamp unworthy of further review. Reports sent to Josiah Meigs, the commissioner of the General Land Office, in 1815 by Edward Tiffin, surveyor-general of the United States, declared the territory as predominantly useless swampland. Tiffin's report stated, "There would not be one acre out of a hundred, if there would be one out of a thousand that would, in any case, admit of cultivation." He continued, "The intermediate space between the swamps and lakes, which is probably nearly one-half of the country, is, with very few exceptions, a poor barren, sandy land, on which scarcely any vegetation grows, except very small scrubby oaks." As a result of this report, school geography books even presented maps of Michigan portraying it as an "interminable swamp."

Gov. Lewis Cass sought to disprove the reports presented by Tiffin and have the previous surveys continued. Writing to Josiah Meigs, Governor Cass shared his opinion that "the quality of the land in this territory, I have reason to believe, has been grossly misrepresented." The high ratings that several surveyors had placed upon Michigan, and the opinion that the land would sell, was also presented to Meigs. After consulting with James Abbott, receiver of the land office at Detroit, Meigs authorized continuance of the surveys in July 1816, as recommended by Cass and Abbott, with preparation for the sale of the land. Although the surveying of Michigan began in 1815 and was not completed until 1831, a land sales office was opened in Detroit in 1818 to sell land in the areas that had been surveyed. Through the current laws, land was to be auctioned at a minimum of 320 acres. Unsold land could be purchased in 320-acre lots for $2 per acre with a required down payment of $160 after the auction. With these requirements, land sales were very slow. A new land act was passed by Congress in 1820, which still required land to be auctioned; however, a minimum of 80 acres of land could now be purchased for $1.25 per acre after the auction. This gave fresh opportunity to many of the less endowed. As sales increased and land was surveyed farther west, a land office was opened in Monroe in 1823. There were settlers who arrived in the territory before land was surveyed and placed at auction by the government. Already clearing land, erecting a cabin, and most assuredly beginning farming, they were referred to as squatters. Their land could still be auctioned, and offered a grand opportunity with cleared land and a cabin already built. The squatters had no legal right to their land. They would intimidate or discourage bidders at the land office by having their rifle under their arms during the auction. The squatters could purchase the property afterwards at $1.25 per acre.

Through an executive proclamation on March 28, 1822, Governor Cass laid out and defined the boundaries of Lenawee County, which encompassed 761 square miles. Still unorganized in relation to government functions, Lenawee remained attached to Monroe County. An act to organize the county of Lenawee was presented on December 26, 1826, to the Legislative Council of the Territory of Michigan. This act also attached all land to which Indian title had been extinguished at the treaty of Chicago to Lenawee County. Michigan was admitted into the Union in 1827. Of the 29 organized counties in Michigan at this time, Lenawee ranked fourth in population. This same year, border lines for townships began in Lenawee with the creation of three townships: Tecumseh, Logan, and Blissfield. Over the course of the next 47 years, townships were established and boundaries changed until 1869, when Lenawee County became home to 22 townships. Although boundaries for townships changed the original territory that was defined by Governor Cass in 1832, Lenawee County was never changed.

With the arrival of settlers in Lenawee County and Michigan as a whole, the necessity of converting trails to roads was recognized by Congress in the 1820s. The Old Sauk Trail, which ran between Detroit and Chicago, passing through the northern section of Lenawee County, was the most valuable inland route for the Native Americans. Most Indian trails were simply a narrow pathway across the land upon which they would walk single file; however, the Old Sauk Trail was much wider and deeper. Many paths branched off into the wilderness along this trail, bringing tribes such as the Foxes, Winnebagoes, Menominees, and Pottawatamies to the meeting point along Lake Michigan near Detroit during times of war and peace. The frontiersmen and French fur traders took advantage of this route long before the arrival of the pioneers. It was no surprise that through an act of Congress in 1825, the trail become the Chicago Military Road, known today as US Highway 12. With the completion of the Monroe Pike in 1835, which ran at a northwest angle connecting Monroe County to the Chicago Road, travel distance was greatly reduced. Prior to the Monroe Pike, those who entered Michigan via the Erie Canal had to make a 60-mile detour to Detroit in order to reach the Chicago Military Road. In 1832, another act of Congress approved surveying for the La Plaisance Bay Military Road, beginning at La Plaisance Bay, the mouth of the River Raisin in Monroe County, passing through Tecumseh, and intersecting the Chicago Military Road in Cambridge Township.

It is important to recognize that a "road" at that time was merely a widened trail. Pioneers frequently followed the Indian trails as far as possible; when they came to a dead end, they would then begin cutting their own paths through the wilderness, seeking their own land. The settlers did have knowledge of farming. Recognizing the types of trees and plants in an area gave an indication of the soil quality. Oak openings, areas in the forest where the trees were sparsely spaced and sunlight poured down upon the ground, were sought by many. Like the prairie lands, these spaces presented cleared land ready to sow and seed. A nearby water source was a necessity, leading many of the first settlers to choose property along rivers and lakes. Whether relocating from New England or coming straight from Europe, these settlers would commonly seek land that reminded them of where they had just come from. Writing to friends and relatives to inform them of the similarity of an area to their homeland or just sharing their impression of the beauty and prosperity, the settlers would often encourage others to relocate to the new territory as well. An example of this is the Irish Hills. The rolling green hills, pastures, and lakes led the first Irish settlers to write home, sharing the news of this new land and its resemblance to Ireland, bringing many family and friends to this part of the county. This region, which stretches into neighboring Hillsdale County, has a strong Irish heritage and became a major tourist attraction. Although the Irish Hills are no longer predominantly Irish, their cultural heritage survives among many local businesses.

It was common for the men to leave their wives and children in Detroit—and later, Monroe—while they explored the new frontier. Yet there were times when entire families would venture out together until they found a piece of land that met their desires; whether forest, prairie, rolling hills, lakes, or streams, they each had their own dreams. Upon locating the right land, the men would return to the land office to purchase the property. After the expense of travel and staying in hotels, many would extinguish all their money by purchasing the land. They now had to create shelter and a field to plant crops in order to be self-sufficient and survive the first winter. This is the point at which pioneering truly began. Through the Pioneer Society of Michigan, the tedious life that settlers led in this territory was documented by those who experienced it. Landmarks throughout Lenawee County recognize the accomplishments of the people who had the courage and determination to endure the hardships of pioneer life, as well as the Native American heritage in this region.

This excerpt from *Illustrated History and Biographical Record of Lenawee County, Michigan*, prepared by John I. Knapp and R.I. Bonner in 1903, strongly reflects the gratitude all of us should have for the pioneers of Lenawee County:

> Many of our present readers can readily imagine, and some can vividly remember their parents, living in a log hut, surrounded by an illimitable wilderness, striving to make a home, and only being able to secure the scantiest food.
>
> Is it possible for the occupants of the hundreds of pleasant and beautiful farm homes and fine estates in Lenawee county to realize that their parents saw nothing but wilderness, roamed at large by bears and panthers and packs of wolves, and screeching catamounts, affording hiding places for thousands of timid deer, where now you see, beautiful landscapes, with herds of cattle and flocks of sheep upon the gentle slopes, and fine homes and orchards upon the hill tops? Are you, as children of those pioneers, who now enjoy all the peace and comfort of this favored land, and occupy those homes, sufficiently impressed with the sacrifices your parents made; with their heroism and their fortitude, their hope and trust? Do you realize what kind of fathers and mothers they were, what they did for you and humanity?

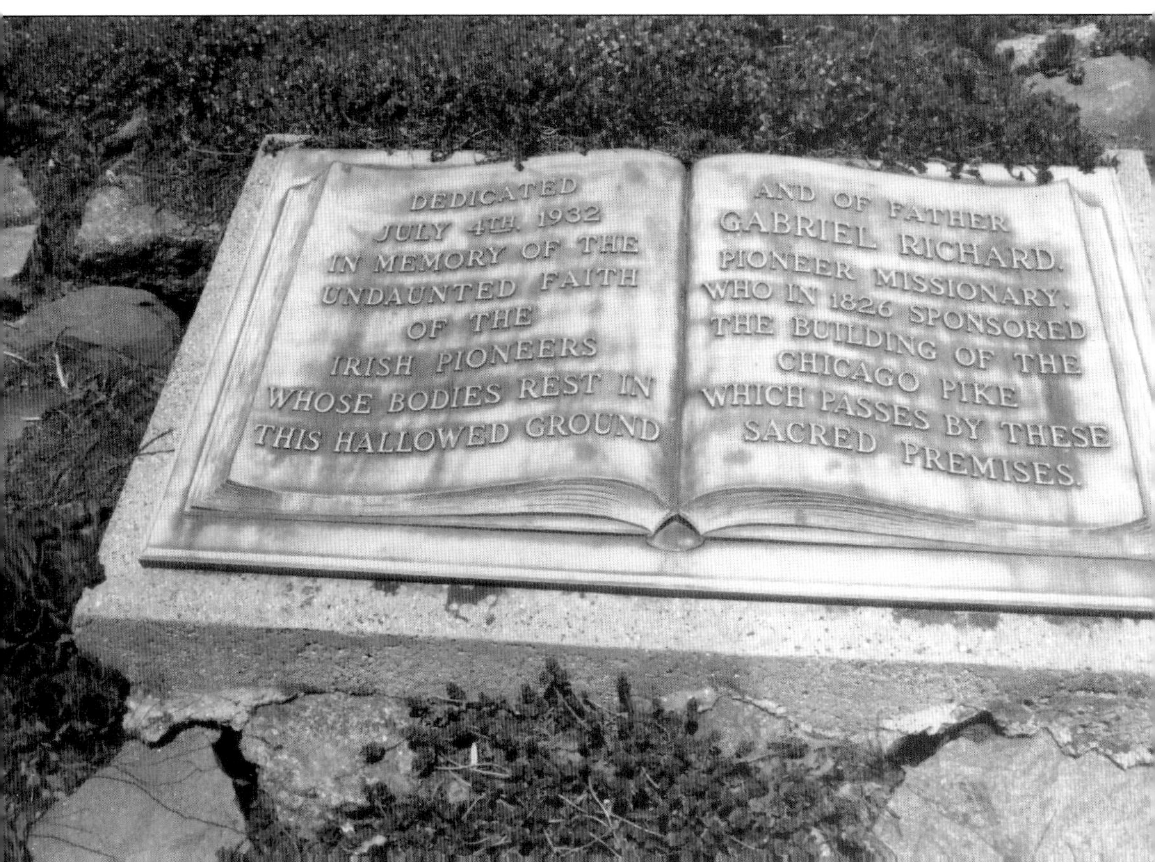

MONUMENT AT ST. JOSEPH'S CEMETERY. Dedicated July 4, 1932, this marker laid in memory of the settlers of the Irish Hills represents the gratitude and respect for the settlers of this region. Located in the cemetery next to St. Joseph's Church in Onsted on US 12, the Old Chicago Road, this marker is laid amongst rocks on a mound overlooking the lake. With many of the earliest settlers of Lenawee County resting nearby in the cemetery next to St. John's Episcopal Church, the oldest Episcopal church in Michigan, the landmark at St. Joseph's Cemetery illustrates the courage and integrity that the settlers of every nationality brought with them as they proudly created the foundation of the communities that are cherished and treasured today.

One

The First Settlers

Musgrove Evans, who had worked as a surveyor in road development in the state of New York, as well as being a land agent for several Quaker families, came to Michigan in 1823 to survey land, and also to seek property for a community. Austin E. Wing, a relative by marriage and a resident of this region, advised Evans as to where the best source of waterpower might be obtained in the new territory, the upper reaches of the River Raisin. Upon locating their desired property along the river, Evans and his group knew that they needed a third party to assist with the management of this development, which would require a sawmill in order to provide lumber for buildings and a gristmill. A third relative by marriage, Gen. Joseph W. Brown, who was a farmer and a miller in Jefferson County, New York, was willing to join the endeavor of building a new settlement in the Michigan wilderness, which led to the creation of the firm of Wing, Evans and Brown.

Austin Wing secured the first land in Lenawee County through the US Land Office in Monroe County in March 1824. A land patent was issued from the federal government and signed by Pres. Andrew Jackson for the west part of Section 27 and the east part of Section 28 in Township 5 south of Range 4 East. In June 1824, they platted the village and named it Tecumseh, in honor of the Shawaneese warrior who was said to have roamed this area. The request to have the county seat placed in the only settlement in the county, a village that had only one log house, was sent to Governor Cass and approved on June 30, 1824. As settlers arrived in the new county, the seat was moved to the village of Adrian on November 1, 1838, providing a more centralized location.

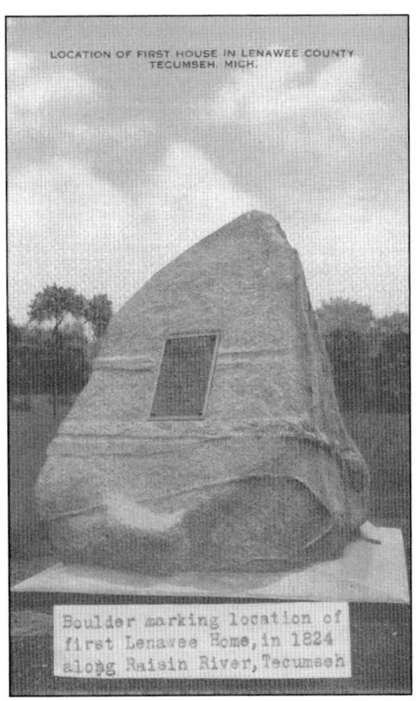

PIONEER PARK MONUMENT OF FIRST HOME IN LENAWEE COUNTY. In 1909, the Pioneer Association dedicated this boulder with a plaque marking the site of the first home built in Lenawee County and one of the first homes west of Monroe County in Michigan. This landmark is located in Pioneer Park in Tecumseh along the bank of the River Raisin. The log home was said to have been 20 feet square and 9 feet in height, with no floor. This rustic log home housed at least 16 people in the winter of 1824–1825. There was neither a chimney nor a fireplace. A bake kettle was used as an oven, with a fire built on the ground inside the cabin. A hole in the bark roof served as a chimney. Mrs. Evans and Mrs. Benson are said to have prepared meals for 15 to 20 people daily throughout the first winter in this home. The next year, a floor was laid, two shanties were added to the house, an outdoor oven was built, and a chimney was put in place, making pioneer living a little easier. (Courtesy of the Tecumseh Area Historical Society.)

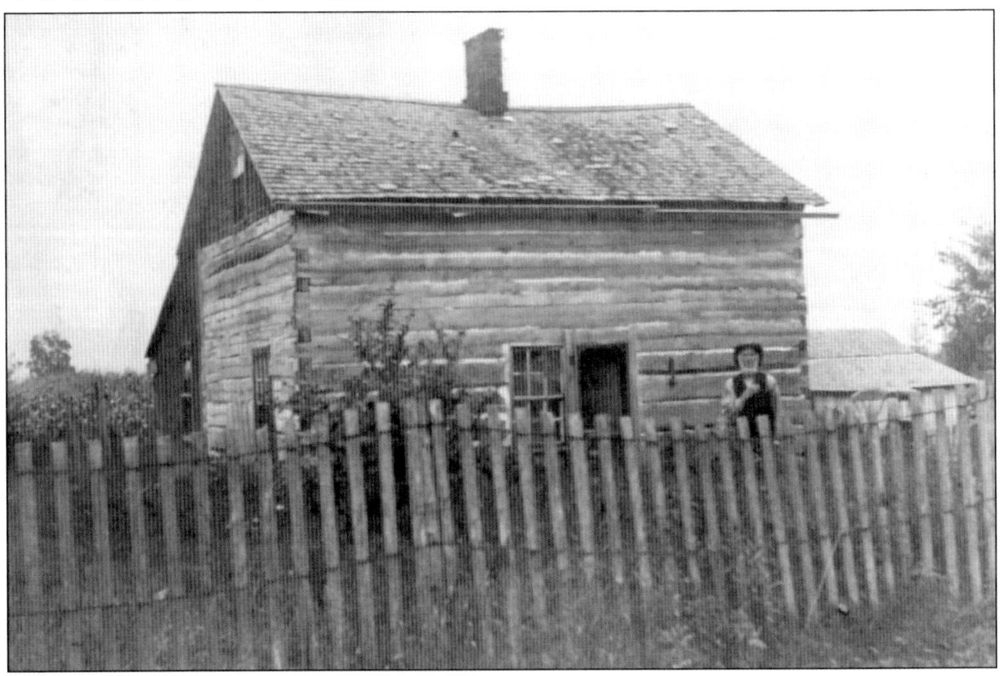

THE BEAL HOMESTEAD IN ROLLIN TOWNSHIP. This log home was the third home built in Rollin Township. Joseph and Porter Beal, at the age of 14, felled the trees, cut the logs to length, and built the home in 1833, within the 40 acres in Section 15 owned by Joseph Beal. The family resided in this home from November 23, 1833, to January 1, 1840. The first township meeting was held here on April 6, 1835. John Somers took occupancy of the home for one year after the Beal family moved on. It was later sold and moved approximately two miles west. This photograph was taken on September 1, 1899. As any home in the wilderness at the time, it would have served as a tavern for land lookers and other weary travelers.

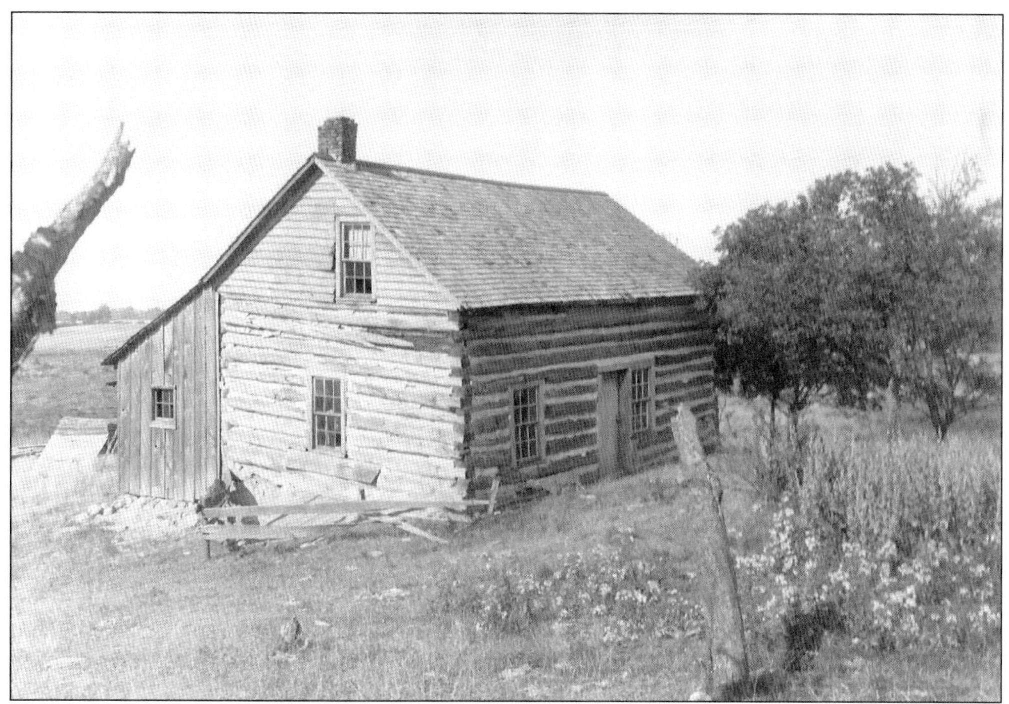

JAMES RYAN HOME. Once located on Morley Road in Woodstock Township, this home shows the common construction method of the settlers. With board and batten technique, clay was often used to pack between the split boards. Cutting the boards to a uniform length and shaving them created shakes, which were used to cover the roof. Openings were cut for the windows and a door. The lean-to addition on the back of the home was often used as additional sleeping quarters; in many cases, it was enough to consider a home a tavern with room for an overnight guest.

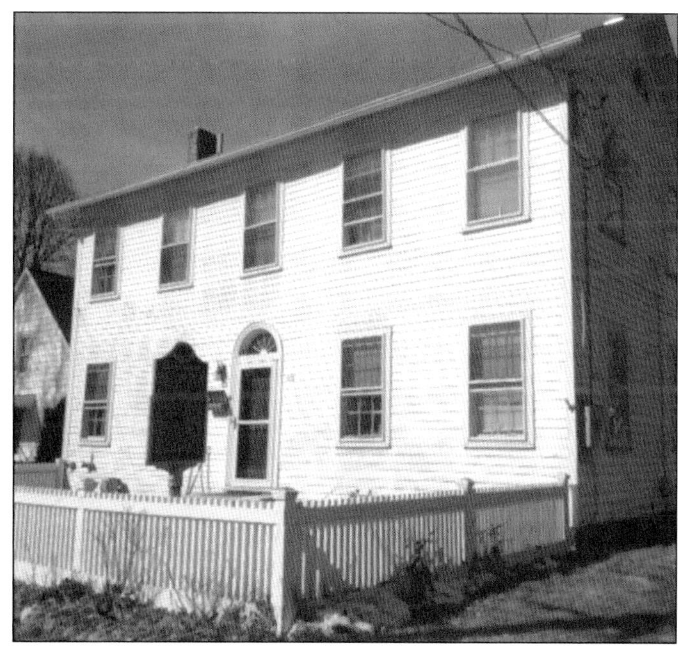

EVANS HOME. This home was built by Musgrove Evans in 1826 and is believed to be the oldest frame house in Lenawee County. By the Fourth of July that year, the frame was standing and the roof completed, which provided the perfect structure for the celebration of Independence Day. The Evans family operated an inn from their home until 1832. The home, first located on Chicago Boulevard, was moved to East Logan Street in 1886, where it is still a private residence. (Courtesy of the Tecumseh Area Historical Society.)

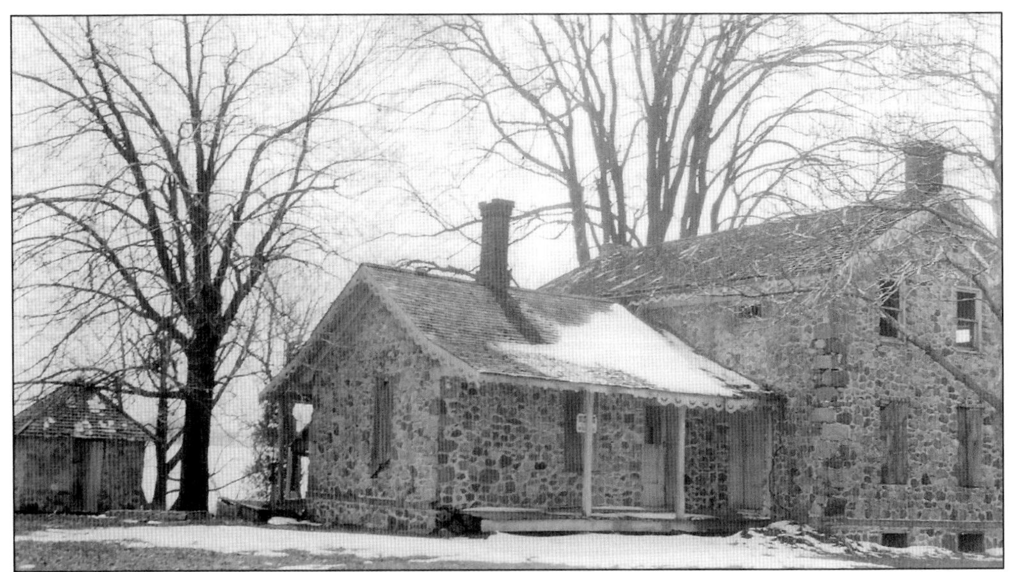

Stone House on US 12 near Evan's Lake. This structure is a reminder of just one of the rugged methods of construction used by the settlers. The house was built on the Old Sauk Trail, now US 12. Several fieldstone structures exist in Lenawee; each of them serves as a reminder of those who created these communities.

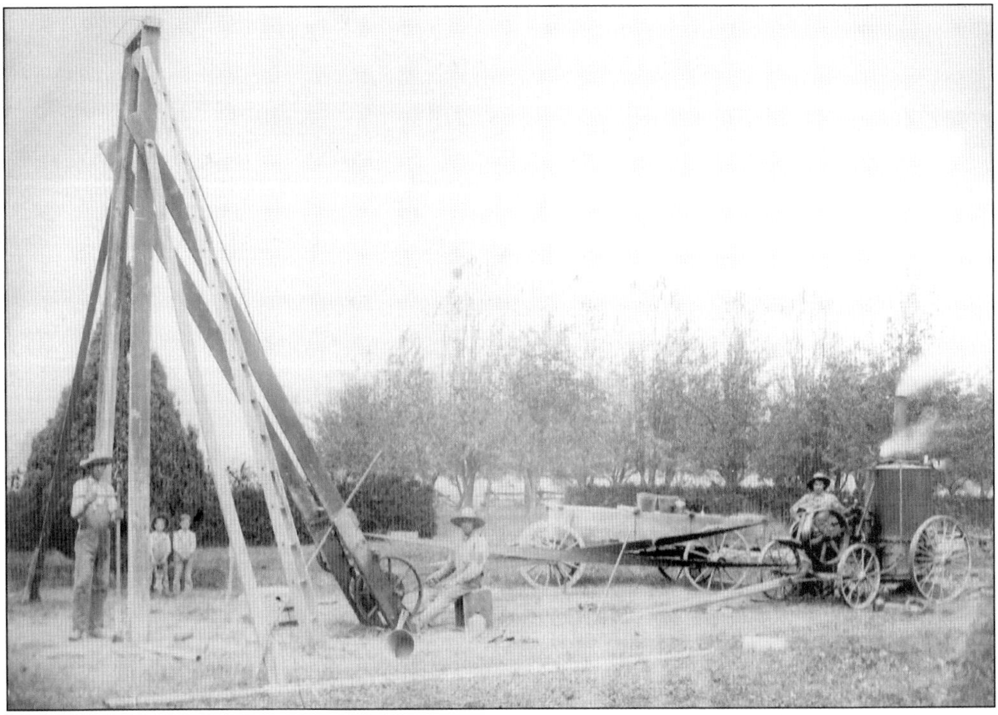

Drilling a Well. Locating a water source was always a major objective for a pioneer home or business. This photograph taken in Jasper, a hamlet in Fairfield Township, during the 1800s shows the setup required to drive a well. The drive point and a screen (perforated pipe) are hammered into the ground. Next, a weighted pipe, which slides over the pipe that is being driven into the ground, is repeatedly raised and dropped until groundwater is reached.

Two

INNS AND TAVERNS

From the time that the first dwelling was built in Lenawee County, every home was a tavern and every cabin was a frontier. Traveling by foot, oxen, and later, wagon or stagecoach, it would be miles and miles of wilderness. Seeing candlelight or the glow of a lantern in a distant window brought relief to many throughout the early years. Whether in need of a meal, shelter, or wagon repair, or being pulled out of the muddy ruts on the roads, those who had settled already were willing to assist the travelers. A few men identified areas on the roads where voyagers would often get stuck in the ruts or break an axle on their wagons. They established taverns at these locations that provided service, for a fee perhaps, to those who were literally "in a rut." The need for accommodations was recognized by several who saw a business opportunity. This influenced the development of inns and taverns, which were built along the main routes, with many becoming stagecoach stops.

Frequently, keeping a tavern merely involved having a space for people to sleep, even if it was on the floor, and food, as described in this excerpt from *The Bean Creek Valley* by James J. Hogaboam:

> Mr. Gregg says: Mr. Cavender moved on his premises, and in March 1835, I went there and built me a log house twenty by thirty feet, took my lumber from Adrian, and moved my family April 16th. Soon after I made an addition of twelve feet to one side, for a cook-room and dining room, and came to Adrian to purchase some groceries—whiskey and brandy—and told them I was going to keep tavern, They thought that was a novel idea, and laughed at me, and had their fun about it. I told them all I wanted of them was to send on the land-lookers; and in June and July I had more customers than I could attend to, frequently from twelve to twenty at a time and one night thirty-five land-lookers.

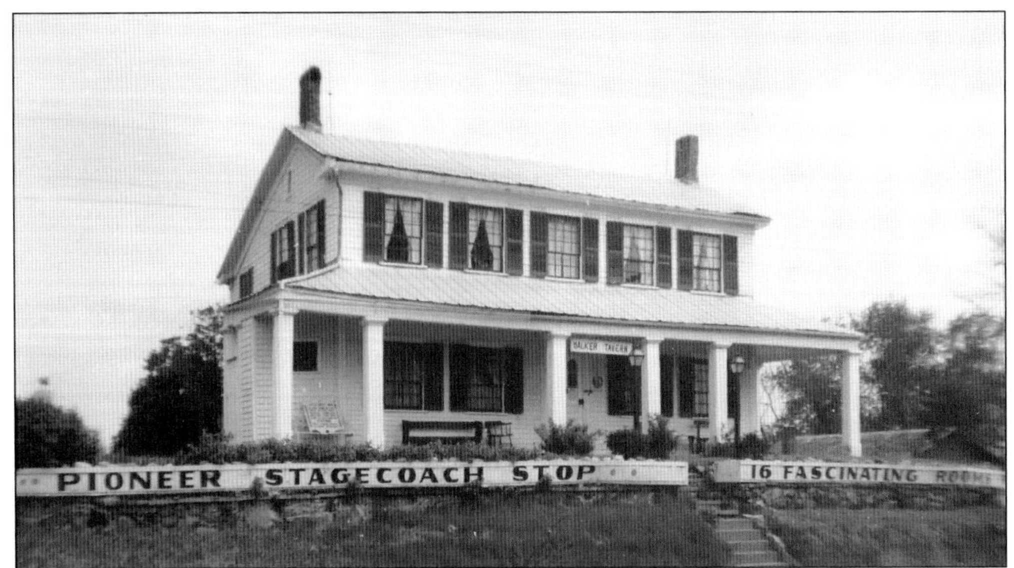

ORIGINAL WALKER TAVERN, CAMBRIDGE JUNCTION STATE PARK. Originally a private residence, Sylvester Walker purchased the property at the intersection of the Chicago Road and La Plaisance Road in 1838 with the intention of opening a tavern for travelers. Many famous visitors, such as Daniel Webster and Ralph Waldo Emerson, enjoyed the home cooking and hospitality. The property served as an inn until 1853. About 1863, the Dewey family purchased the premises for their private use. In the early 1970s, the property was purchased and restored by the Michigan Department of Natural Resources. Now a part of Cambridge Junction State Park, the Walker Tavern is one of the oldest stagecoach stops remaining.

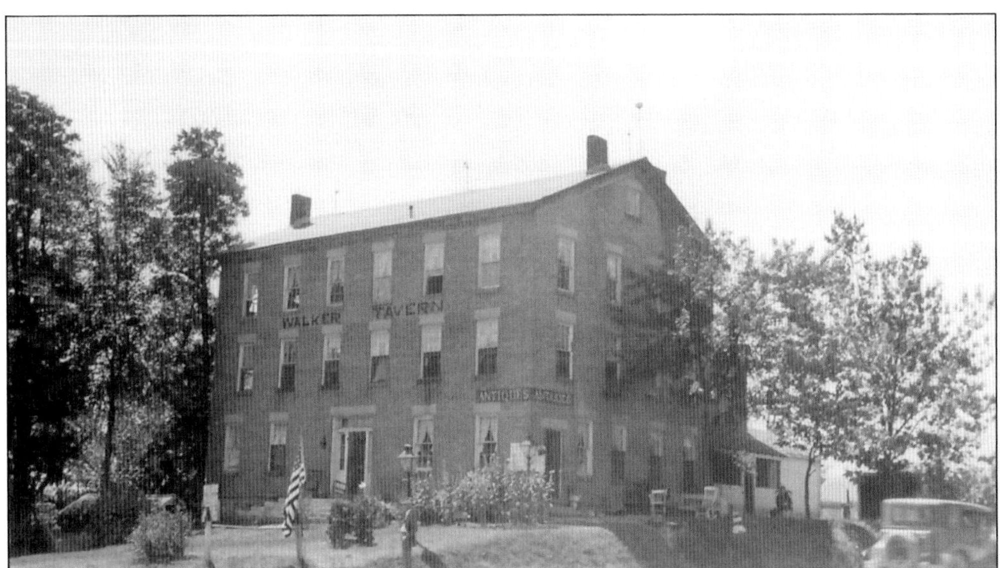

WALKER TAVERN. Walker's success as an innkeeper gave him incentive to build a second tavern across from the original location in 1854. The three-story brick structure was built with 28 rooms. The third floor was a ballroom, the second floor provided sleeping quarters for guests, and the first floor was a public area. This included a dining room, post office, and barbershop. Now privately owned, the newly renovated building serves as a wedding venue and event center.

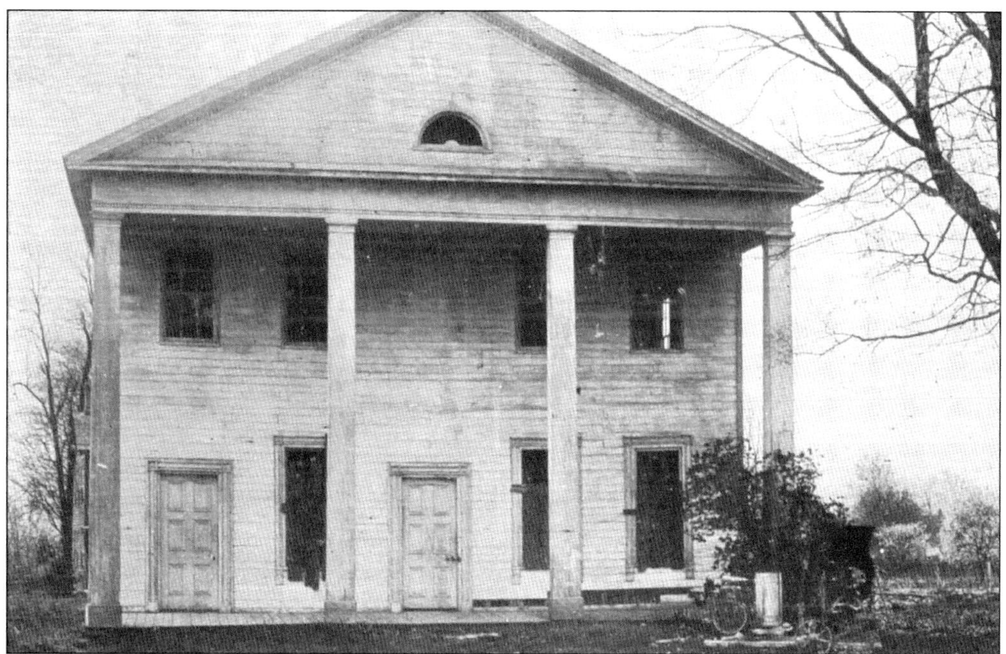

Peninsular House in Tecumseh. In 1827, Gen. Joseph Brown built the Peninsular House to provide service as a hotel for the patrons of his stage line, which ran from Detroit to Chicago. Originally located south of the Red Pond Bridge in Tecumseh, it was dismantled in 1911, and the quality lumber was sold.

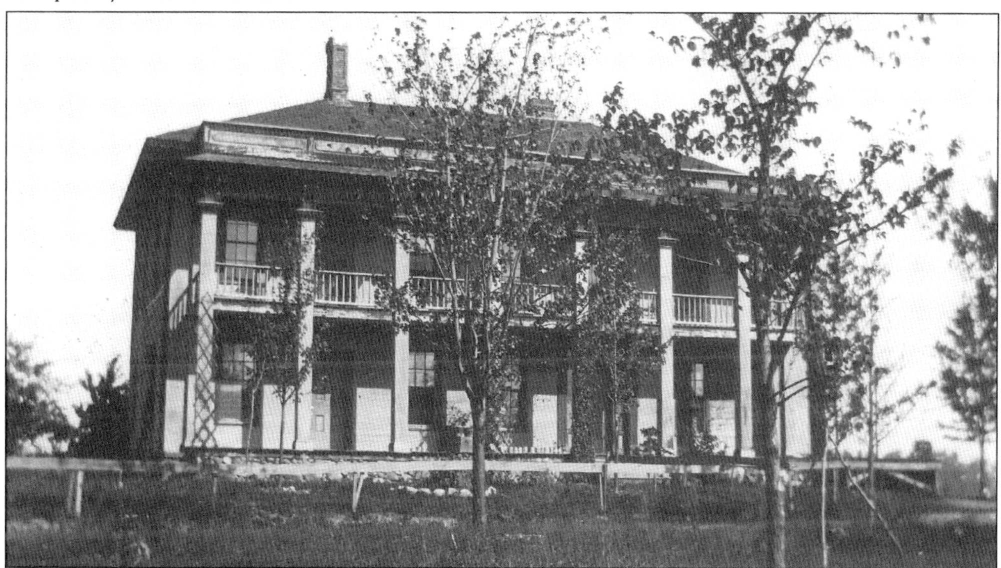

Davenport House. Originally, a log tavern built by Henry W. Sisson in 1834 stood on this site on the Old Sauk Trail, a few miles east of the Cambridge Junction in Franklin Township. John Davenport bought the property in 1839 and built this structure, which still stands today, to serve as a stagecoach stop and inn. In 1864, upon purchase by Henry Lancaster, the inn became known as the Lancaster House. Services later included a post office and general store. Stagecoaches continued to stop as late as 1900. The Bauers purchased the hotel in 1930, naming it Bauer Manor. The Van Dorens took ownership in 1965, converting it to a restaurant.

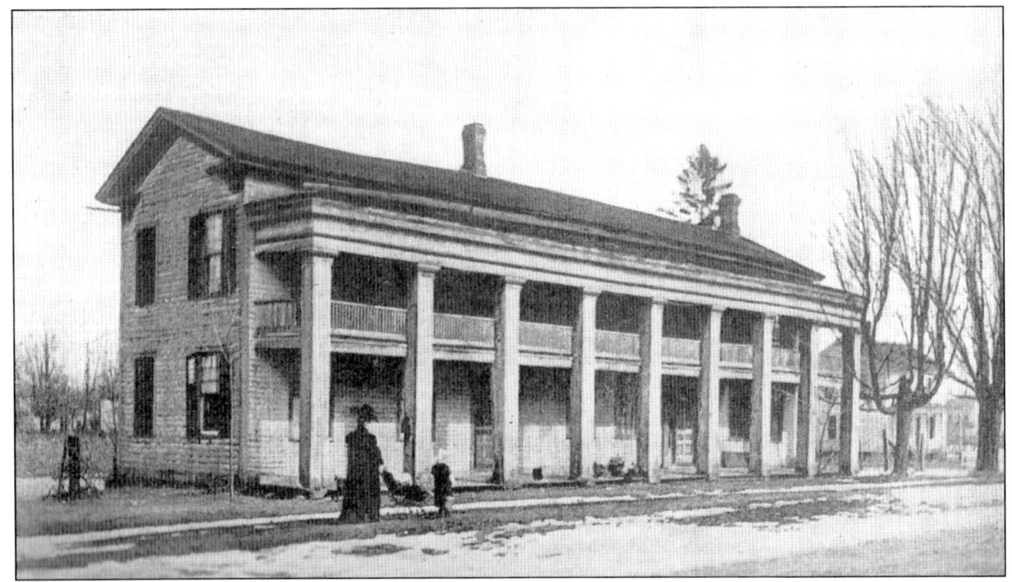

Eagle Tavern in Clinton. Built around 1830 by Calvin Parkhurst, this building changed hands and became known as Park Tavern and later the Eagle. During the Civil War, the name was changed to the Union Hotel, with many soldiers stopping on their way to and from the front lines. The inn was one of the first stagecoach stops between Detroit and Chicago. The ballroom provided entertainment for guests and local residents for many years. Quality timber was used to construct the inn, predominantly black walnut, including the interior woodwork. Every room was filled each night, with beds spread out in the ballroom or in the office when more guests arrived.

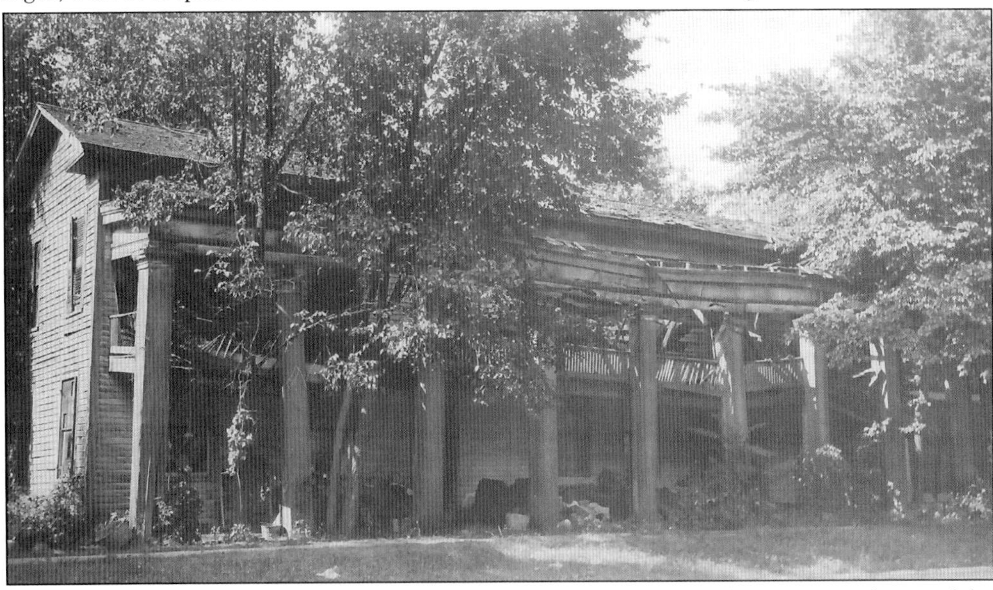

Eagle Tavern in 1927. This photograph, taken in the 1920s, shows the weary condition of the Clinton Inn originally located on the Chicago Road. In 1927, Henry Ford purchased the inn. The building was dismantled and reassembled at Greenfield Village, reopening to the public on October 21, 1929. Great care was taken to utilize as much as possible from the original structure. Many of Mary Ella Smith's personal belongings were put on display in the building, including her piano, upon which she gave piano lessons.

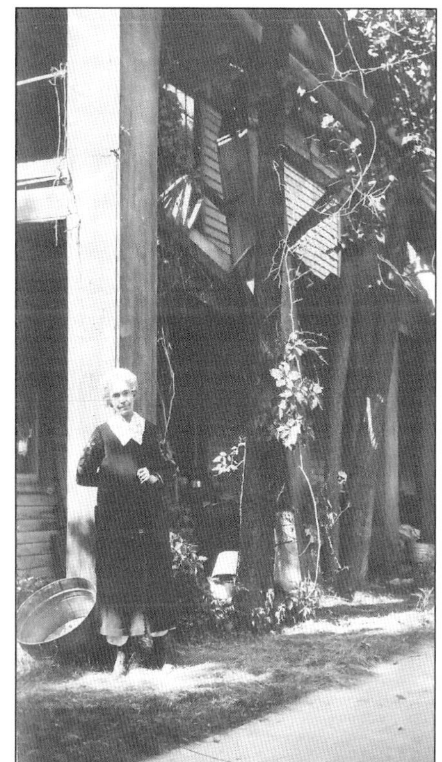

Mary Ella Smith in front of the Dilapidated Eagle Tavern. Seen here is Mary Ella Smith outside the dilapidated Eagle Tavern in 1927, at the time it was purchased by Henry Ford. Her grandparents had purchased the tavern in 1833, and their daughter Mary Ann Muir and her husband, Walter Smith, took over the business, later leaving it to Mary Ella. She lived here until Ford bought the property.

Fairfield House. Located on South Adrian Highway, almost at the Ohio border, this inn provided a resting point for travelers, whether they wanted an overnight stay or merely a good meal to carry them through the distance ahead, as fresh food was always available. The Fairfield House was destroyed by fire in 1907.

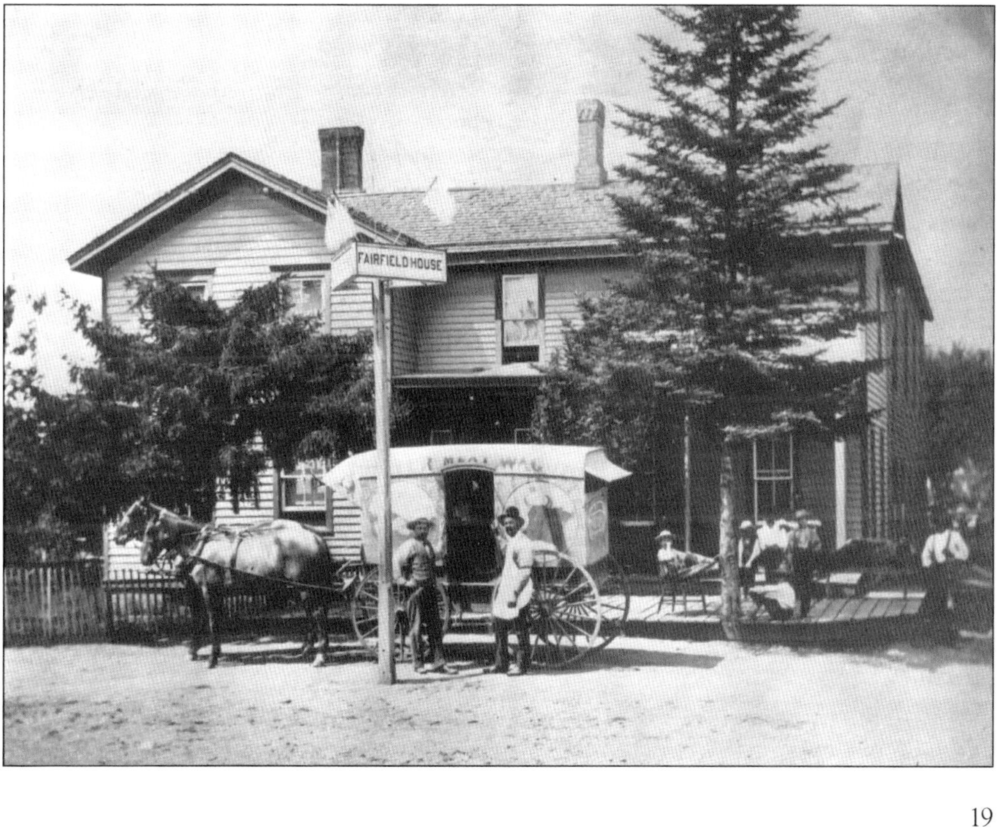

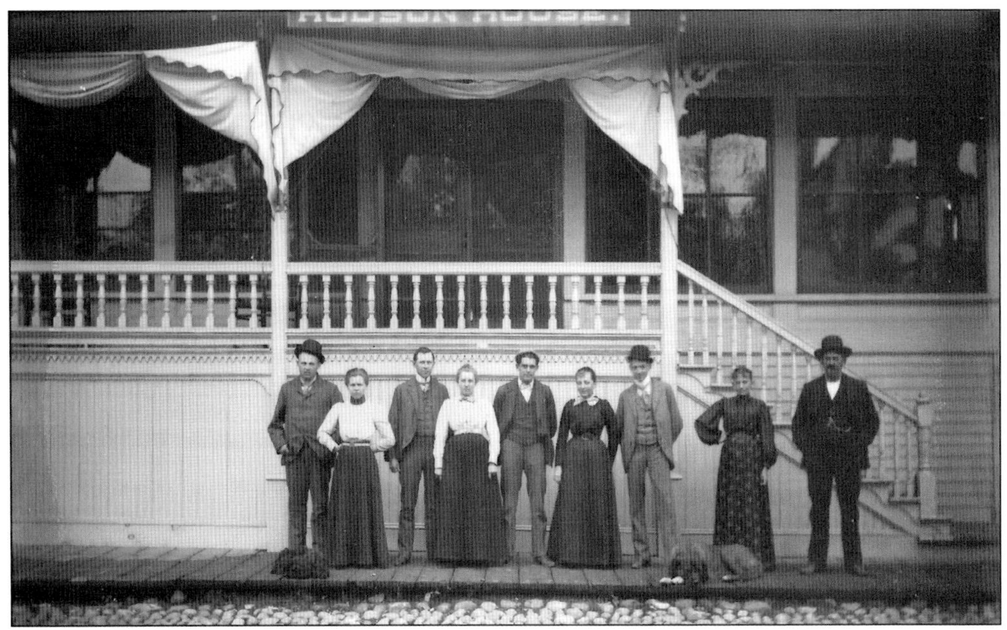

Hudson House. Located on Church Street in the village of Hudson, the Hudson House was also known as Lyon's Hotel in 1862 and the Wilson House in 1864. This establishment was noted for providing good fare and lodging. A large feed stable was available. In 1871, Wilson exchanged the hotel with L.E. Halram for a farm near Wayne, Michigan. J.F. Bell took ownership in 1880, followed by A.H. Lane in 1885, and then C.W. Parker in 1916. The hotel was operated as a cafe in 1936.

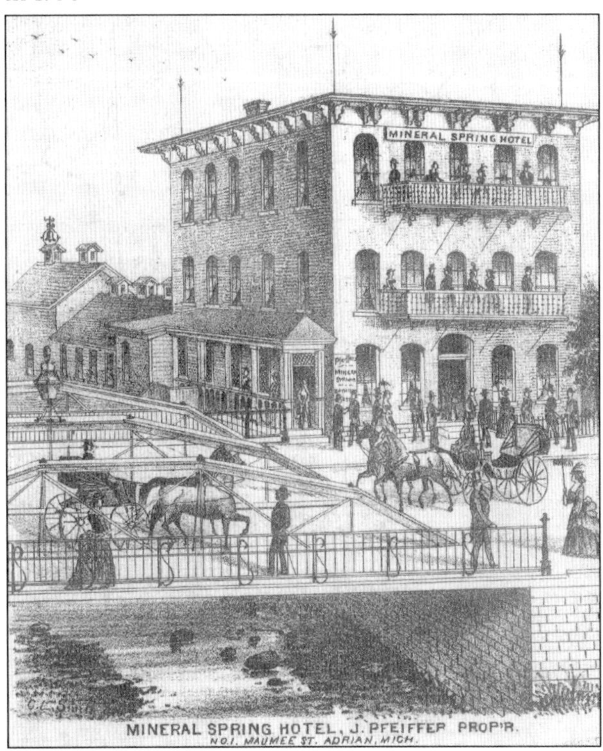

Mineral Springs Hotel in Adrian. This hotel was built in 1874 on the edge of the River Raisin on Maumee Street. Using the mineral spring to entice customers, it was considered a healing house, with fresh water available. It was renamed the Commercial Hotel in 1890; for many years, it has been known as the West Maumee Trading Company.

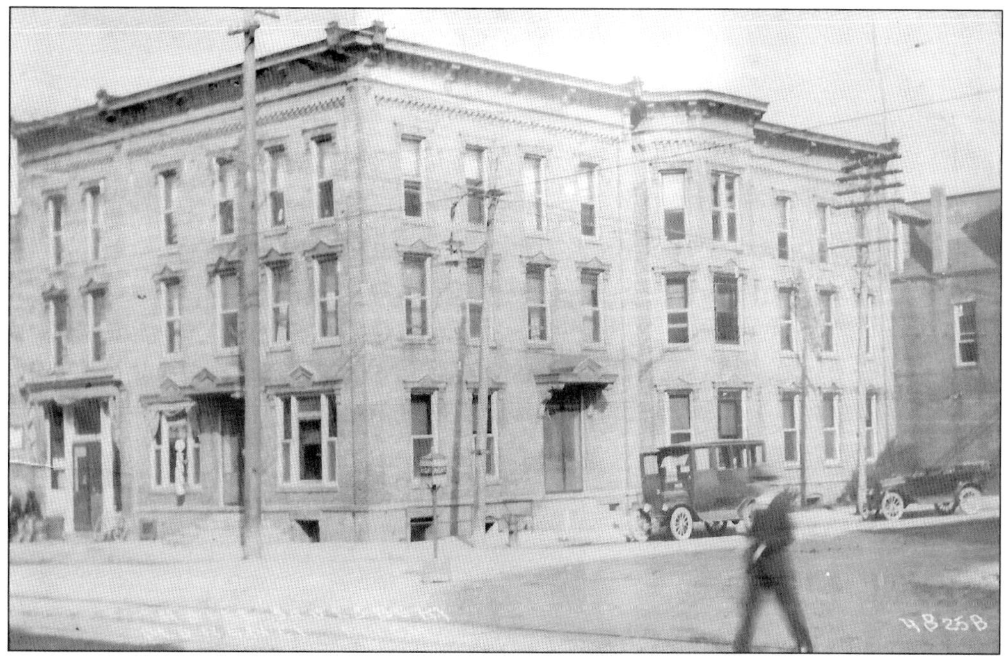

The Hotel Saulsbury in Morenci. Located on Main Street in the city of Morenci, the Saulsbury Hotel offered luxurious comfort to its guests. Built in 1889 by Cary S. Saulsbury, this hotel accommodated many businessmen and travelers. With failing health after 10 years of proprietorship, Saulsbury rented the building out for a few years and eventually sold it.

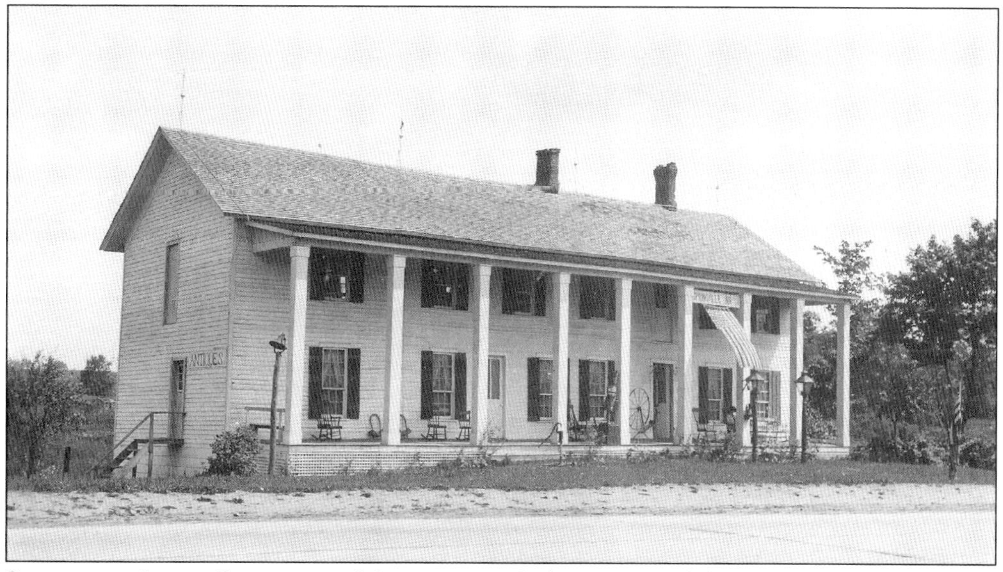

Springville Inn in Springville, Michigan. With the creation of the La Plaisance Bay Military Road, a second stagecoach route was available. This road intersects the Chicago Military Road in Cambridge. Springville, named for the abundance of springs in the area, was settled west of Cambridge Junction around 1832. Abram Butterfield built a tavern shortly thereafter to accommodate the pioneers and weary travelers on the La Plaisance Bay Military Road three miles south of the Chicago Military Road. The inn became a community gathering area. The settlers met at this site in 1835, organizing the township and naming it Cambridge.

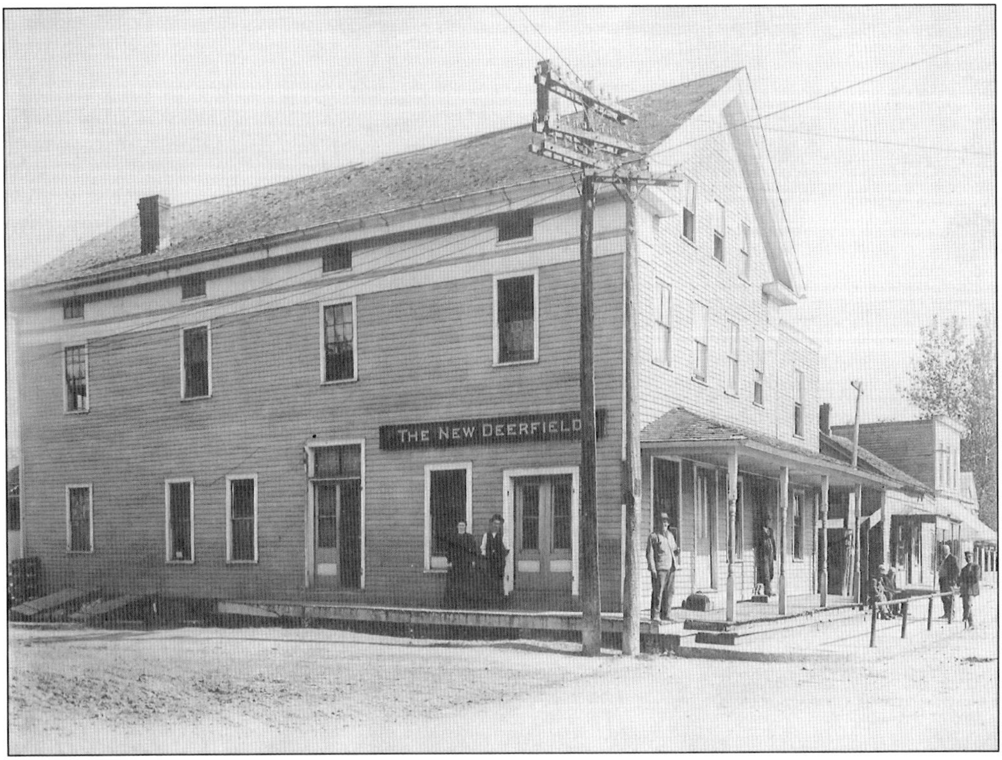

THE NEW DEERFIELD HOUSE. Originally known as the Deerfield House, this hotel was built around 1850. With Joseph Hudson as proprietor in 1894, it was renamed the Hudson House and became known as the New Deerfield by 1900. Charles Breningstall purchased the property in 1909. In 1968, it was converted to a one-story structure. Throughout the years of passenger trains arriving at the Deerfield depot, the hotel maintained a flourishing business.

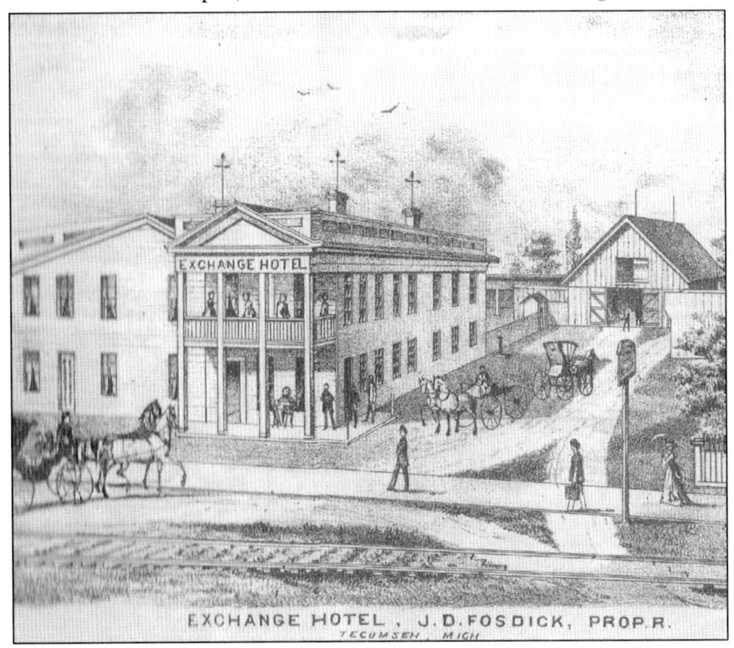

TECUMSEH EXCHANGE HOTEL. Once located on Evans Street in Tecumseh, the Michigan House, also an inn, stood on this site. Destroyed by fire in 1858, the Tecumseh Exchange Hotel was built in its place that same year. The railroad was a major source of guests, and the hotel provided lodging until about 1900.

Three

Gristmills and Sawmills

To meet the needs of a frontier community, the first settlers arrived with the intentions of building a gristmill and a sawmill. Reducing wheat to flour and corn to meal was a necessity, with mass production a major goal. Many traveled for days to reach the nearest mill, then waited in line to have their wagonloads ground. With ample water supply throughout Lenawee County, hydraulic power was the common source of energy. Pioneers brought knowledge and innovation from the eastern states and Europe with them. Whether seeking rapid water flow or building waterwheels or dams, they worked together, sharing skills and techniques that led to substantial improvements in technology. As the boundaries of settlement expanded, gristmills were a part of every neighborhood.

While the first home was made of logs or split wood, the settlers anxiously awaited the presence of a sawmill to turn their logs into cut boards. Many times, a barn would be the first frame structure built, followed by a frame house. The sawmills brought opportunity to build schoolhouses, churches, and courthouses, changing the image of the community from a frontier to a village or city. The industrialization of milling wheat, corn, oats, and even wool had a large effect on the economy and development of communities within the county. According to the Michigan census, Lenawee County had 14 gristmills and 17 sawmills in 1837, with an increase to 17 gristmills and 54 sawmills by 1854. The Clinton Woolen Mill was organized in 1866 and continued operation until 1957. Another need was for cider and vinegar mills, with the abundance of orchards in the area. Mill privileges had to be purchased for the parcels upon which the mill would be located.

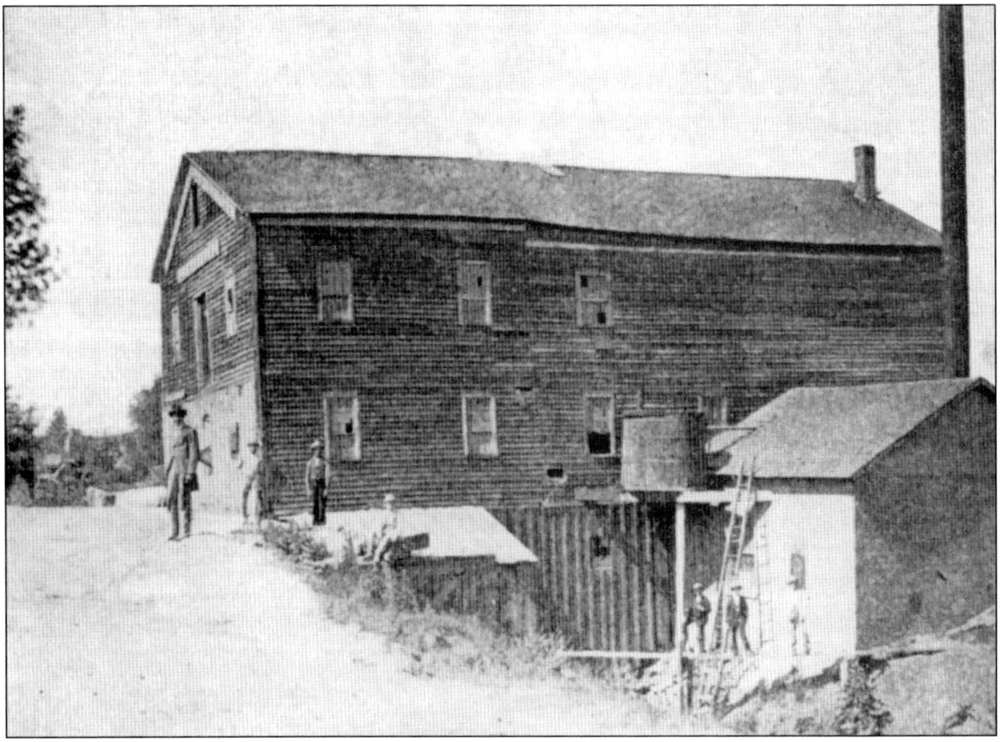

OLD RED MILL. On the north side of Adrian, past the Bent Oak Bridge, the Old Red Mill was built in 1829 by Addison Comstock and Isaac Deane. This was the second flouring mill west of Monroe and Toledo. It was north of the city of Adrian on the River Raisin. As people continued to settle, more gristmills were needed, with some farmers still traveling over 50 miles to have their wheat ground in Tecumseh.

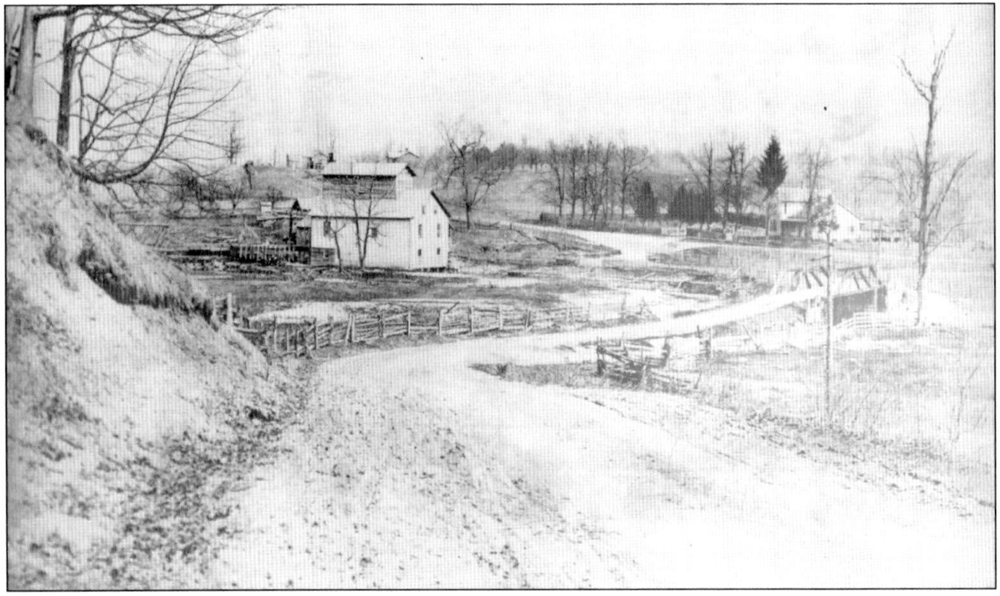

HOOKS MILL. Once located on Wolf Creek Highway a few miles northwest of Adrian, this mill was built by Edward and Thomas Hook in 1836.

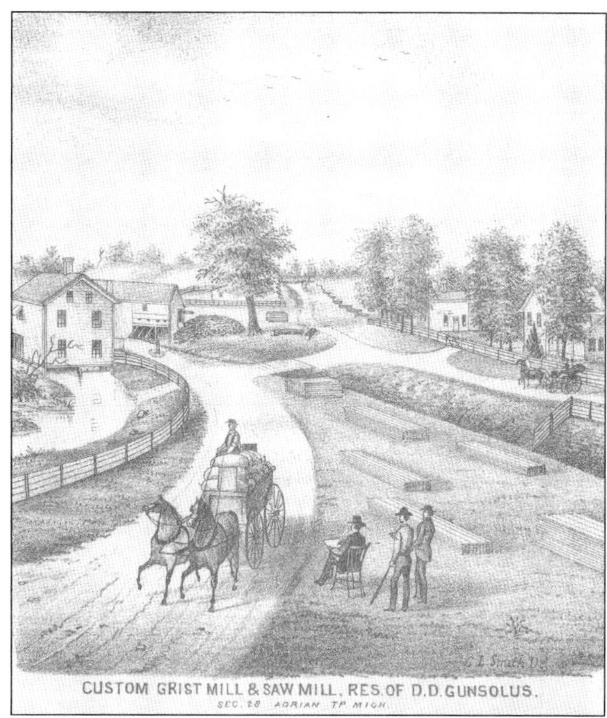

DANIEL D. GUNSOLUS CUSTOM GRISTMILL AND SAWMILL. Located in Adrian Township in the late 1800s, the D.D. Gunsolus gristmill and sawmill accommodated the needs of each customer with customized service for processing grain, cutting logs, and selling lumber. Daniel and his wife, Elmina, were both natives of Pennsylvania.

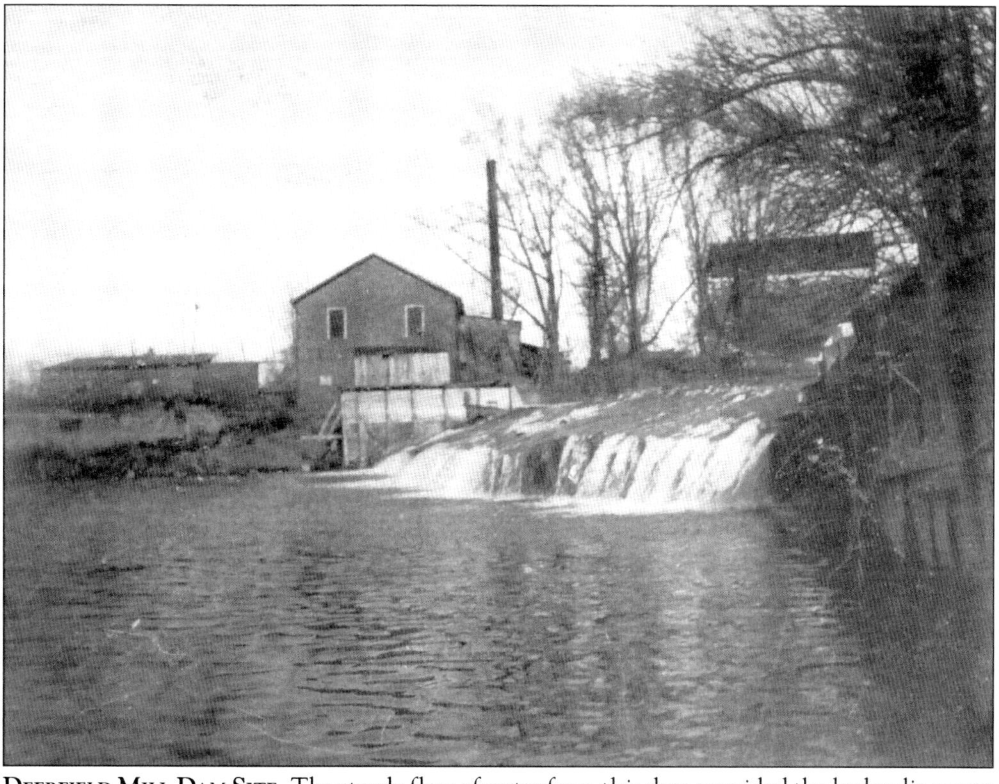

DEERFIELD MILL DAM SITE. The steady flow of water from this dam provided the hydraulic power that operated the Deerfield Grist Mill.

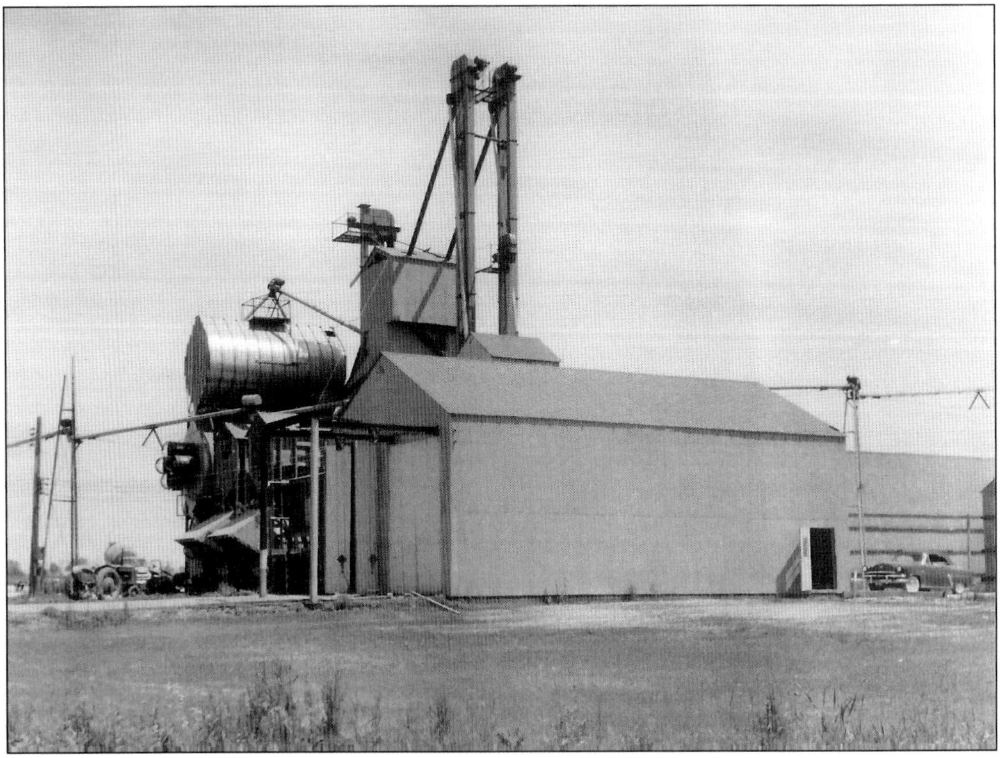

HADY & SONS ELEVATOR. Used for storage of processed grain of farmers in the Blissfield area, this elevator was owned by Hady & Sons.

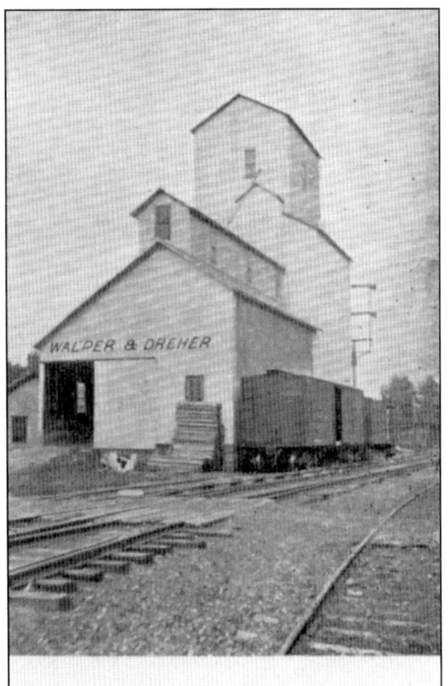

BRITTON ELEVATOR. Originally located in Ridgeway, this elevator was moved across the railroad tracks in 1895 due to the advantage of a direct loading dock on the Wabash Railroad. The structure was moved on two flatcars with fellow Brittonians holding guy ropes on each side to stabilize it as it was pulled along the rails by engine No. 25, with engineer Joe Beatly in control. The elevator was run by real horsepower, with a horse in the basement powering the machinery that moved the grain to different parts of the elevator. Fire completely destroyed the elevator on October 7, 1956.

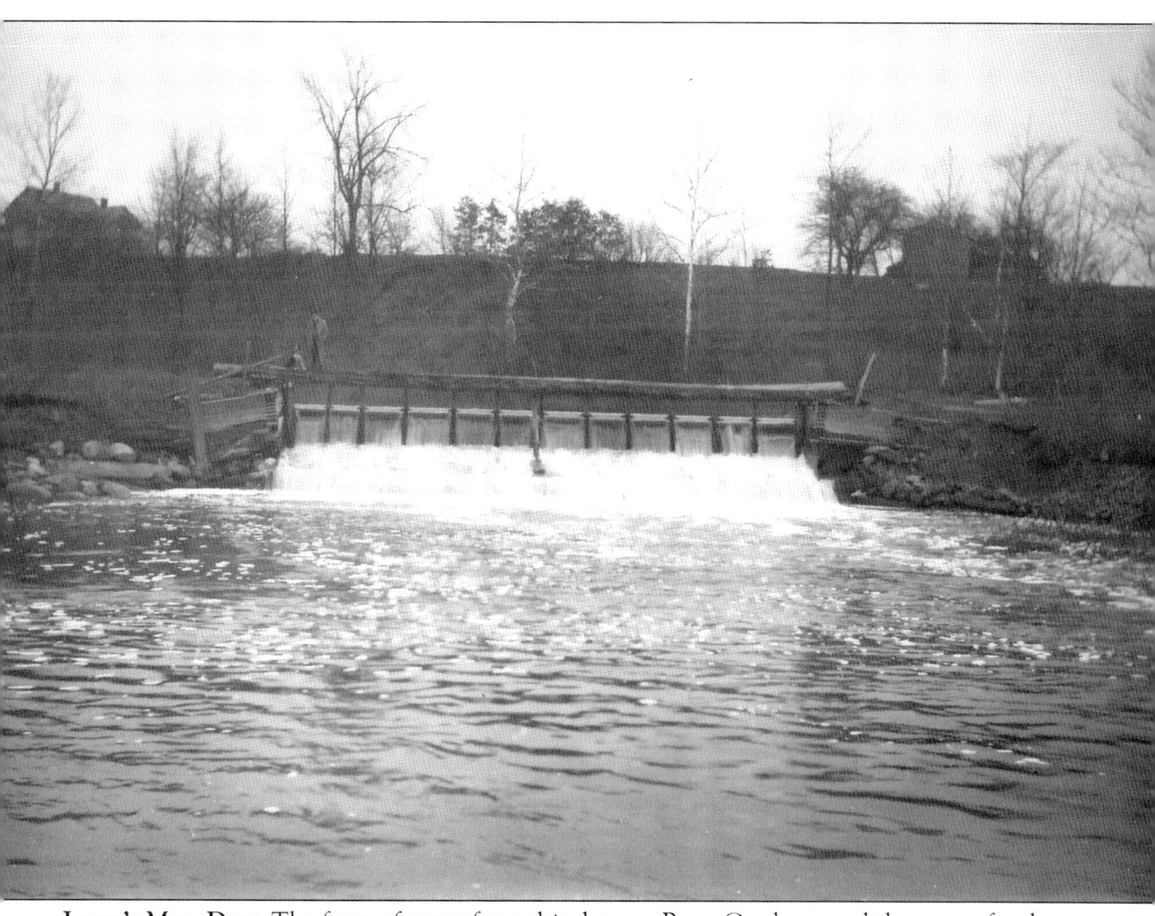

Lowe's Mill Dam. The force of water from this dam on Bean Creek created the power for the grinding mill for decades. First-class quality flour was guaranteed with the use of a separator for cleaning and scouring wheat, as mentioned by E.W. Kefuss in the *Hudson Post Gazette* in June 1897.

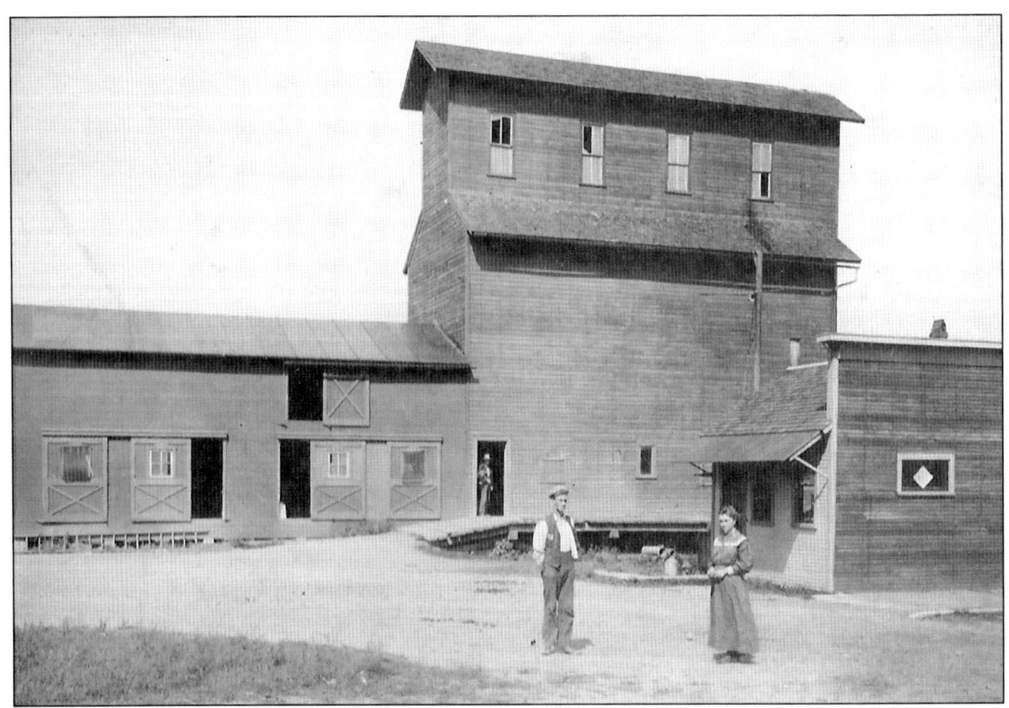

Sickner & Shuger Grain Elevator. This grain elevator located in Onsted provided storage for area farmers. Henry J. Sickner and B. Shuger were in charge of the facility.

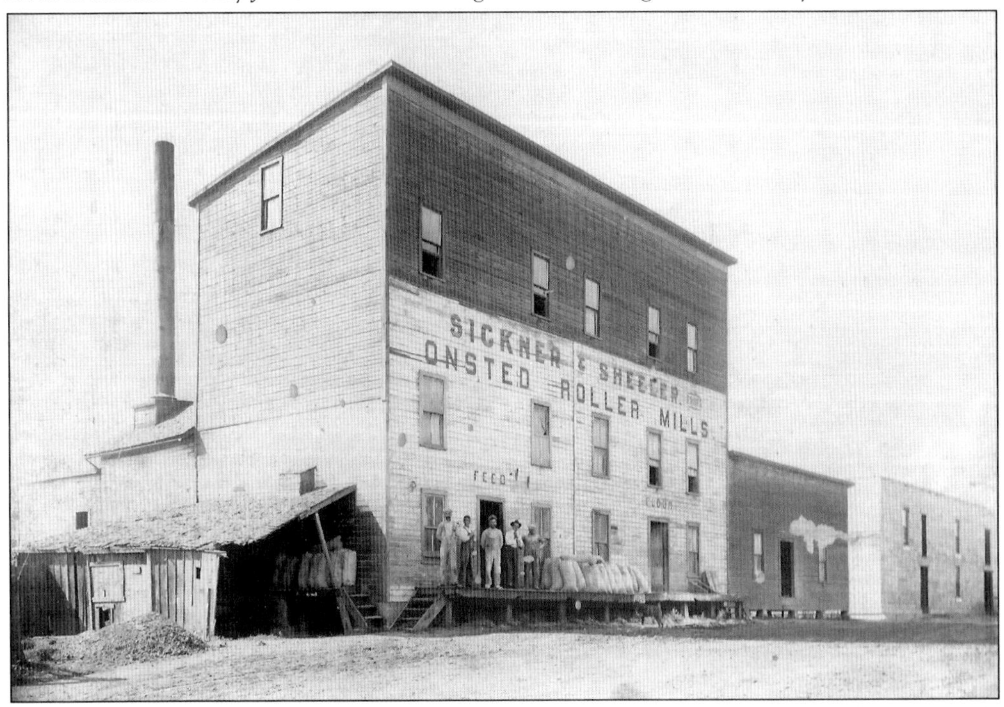

Sickner & Sheeler Onsted Roller Mills. This photograph was taken sometime between 1907 and 1910. William Sickner is believed to be the man standing in the doorway in the center of the group of men. Feed and flour production were the main endeavors of this business.

G. J. Schultz

Proprietor of the

BLISSFIELD

Water Mills

Dealer in All Kinds of Flour, Feed and Grain.

Blissfield, Michigan.

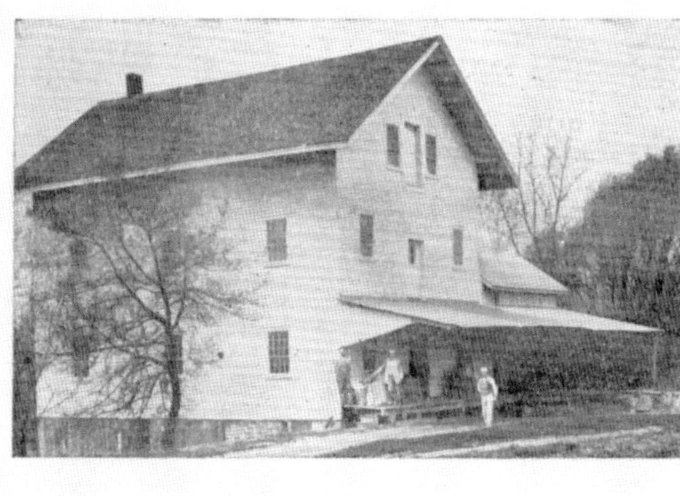

G.J. Shultz Water Mills. G.J. Schultz prided himself on producing several varieties of flour and grain for the community. Maintaining water quality and obtaining higher levels of purity through the grinding process was the business's main objective.

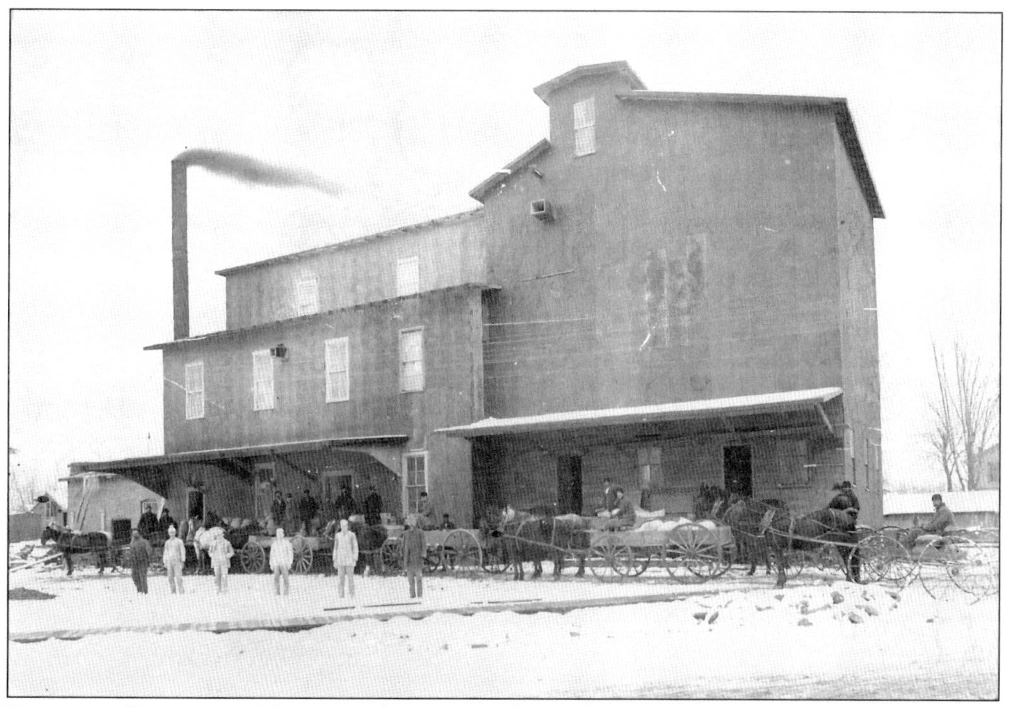

Blissfield Elevator. The grain elevator was located on North Lane Street in Blissfield in 1910. The elevator manager, Hugh Luce, is second from the right, with Willis Hall third from the left.

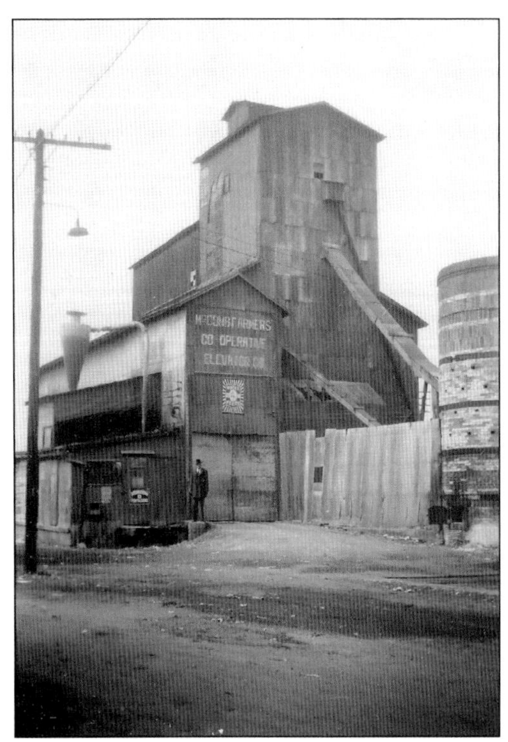

Deerfield Grain Elevator. This elevator was built in 1908 by W.F. Weisinger and Dale Munson. The Karner brothers sold the structure to the Deerfield Cooperative Association in 1908 for $16,000; they also sold the grain on hand for $2,243. An addition was made to store poultry, eggs, cream, feeds, and seeds. The facility continued to change hands, with the co-op selling it to J.J. Walper, who sold it to William and Carl Karner. It continued to be managed by a board of directors through the 1970s.

Blissfield Consolidated Millworks. An example of advancement in agricultural industrialization, this photograph taken in 1960 shows Blissfield Consolidated Millworks, which is a part of Michigan Agricultural Commodities today, still serving farmers by processing their crops.

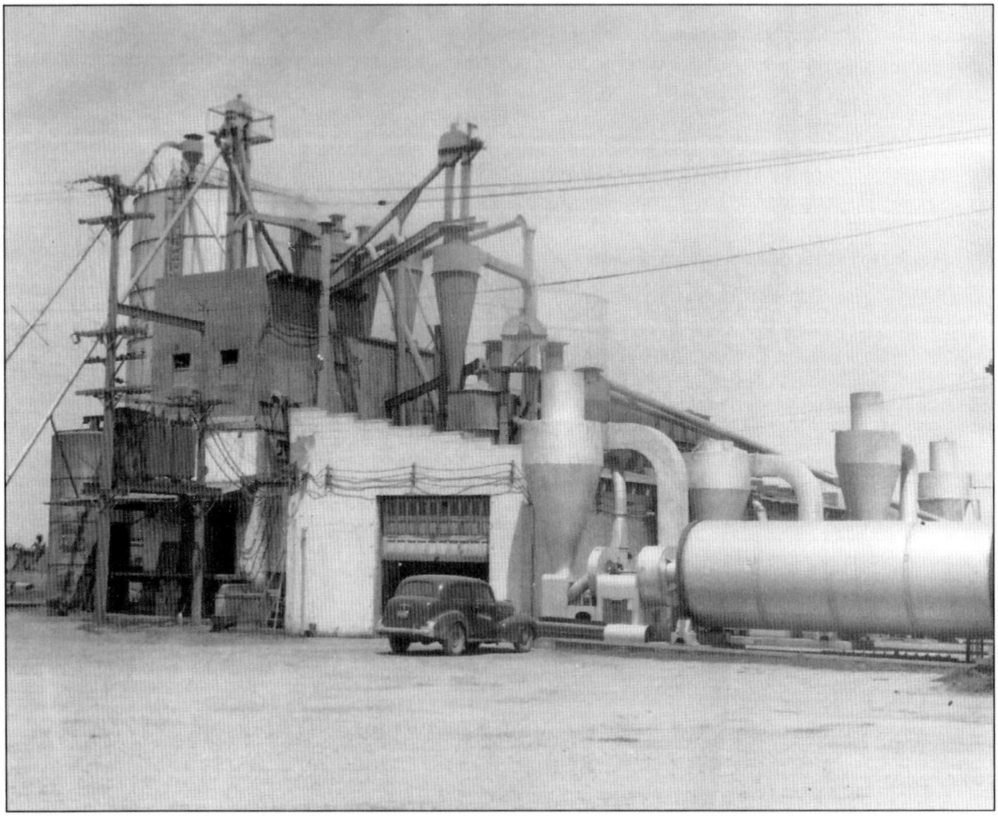

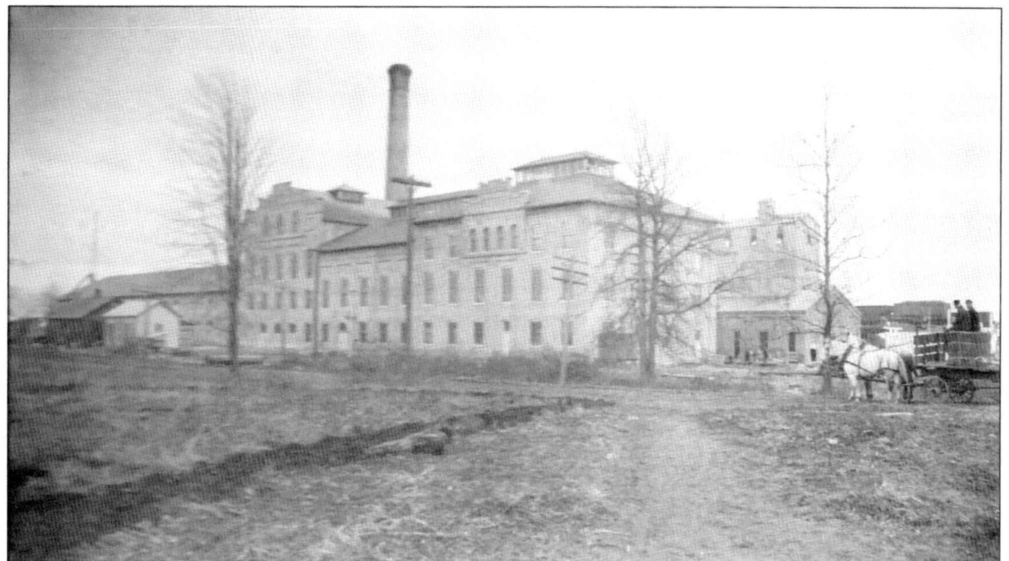

CONTINENTAL SUGAR COMPANY, EARLY 1900S. Riga and Ogden Townships had an extraordinary yield of sugar beets, as well as the largest percentage of sugar output from the crops of any county in Michigan in the late 1800s. In 1905, the Continental Sugar Company of Fremont, Ohio, built a mill in Blissfield to process sugar beets. This inspired farmers in surrounding townships to also grow sugar beets.

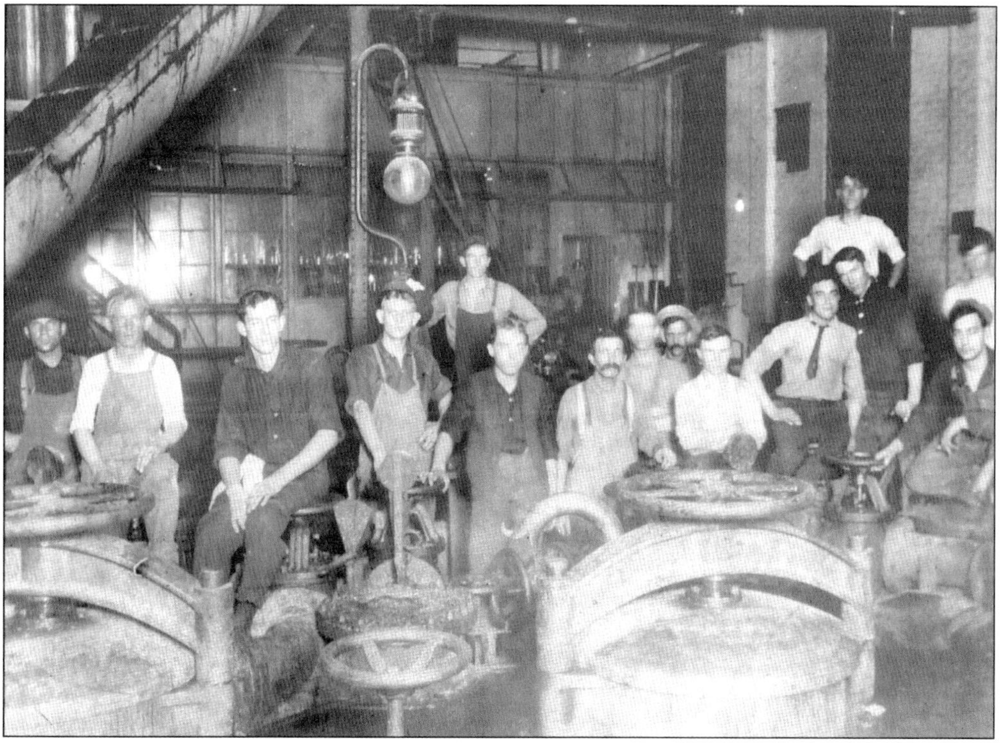

CONTINENTAL SUGAR COMPANY EMPLOYEES. Employees are shown inside the factory located in Blissfield. Sugar beets were washed, sliced, juiced, and then dried to create pure granulated sugar at this plant.

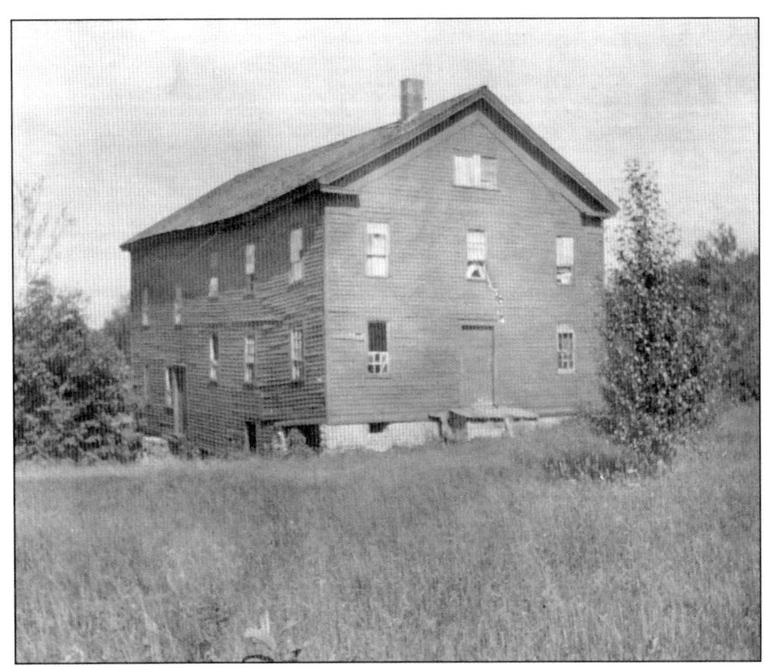

Quaker Mill in Rollin Township. In the early winter months of 1836, this mill, located in the Bean Creek Valley, was put into production by Joseph Beal. A member of the Society of Friends—or the Quakers, as they are commonly known—Beal named the mill in honor of the Quaker society of which he was a part.

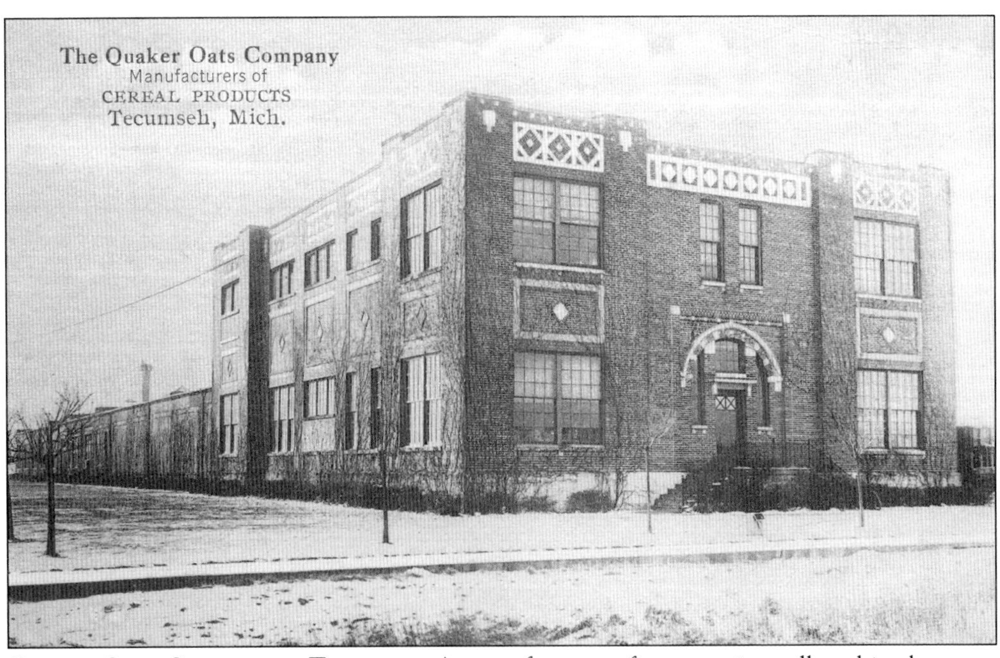

Quaker Oats Company in Tecumseh. A manufacturer of macaroni noodles, this plant was purchased from Uncle Sam's Macaroni Company by the Quaker Oats Company, located in Tecumseh, in 1911. The plant closed in 1960 after being purchased by the Tecumseh Corrugated Box Company.

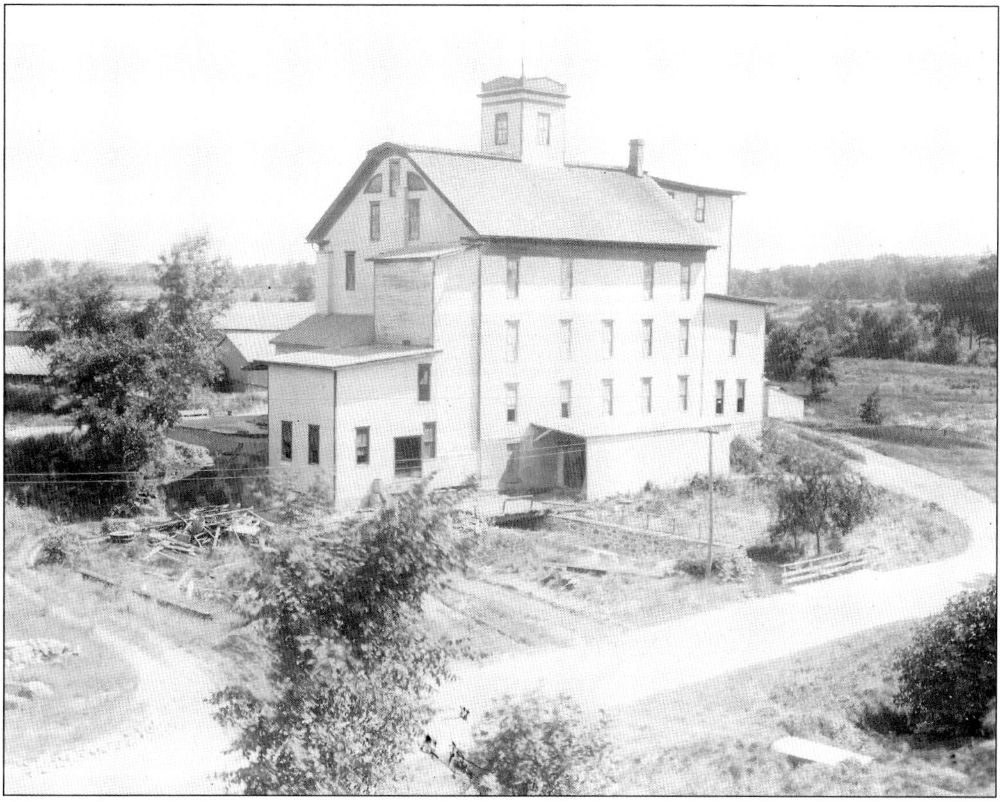

Globe Flouring Mill, Tecumseh. Founded in 1832 by Stillman Blanchard for the production of flour, the Globe Mill was located on Globe Pond in Tecumseh. William Hayden purchased the mill in 1858. Beginning in 1881, Globe flour was shipped worldwide. Damaged by fire in 1898, the mill was reconstructed and renamed the William Hayden Milling Company. Hayden also created a new flour brand, 1900, at this time.

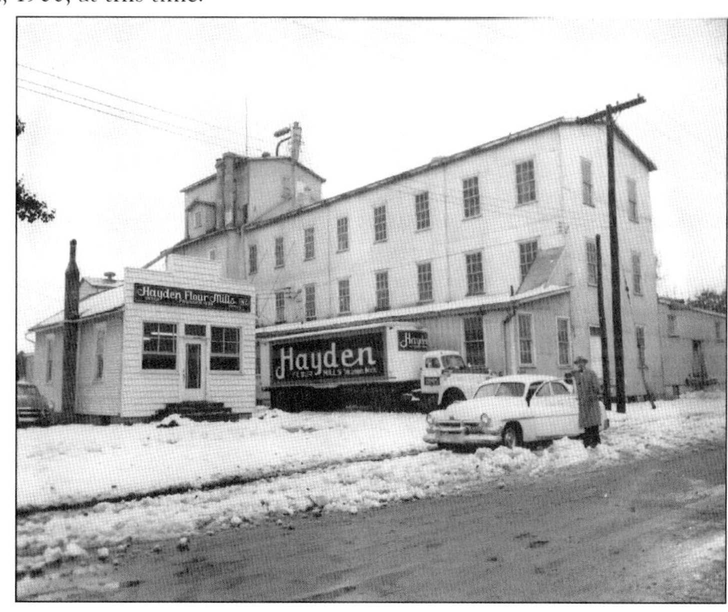

William Hayden Milling Company. Founded in 1835, this photograph taken in 1951 shows a sign of continued success by the Hayden family with their new location at 314 South Pearl Street in Tecumseh. It was operated that year by Perry Hayden, the grandson of the founder of the milling company.

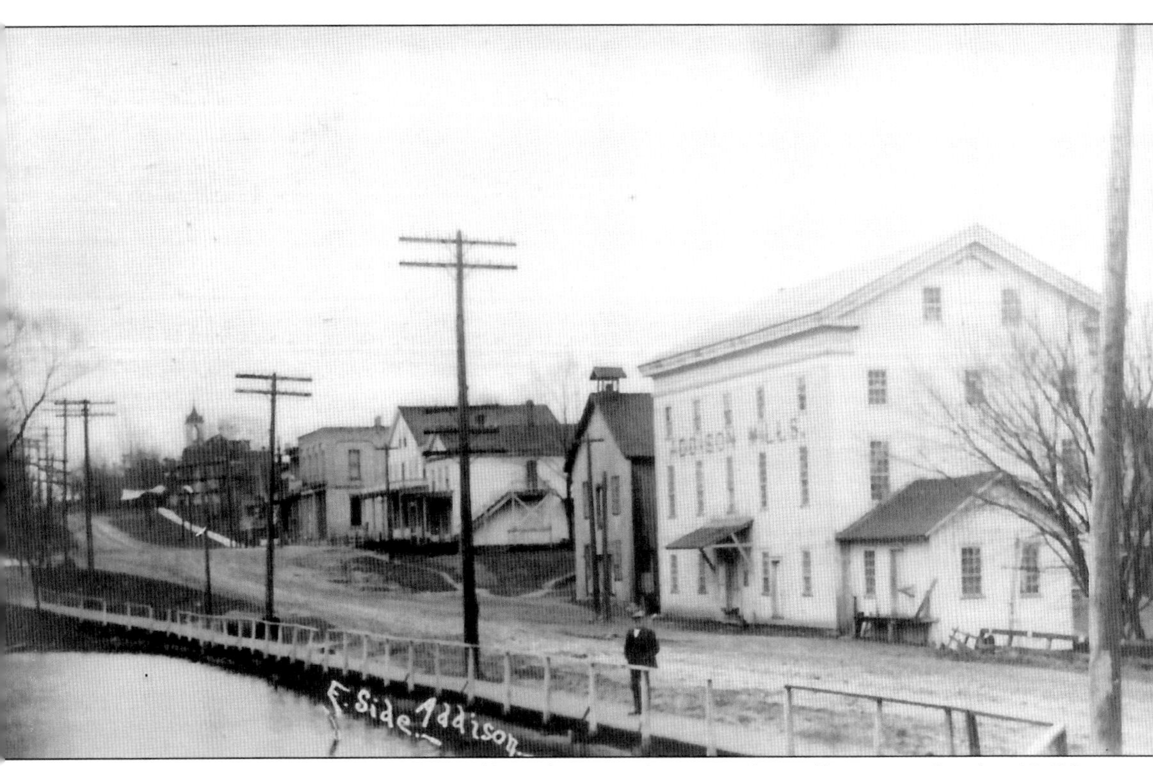

ADDISON FLOURING MILL. With a mill pond to provide power, this mill was completed in 1848 by Darius C. Jackson. Having control of the water levels in the mill pond also meant control of the water levels in Bean Creek and Devil's Lake. The mill provided many products, including quality baking flour. As government regulations changed, the mill had to cease production of flour and switch to livestock feed and dog food. The mill shut down completely by the early 1970s. The vacant building was demolished in 1980, leaving only the pond to bring back memories.

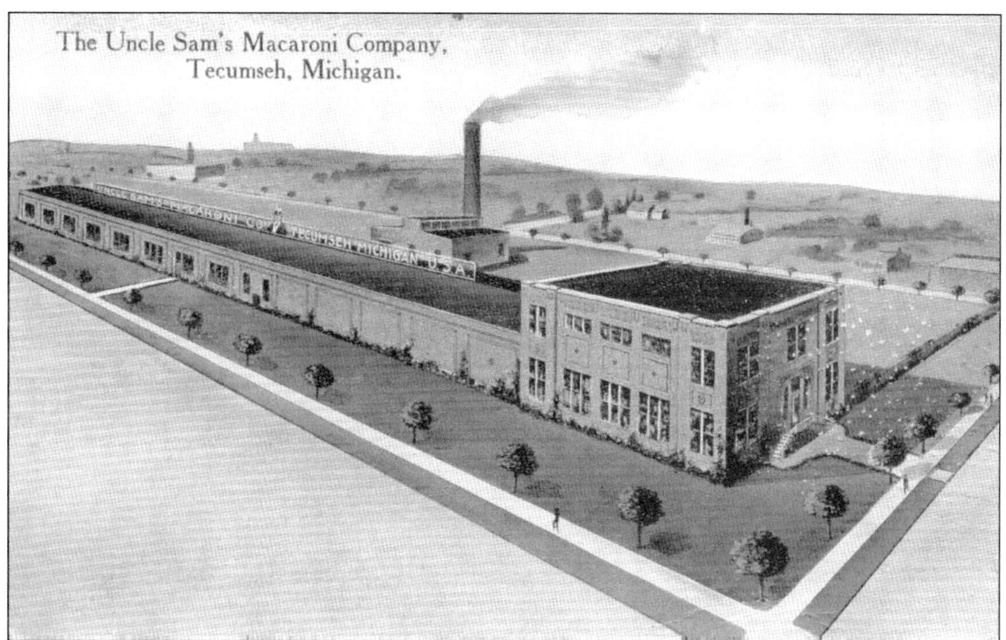

Uncle Sam's Macaroni Company. In 1904, the Michigan Macaroni Company purchased what was a steam-powered flour mill on North Maumee Street. The structure was originally a Presbyterian church that the Heck brothers purchased in 1891 after their mill on the Red Pond burned to the ground. They created the first non-water-powered mill in the area when they converted the old church into a mill. Uncle Sam's Macaroni Company emerged.

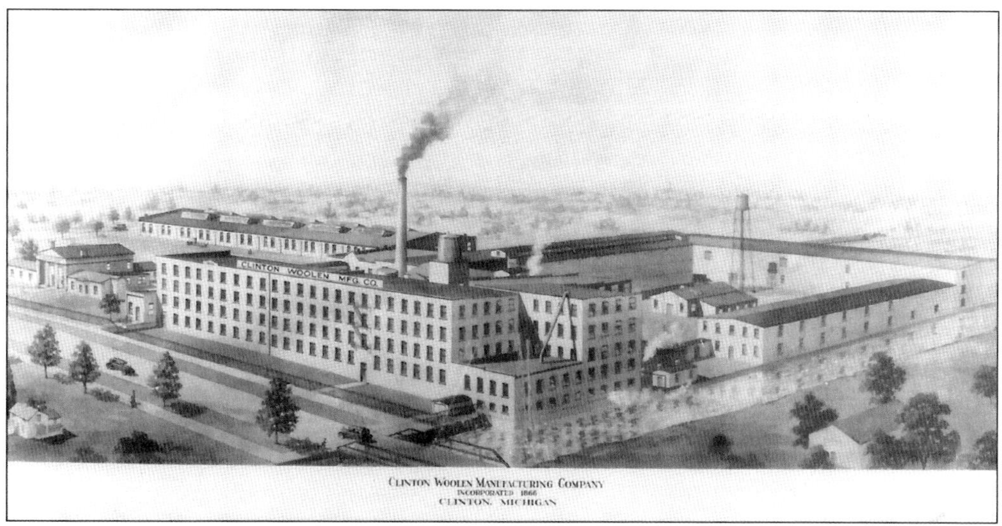

Clinton Woolen Mill. Built in Tecumseh on US 12 in 1867, the Clinton Woolen Mill created a fine product of cloth ready for market. They advertised plain and fancy cashmeres, with W.S. Kimball and A.C. Huntington as superintendents. In 1886, fire destroyed the premises; however, the mill was rebuilt within a year. The plant created woolen cloth for the armed forces during World War II. The operation continued until 1957 as one of the last woolen manufacturers in this region. The vacant mill was later demolished.

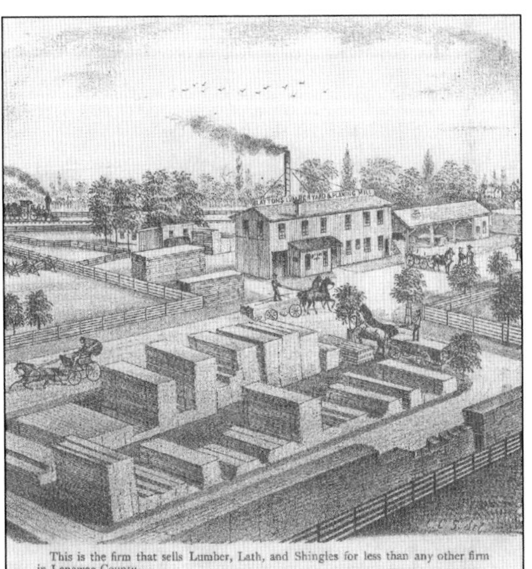

A.W. SLAYTON & COMPANY, TECUMSEH. This lumber yard advertised the benefit of having a side track from the railroad run right into its yard. With this advantage, it could keep prices down and easily ship in bulk.

JOHN H. FRITZ SAWMILL AND RESIDENCE. Operating in Riga Township, John Fritz provided lumbering services as well as the sale of cut lumber.

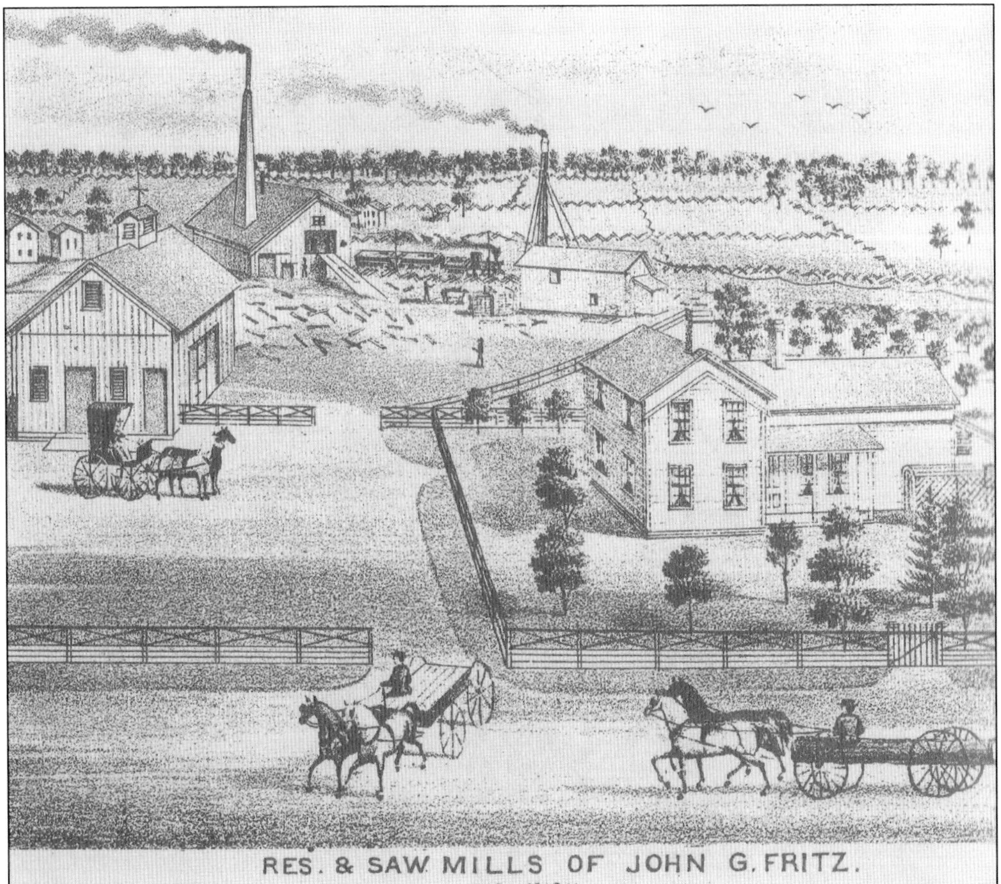

RES. & SAW MILLS OF JOHN G. FRITZ.
RIGA. MICH.

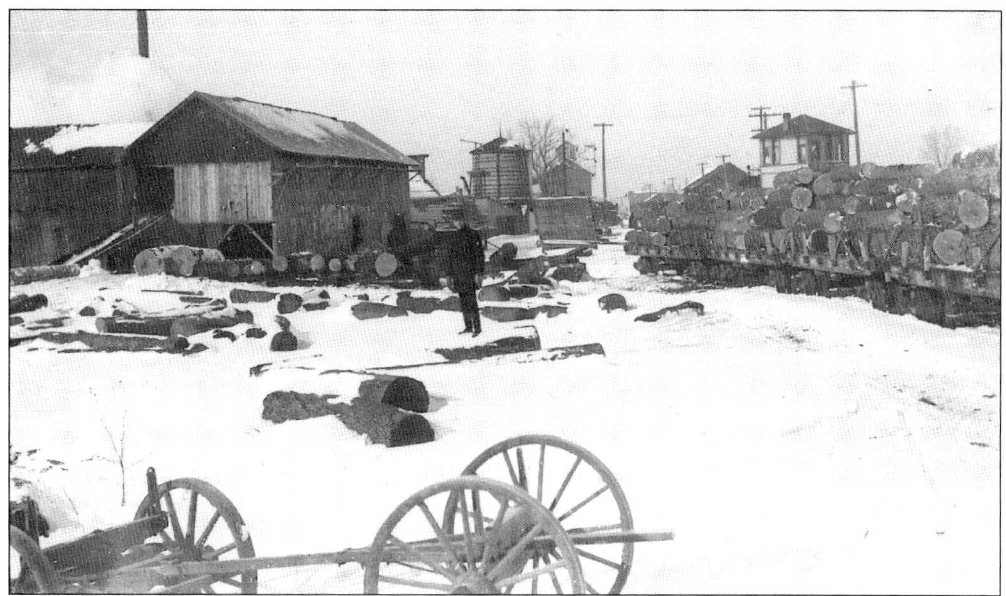

Sam Kniffin Sawmill. This sawmill began operation in 1865 next to the Wabash Railroad tracks in Britton. While upgrading the equipment, the mill was rigged with the latest buzzsaw, a planing department, and other equipment for finishing lumber. This photograph taken January 26, 1898, shows the building where workers once had quite a fright when Will Larabee's chest was sliced so deeply by a saw that they could see his heart beating. Larabee survived. Andrew Gogolin is pictured here in 1893.

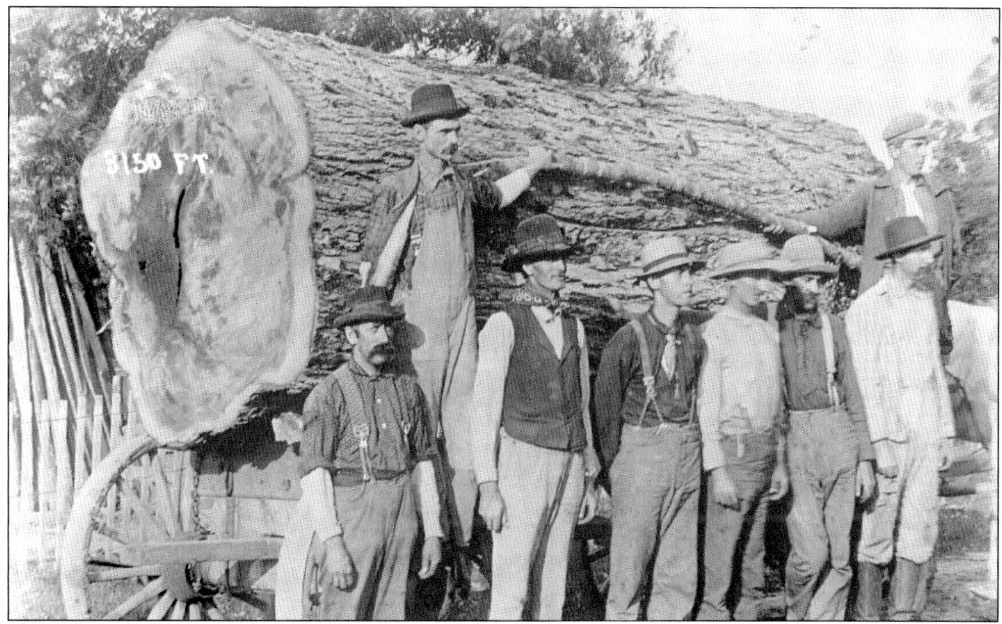

Log Cut on Raymond Farm. This log cut on the Raymond farm in Rollin Township represents 3,150 feet of board lumber. The skill and hard labor that was required—not just to cut and fell the tree without modern machinery, but also to raise the massive logs onto a wagon or railcar—is to be respected. The quantity of lumber that existed in the virgin forests when the settlers arrived was immeasurable.

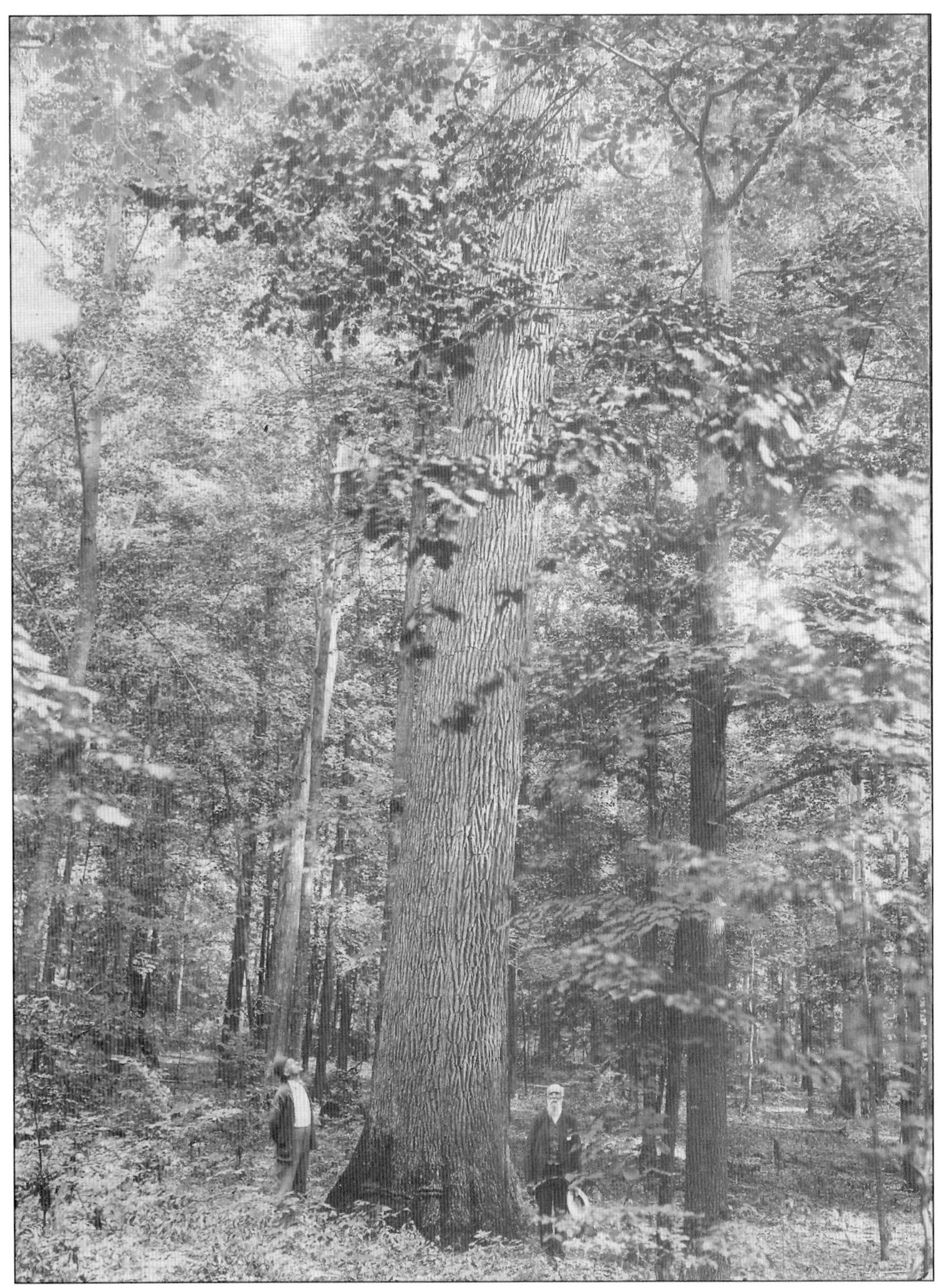

George Horton Gazing at a Tree. This image of George Horton standing on his property in Seneca Township, gazing upward, is said to represent his wonderment toward what stories that mighty oak tree could tell. Through reforestation and conservation, Horton strove to save the oldest quality trees that existed, as well as other artifacts of nature. This tree was believed to be one of the oldest in Lenawee County when this photograph was taken in 1902, with a circumference of 23 feet at the point for cutting.

Four

WAGONS AND CARRIAGES

As settlement increased throughout Lenawee County, opportunity for new businesses, including the manufacturing and repair of wagons, carts, and carriages increased as well. With the rugged trails and muddy roads, there was a need for service in every community. An attempt was made to improve the roads in the early 1800s with the creation of a corduroy road. This method involved filling depressions or swampy portions of a road with logs of various lengths and filling gaps with brush. This type of road could be dangerous for people and horses and even cause damage to wheels and axles by the slipping or rolling of the logs.

The next approach was the creation of a plank road. Boards of uniform length and thickness were laid across the width of the road, with stringers placed parallel to the length of the road. Initially, the roads would be very smooth, especially if ditches were created on each side for proper drainage. The Michigan legislature granted charters to private companies for the creation of timber roads in 1837. Charters granted in 1844 included a route near Sylvania, Ohio, to Blissfield, Michigan. A plank road law was passed by the Michigan legislature in 1848, which allowed any company to build a plank road as long as the construction met the specifications presented by the state law. This law also regulated tolls for the plank roads, not just for vehicles, but livestock as well.

These smooth roads delivered convenience in travel for a while. Within a few years, the boards would warp or rot, creating the necessity of replacement. In time, the cost of maintaining the toll roads would outpace the income from the tolls. Filling the gaps in the road with gravel instead of replacing the planks led to even more hazardous travel. Eventually, all of the planks were removed, or perhaps left to decay, and replaced with gravel. Even with this effort to improve transportation, the business of building and repairing the vehicles of the pioneers prospered into the 20th century.

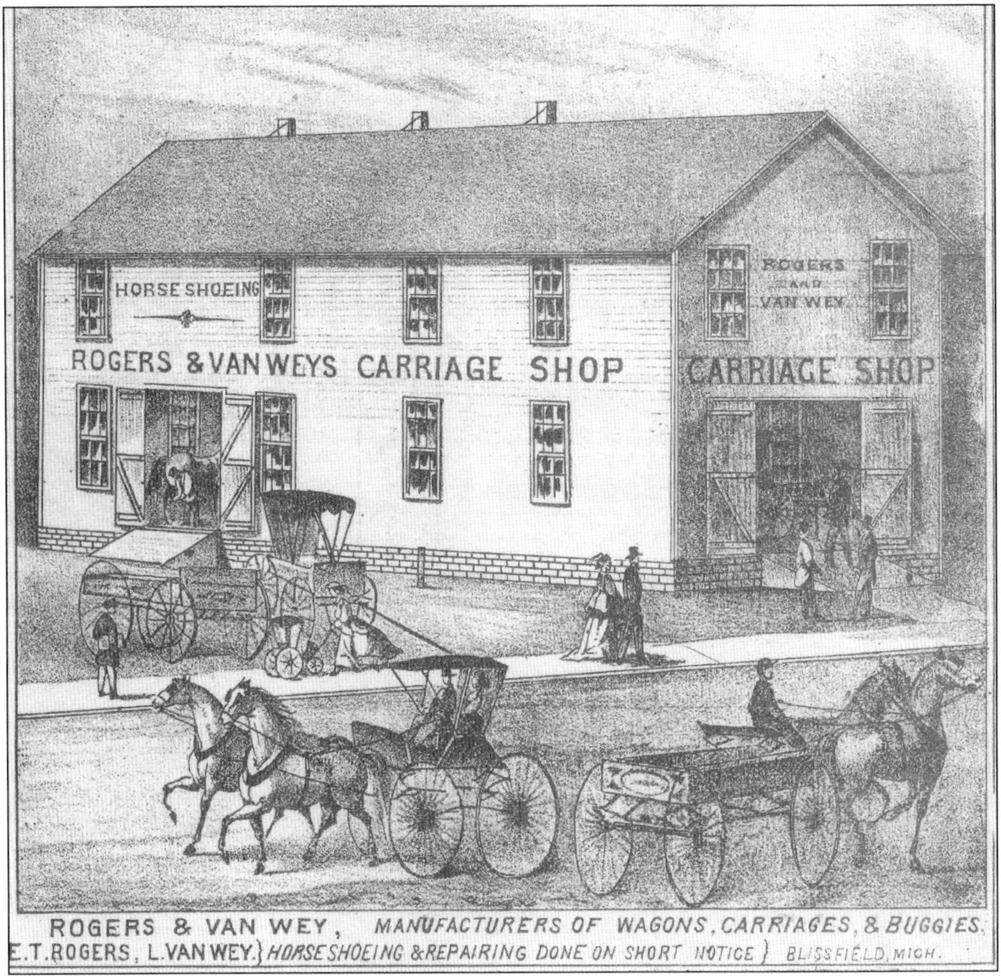

ROGERS & VAN WEY, MANUFACTURERS OF WAGONS, CARRIAGES, & BUGGIES.
E.T. ROGERS, L. VAN WEY.} HORSESHOEING & REPAIRING DONE ON SHORT NOTICE} BLISSFIELD, MICH.

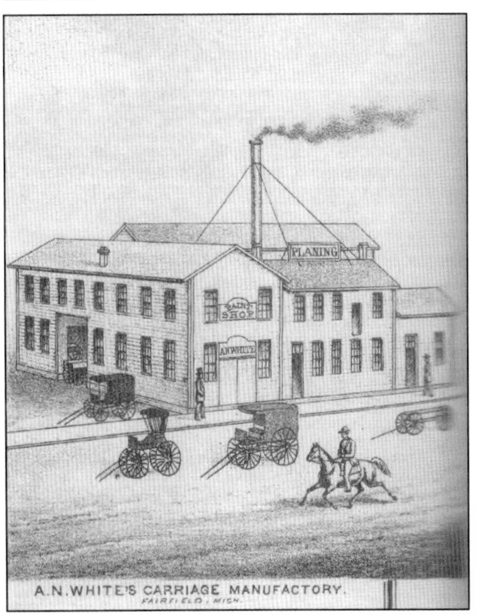

ROGERS & VAN WEY CARRIAGE SHOP, BLISSFIELD. Owned and operated by E.T. Rogers and L. Van Wey, this business manufactured carriages, buggies, and wagons. "Horseshoeing done on short notice" was advertised on the side of their building in Blissfield.

A.N. WHITE, CARRIAGE MANUFACTURER, FAIRFIELD. A.N. White settled in Fairfield in 1857. A wagon maker by trade, he built the A.N. White Carriage Factory, sawmill, and gristmill in 1861 on the west side of Main Street, north of Grandy Street. The factory and mills burned in 1865. White rebuilt the factory and a steam planing mill with an upgrade of equipment. In 1873, he converted to making cheese boxes. Upon his death, his two sons continued the business until 1900, when the last boxes were made. In 1926, all merchandise was liquidated and the building was sold and then razed.

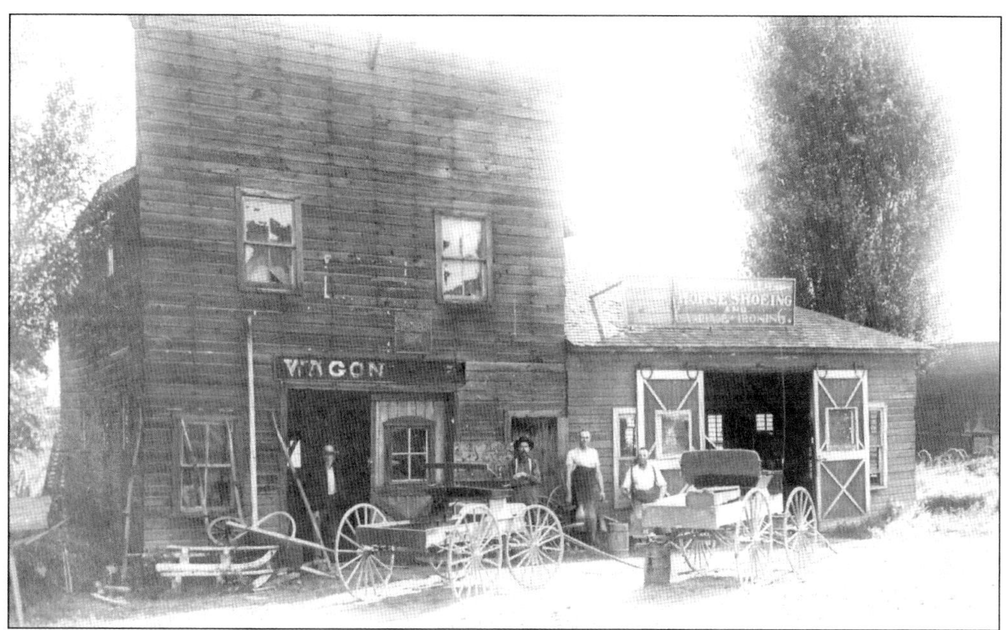

Onsted Wagon Works. Horseshoeing and carriage ironing are services posted for this repair and maintenance shop near the Old Chicago Trail on the northern side of Lenawee.

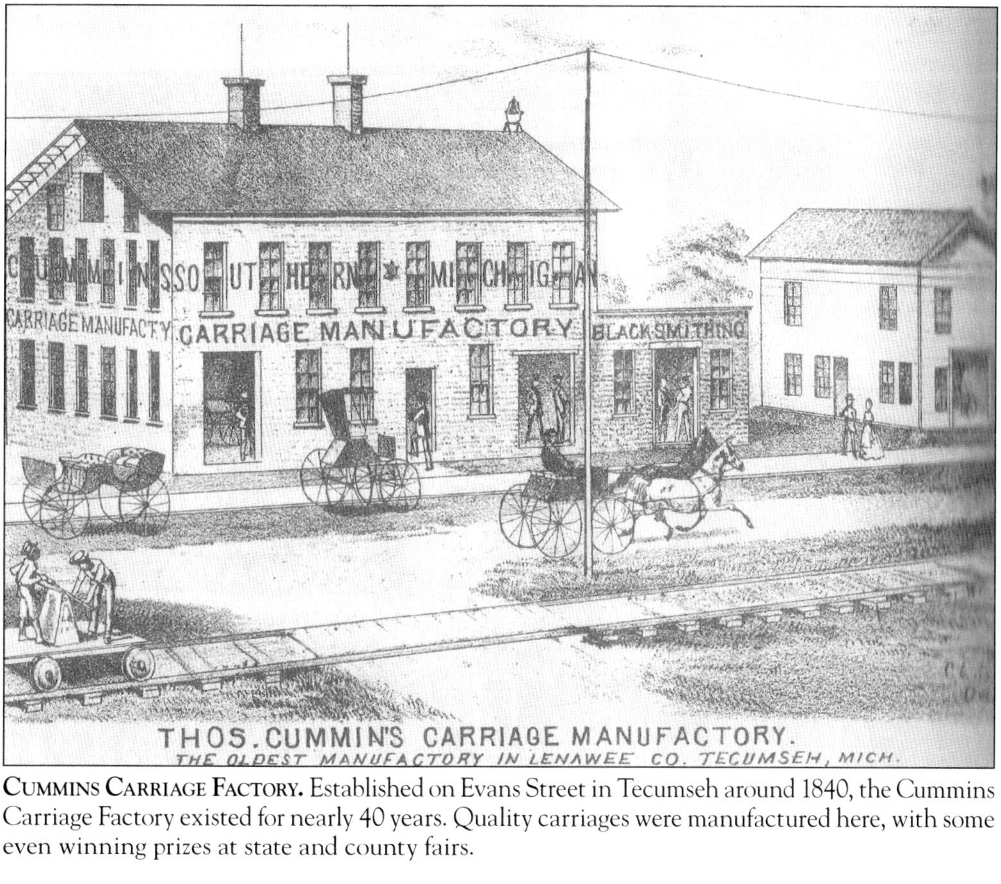

THOS. CUMMIN'S CARRIAGE MANUFACTORY.
THE OLDEST MANUFACTORY IN LENAWEE CO. TECUMSEH, MICH.

Cummins Carriage Factory. Established on Evans Street in Tecumseh around 1840, the Cummins Carriage Factory existed for nearly 40 years. Quality carriages were manufactured here, with some even winning prizes at state and county fairs.

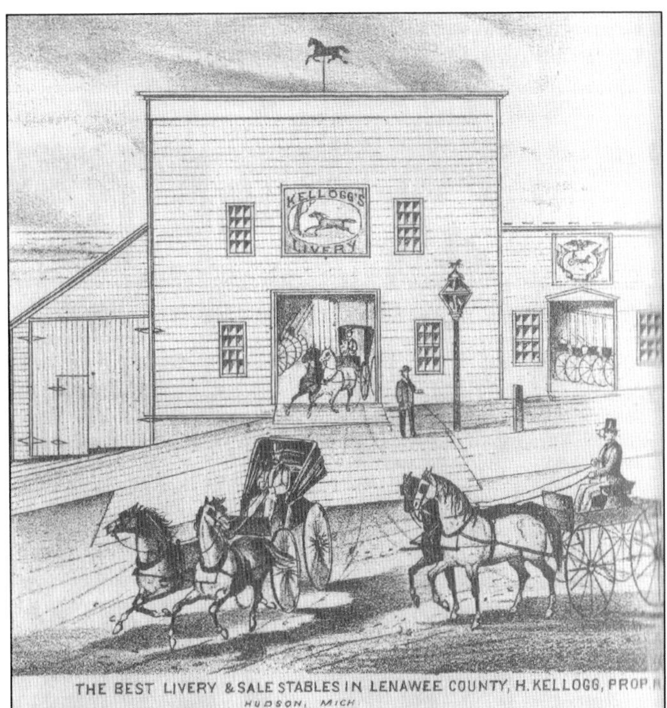

KELLOGG LIVERY & STABLES, HUDSON. Established by Henry Kellogg, the livery and stables led to a specialized line of handmade harnesses. Henry's son Charles continued with the business of manufacturing harnesses into the early 20th century. (Courtesy of Hudson Museum.)

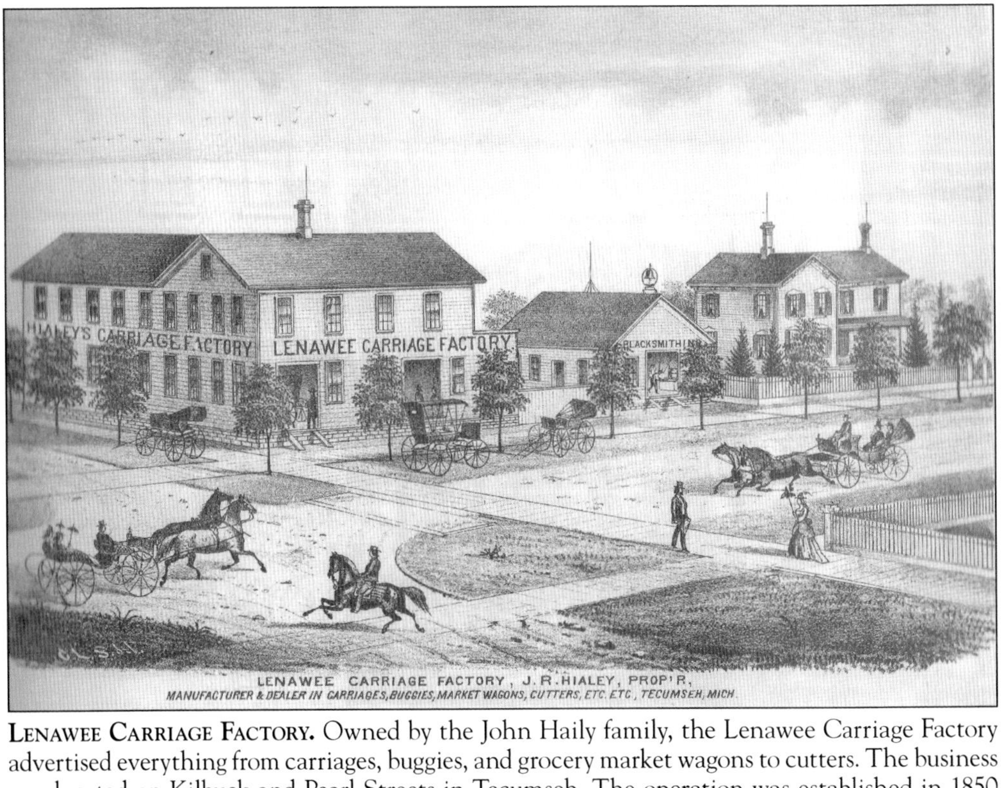

HIALEY'S CARRIAGE FACTORY
LENAWEE CARRIAGE FACTORY
BLACKSMITHING

LENAWEE CARRIAGE FACTORY, J. R. HIALEY, PROP'R,
MANUFACTURER & DEALER IN CARRIAGES, BUGGIES, MARKET WAGONS, CUTTERS, ETC. ETC., TECUMSEH, MICH.

LENAWEE CARRIAGE FACTORY. Owned by the John Haily family, the Lenawee Carriage Factory advertised everything from carriages, buggies, and grocery market wagons to cutters. The business was located on Kilbuck and Pearl Streets in Tecumseh. The operation was established in 1850 and continued into the 20th century.

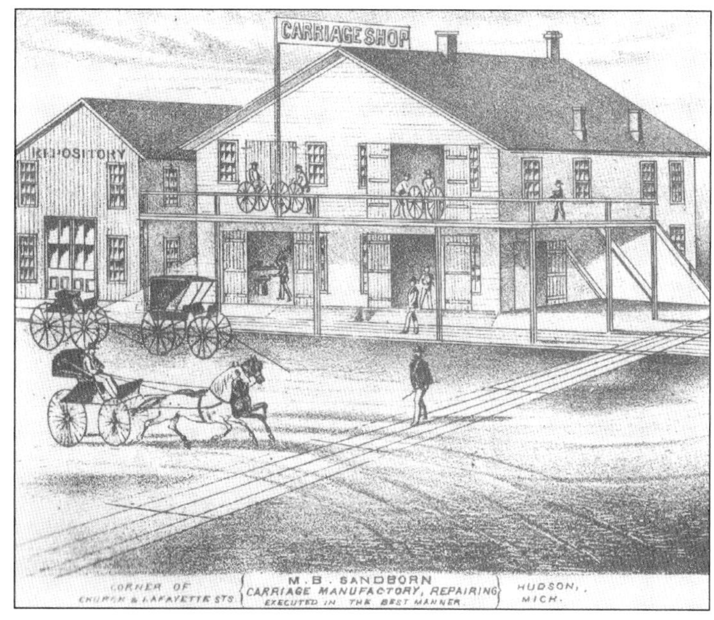

SANDBORN CARRIAGE SHOP, HUDSON. Located on the corner of Church and Lafayette Streets in Hudson, this business specialized in carriage manufacturing and repair.

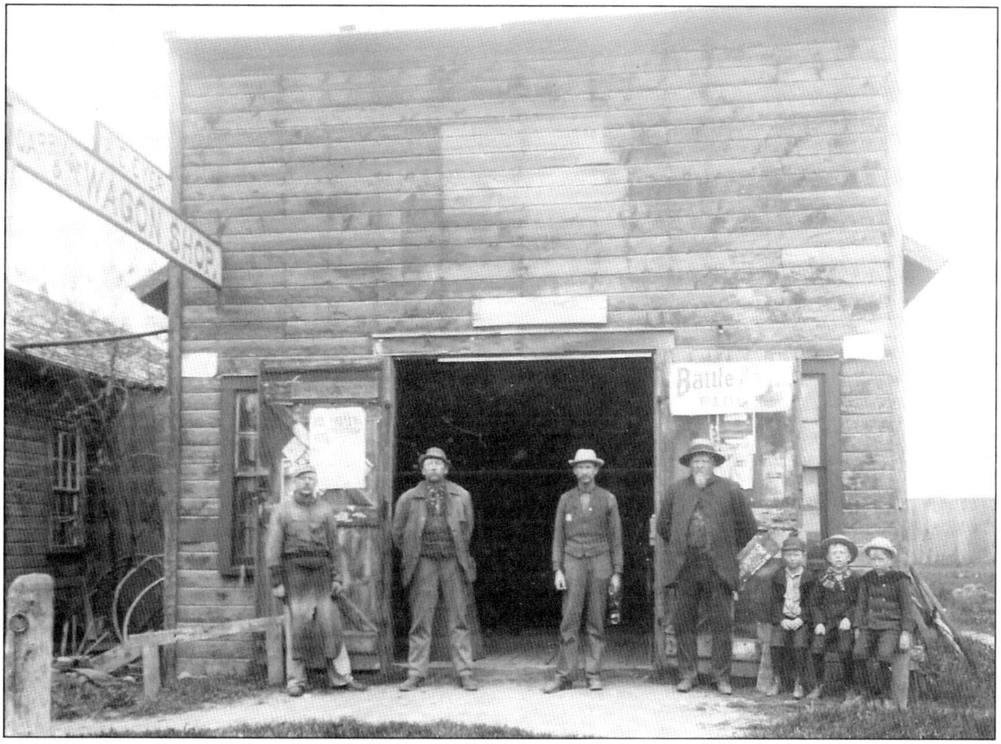

ADDISON CARRIAGE & WAGON SHOP, C. 1860. Manufacturing carriages and wagons was the primary service of the Addison Carriage & Wagon Shop. With a location on the Jackson-Hudson stagecoach route in Woodstock Township, it provided service to a wide range of communities. For decades, this was the only provider of carriage and wagon service in this area, approximately 20 miles northwest of Adrian.

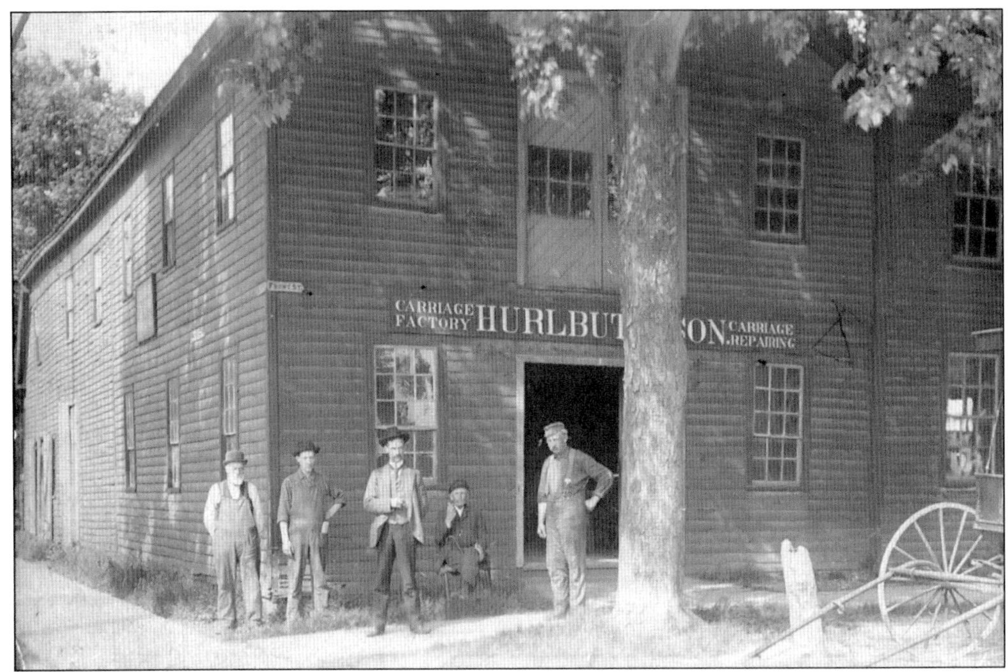

Hurlbut & Son Carriage Shop. John Hurlbut began his business in 1862 shortly after migrating from Palmyra, New York, with his brother. The business was built on the northeast corner of North Main and East Front Streets in Adrian and consisted of two sections that were connected. This family business produced open grocery store delivery wagons, carriages, and cutters. When his sons John Jr. and Willis reached working age, John formed a partnership with the boys and his own brother, Silas.

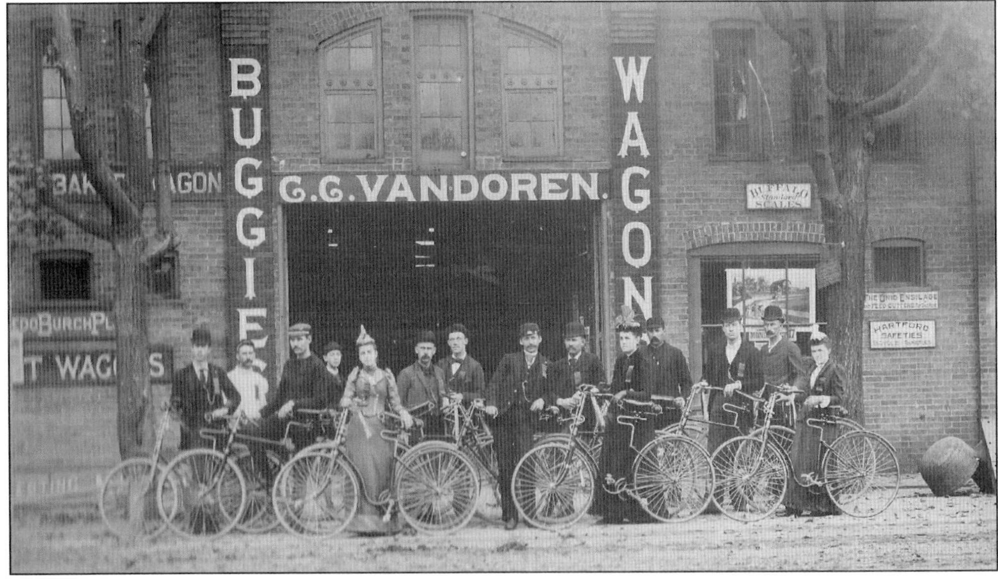

C.C. Van Doren Buggies & Wagons. Located in Adrian, the Van Doren shop built and serviced buggies and wagons. The Adrian Bicycle Club is shown in front of the shop. Commodities used with the carriages, such as soft seats and wheels, were needed for bicycles as well. The Lenawee and the Hillsdale were two models of bicycles made in the county.

Five

Dairy and Produce Industries

Arriving in untouched territory, some settlers were fortunate enough to have some livestock, such as a cow, sheep, horse, oxen, or perhaps a hog and a few chickens. The first settlers still had to rely on the land as their main source of food, and started planting as soon as possible. With a variety of soils throughout the county, determining the compatibility between the soil and the crops was important. Those settlers who entered from Toledo had to trudge through the Cottonwood Swamp in what are now Riga and Ogden Townships. The clay and muck was of unknown depth, and dense forests were filled with monstrous cottonwood trees up to nine feet in circumference, as well as hickory and soft maple trees. Predominantly German settlers entered into this area. The settlers had an enormous task of draining and tilling the fields, as well as ditching the roads. In time, their efforts created the most fertile soil, with the State Tax Commission declaring Riga the best agricultural township in the state, with Ogden ranking second. By 1900, Lenawee County held the highest level of agricultural wealth in the United States. With fertile fields available to produce feed for livestock, the science of dairying developed into mass production of cheese and butter, as well as a massive population of cows. Lenawee soon became the leader in manufacturing cheese and butter in Michigan at the beginning of the 20th century.

At the same time, the mass production of sugar beets, corn, and more potatoes than the regions recognized as "potato districts" in northern Michigan developed. Many celery beds were present; however, it was the work of the Prairie Celery Company and Tecumseh Celery Company that turned the swampland into profit, making Tecumseh the celery capital of the world in the late 1800s. Perry Hayden's Dynamic Kernel Project created the world's smallest wheat field in 1940 with assistance from Henry Ford's staff in Tecumseh. Many orchards, vineyards, and berry farms were also developed. The Adrian Horticultural Society was established in the 1840s, bringing organization to the industry and making Lenawee known as a large producer of quality fruit. Later known as the Lenawee Horticultural Society, the members joined with the Lenawee Agricultural Society, creating the first Lenawee County Fair in 1839.

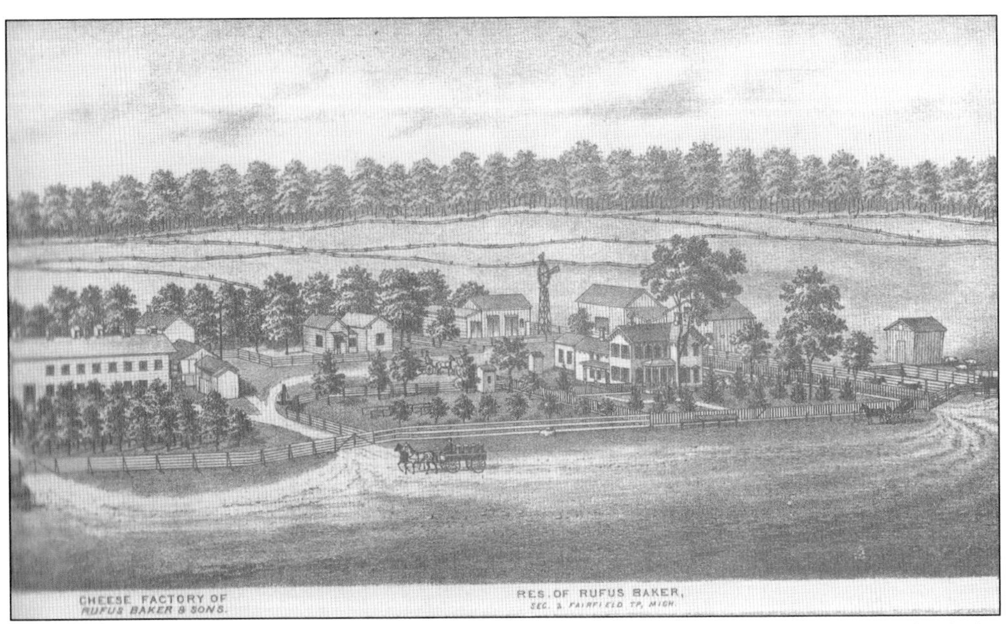

RUFUS BAKER CHEESE FACTORY. After several years of farming in Lenawee, Rufus Baker built the Fairfield Cheese Factory in 1866. This was the first cheese factory to be operated in Michigan, opening just four days prior to Samuel Horton's establishment. With his son E.L. Baker joining him in business, the name was changed to Rufus Baker & Son. They opened a wholesale cheese store in Adrian in 1872. With the addition of L. Ladd to the company in 1874, the name again changed, this time to Rufus Baker & Company. The business continued until December 1878.

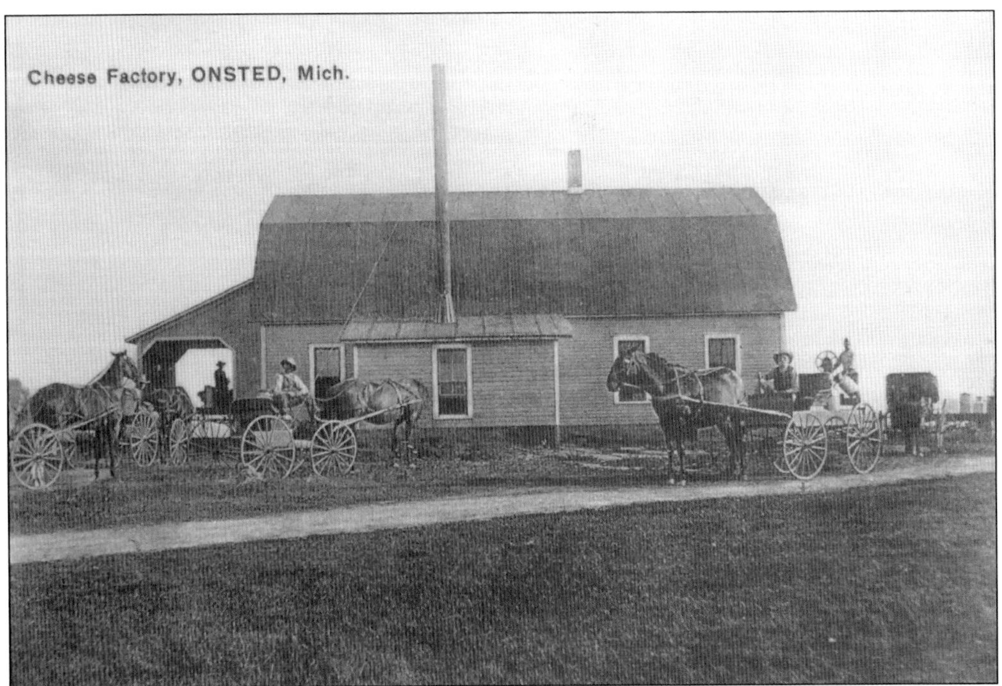

ONSTED CHEESE FACTORY. Operated by L.R. Connor in the late 1800s, this small facility, like many others, processed soft cheese.

Raisin Union Cheese Factory. One of several branches of the Baker Family Cheese Industry, this was located in Raisin Township. Jacob Baker was noted as the secretary at this location. A receipt signed by Rufus Scott of Watertown in Jefferson County, New York, and Baker shows Walter Scott's patent cheese turner being sold to Raisin Cheese Manufacturing Company of Raisin in Lenawee County, Michigan, for $32 on August 19, 1870.

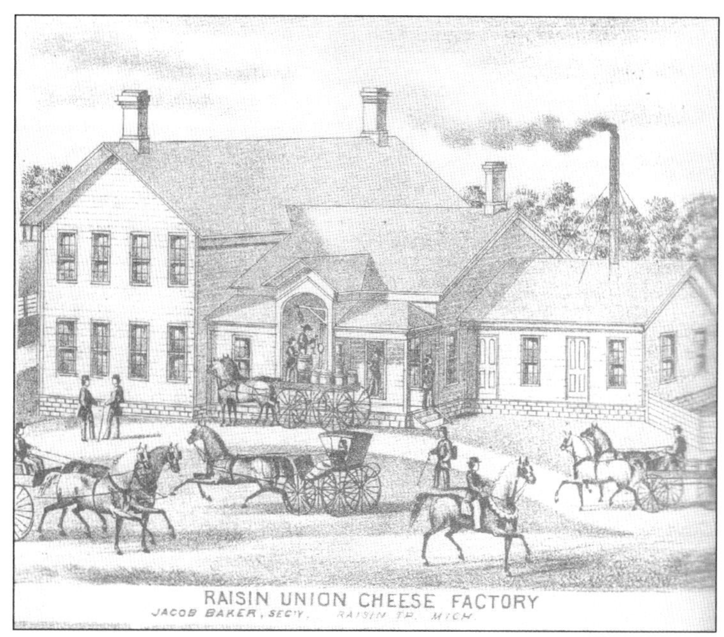

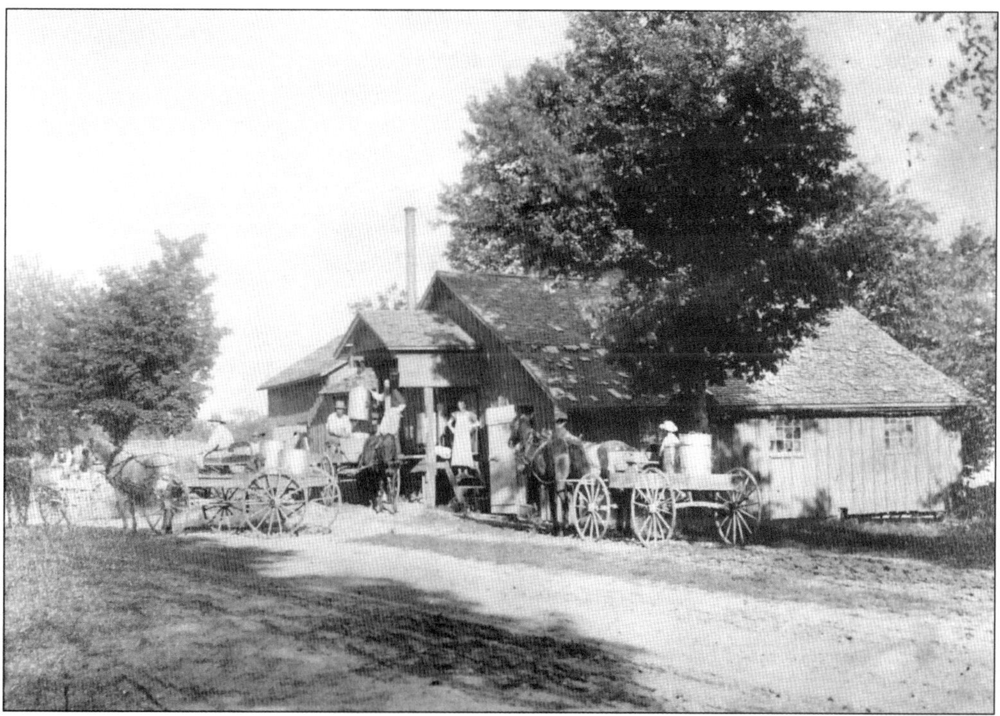

Fairfield Creamery. Essentially serving as a skimming station, the Fairfield Creamery served the farmers on the south end of Lenawee County.

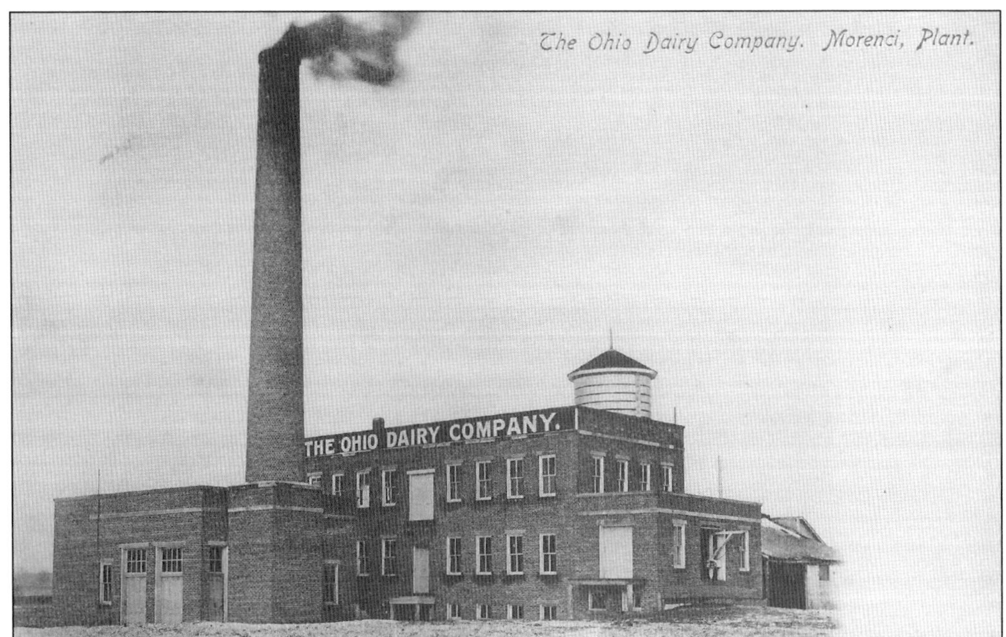

Ohio Dairy Company. In 1902, the Ohio Dairy Company purchased the Morenci Creamery, which contained a plant built in 1900 that was converted to produce sweetened condensed milk. A new plant was built in 1905. Production continued until 1950, with peak operations producing 180,000 pounds of milk per day. Several dairy processing plants developed throughout Lenawee, which benefited the farmers with higher prices paid for their milk; it caused many of the smaller creameries to close their doors forever.

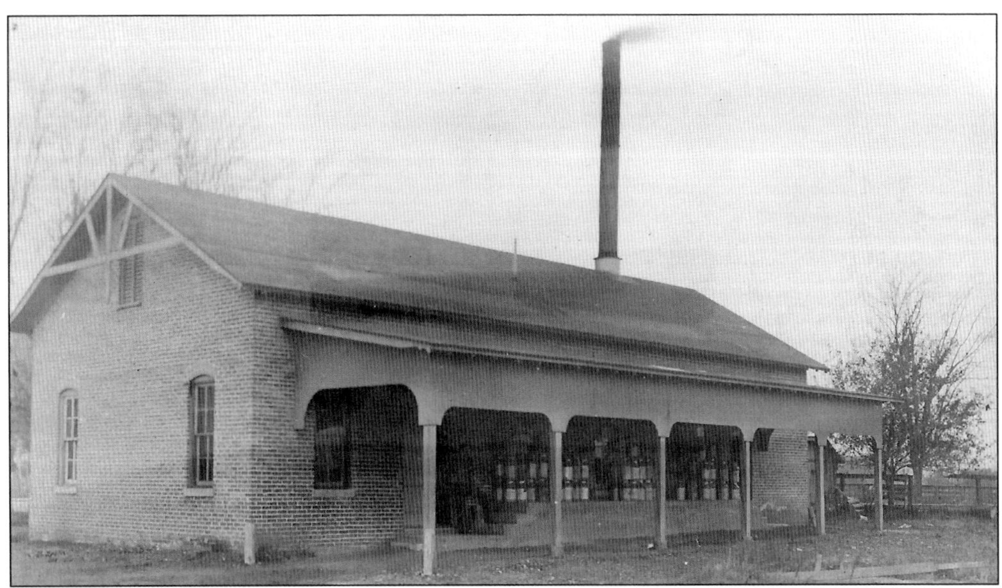

Blissfield Creamery Company. E.C. Keeler was in charge of this creamery in Blissfield. Many jugs can be seen on the platform of the skimming station.

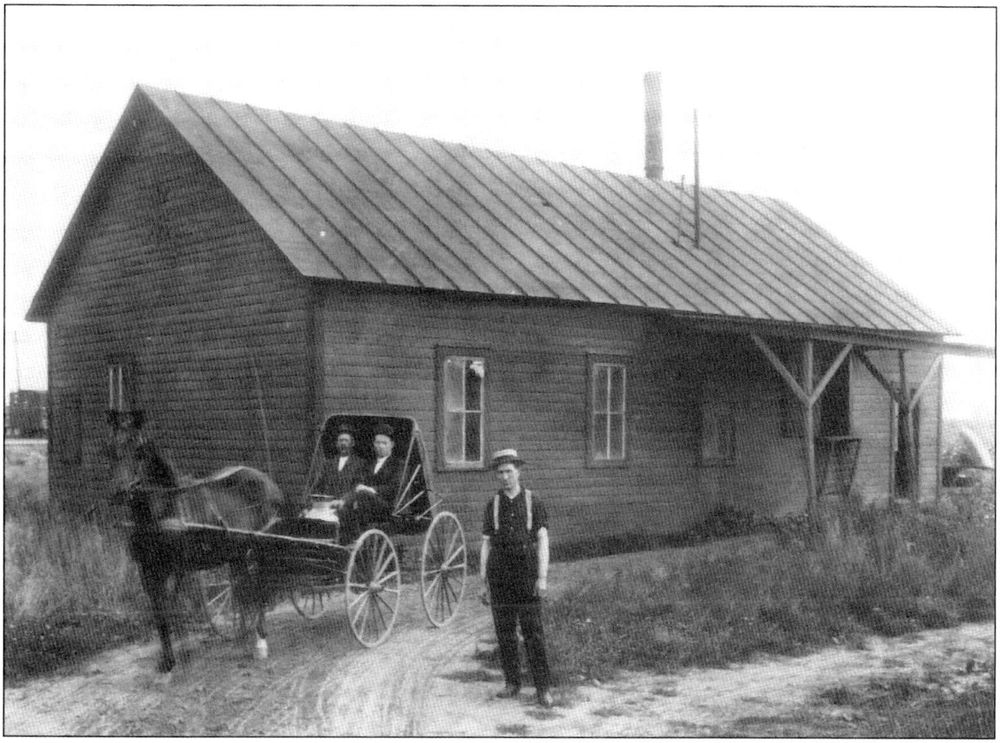

CLOVERLEAF CREAMERY COMPANY. About 1892, William Calhoun stands in front of the creamery as customers sit in their carriage with a jug of milk. Delivering the milk to the creamery was a daily task that had to be performed promptly. Most every community had a creamery by the turn of the 20th century. Located in Holloway, George Holloway was the owner of this business.

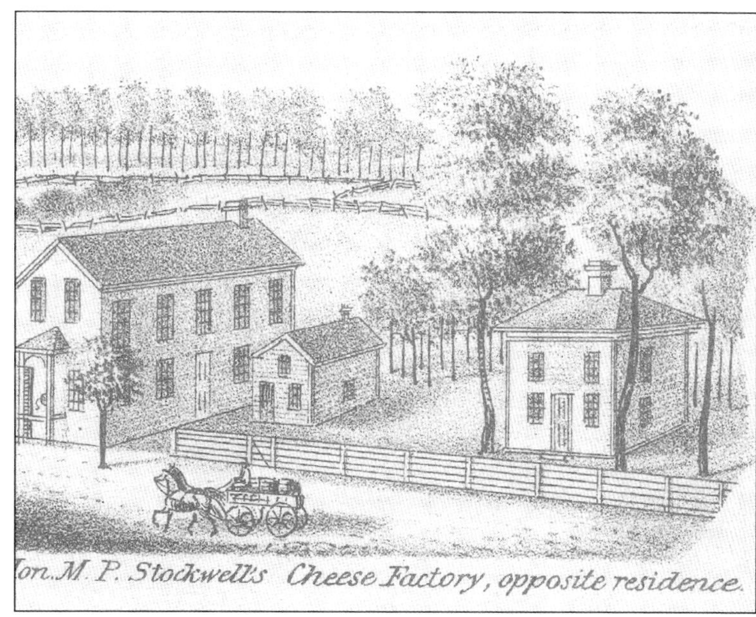

STOCKWELL'S CHEESE FACTORY. Located in Dover Township, the Stockwells began with a small farm and a log house in 1856. They established the Dover Center Cheese Farm in 1869 and operated it until 1883. Their success was illustrated by their beautiful home, which was built in 1856, and by what had become a 290-acre farm.

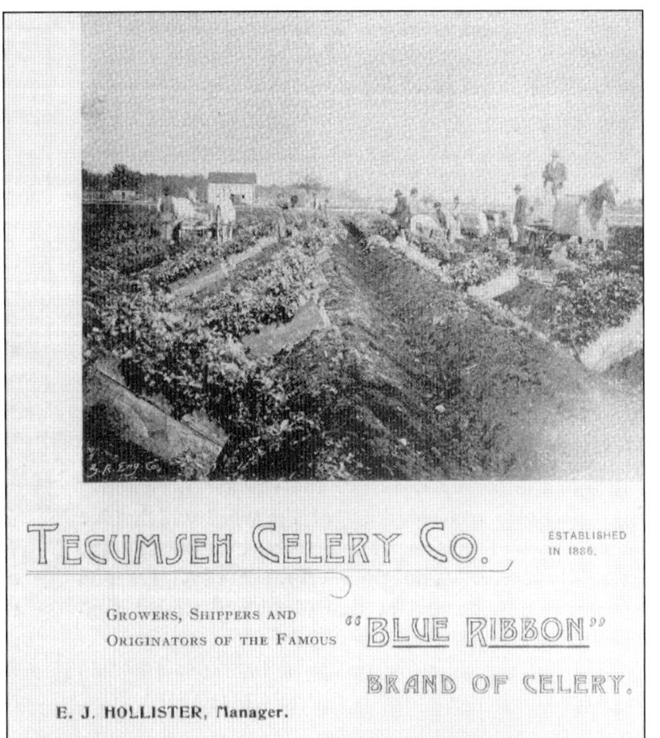

TECUMSEH CELERY COMPANY. Established in 1886, the Tecumseh Celery Company advertised as "Growers, shippers and originators" of their unique blue-ribbon brand of celery. E.J. Hollister was the manager of the company. (Courtesy of the Tecumseh Area Historical Museum.)

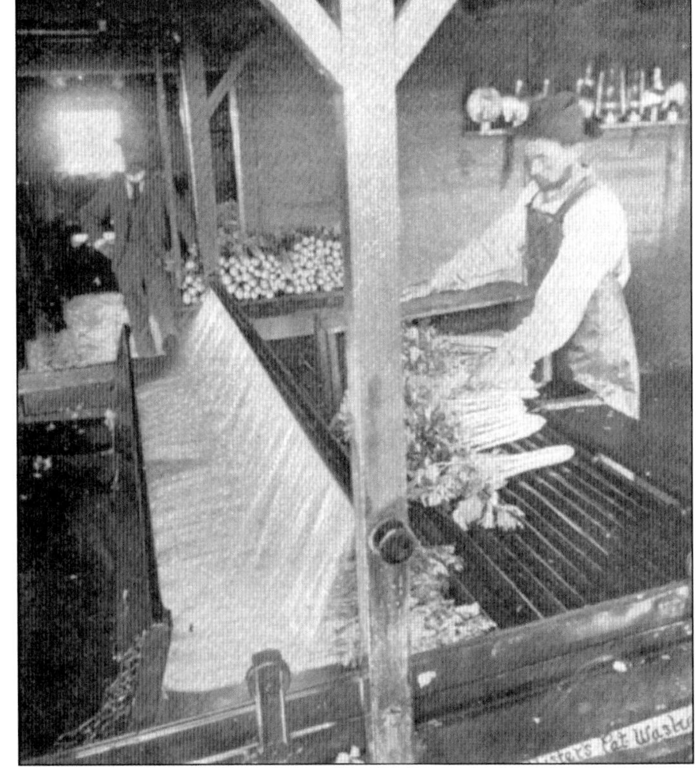

TECUMSEH CELERY WASHER. This photograph from the Tecumseh Celery Company shows the process of thoroughly rinsing the bundles of celery, preparing them for market. (Courtesy of the Tecumseh Area Historical Museum.)

THE PRAIRIE SIDE CELERY CO.

. . . TECUMSEH, MICH.

ESTABLISHED, 1893.

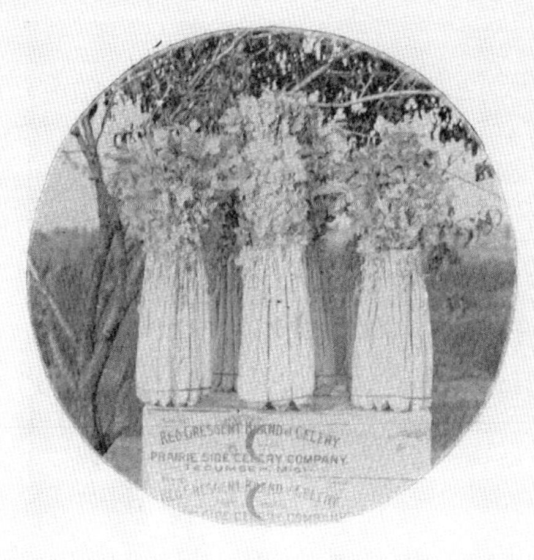

Producers of the Celebrated

Red Crescent Brands of Celery.

Unequaled for . . .
CRISPNESS, FLAVOR AND BEAUTY.

20

PRAIRIE SIDE CELERY COMPANY. Also located in Tecumseh, the Prairie Side Celery Company was established in 1893. The Red Crescent Celery brand was grown on their farm. (Courtesy of the Tecumseh Area Historical Museum.)

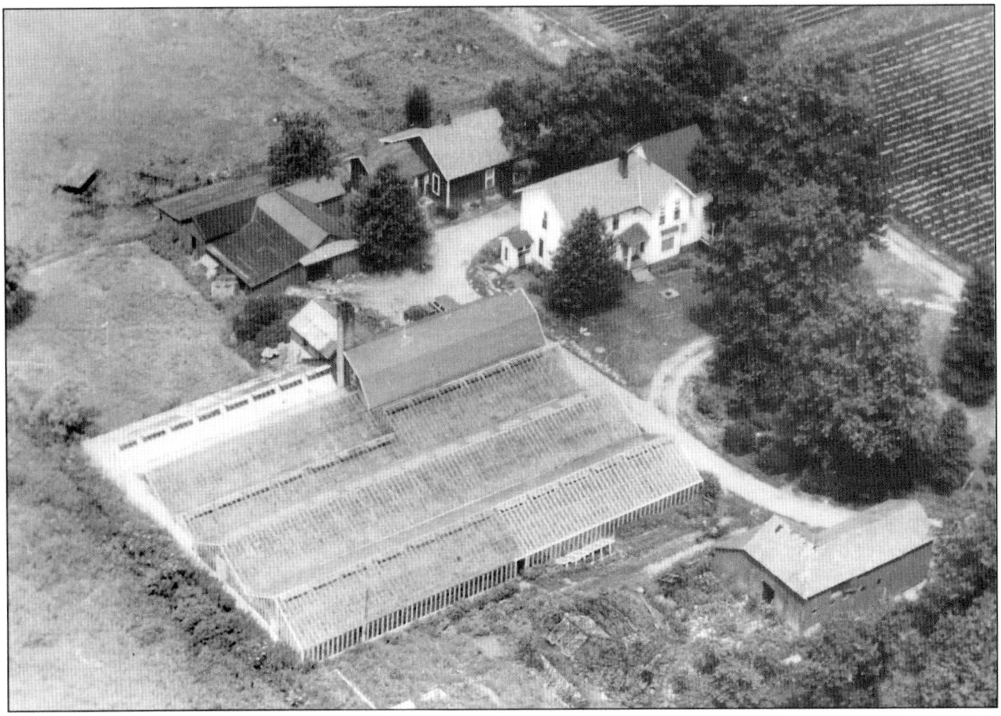

ORSON LOVELAND GREENHOUSE AND CELERY FARM. For over a century, nearly everyone in the area had a celery patch; they are even marked on old maps. This farm, once located on East Carlton Road just west of Ogden in Palmyra Township, provided an abundance of celery for market.

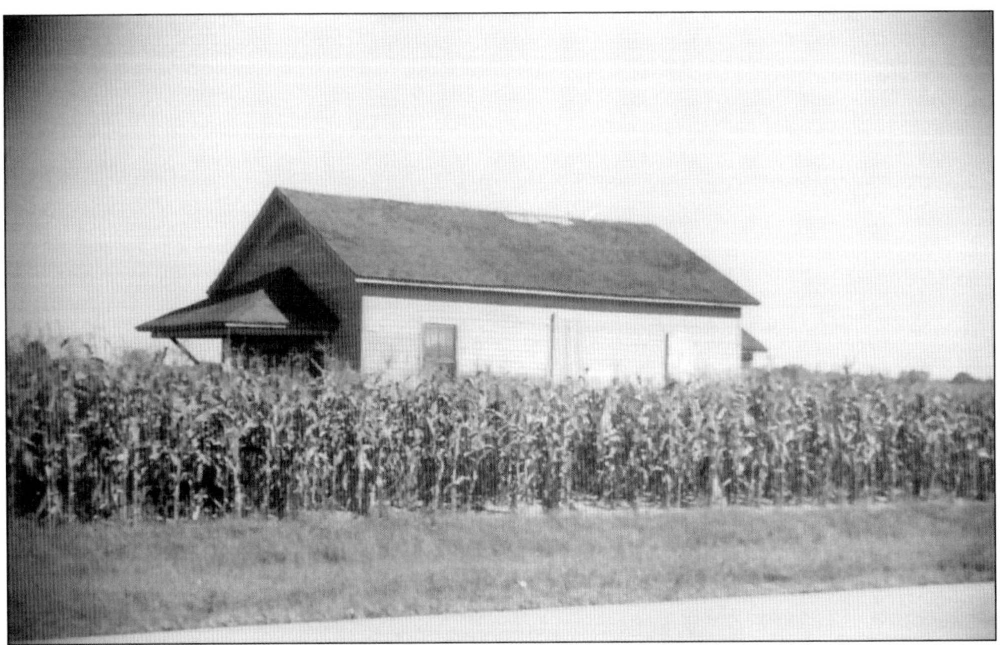

MEDINA BEAN PATCH. This small bean patch in Medina Township may appear to be more of a garden than a farm. Many families produced crops in smaller quantities to meet their needs, with perhaps some left over for market.

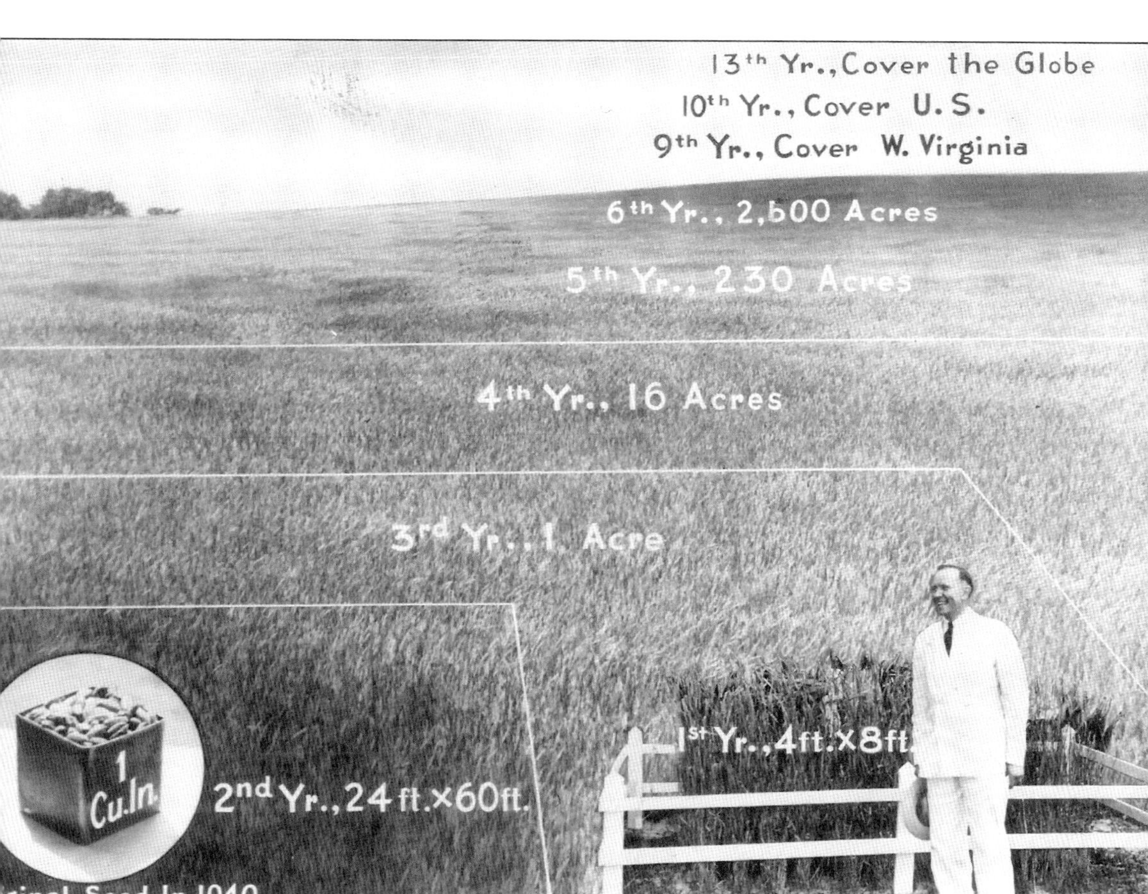

Perry Hayden Dynamic Kernel. On September 26, 1940, Perry Hayden planted a small wheat field, a four-by-eight-foot spaded garden, in which he planted one cubic inch of seed— exactly 360 kernels of certified Bald Rock soft red winter wheat. The first harvest netted 50 cubic inches of kernels, or 18,000 kernels. The project drew interest, bringing crowds each year to the planting and harvest. One tenth of the kernels were tithed to the church by Hayden, with the rest being planted each year. The project was to continue its cycle for six years.

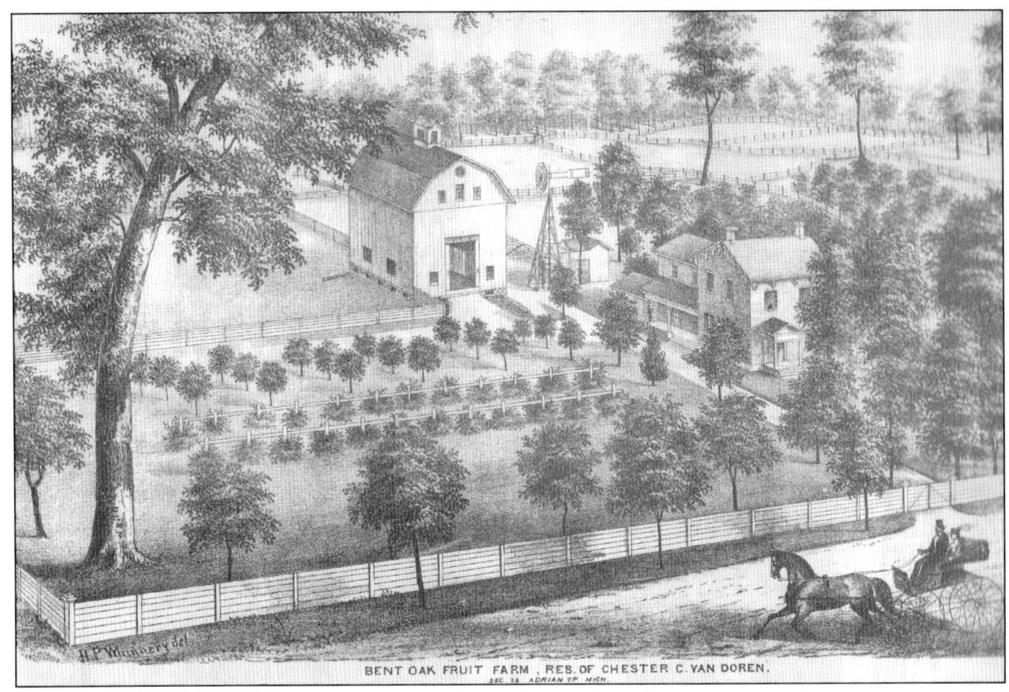

BENT OAK FRUIT FARM. It was customary for settlers to have fruit trees on their property within the first year or two of relocating. Whether buying trees to plant for fruit for market or home consumption, the Bent Oak Fruit Farm in Adrian Township provided convenience for many.

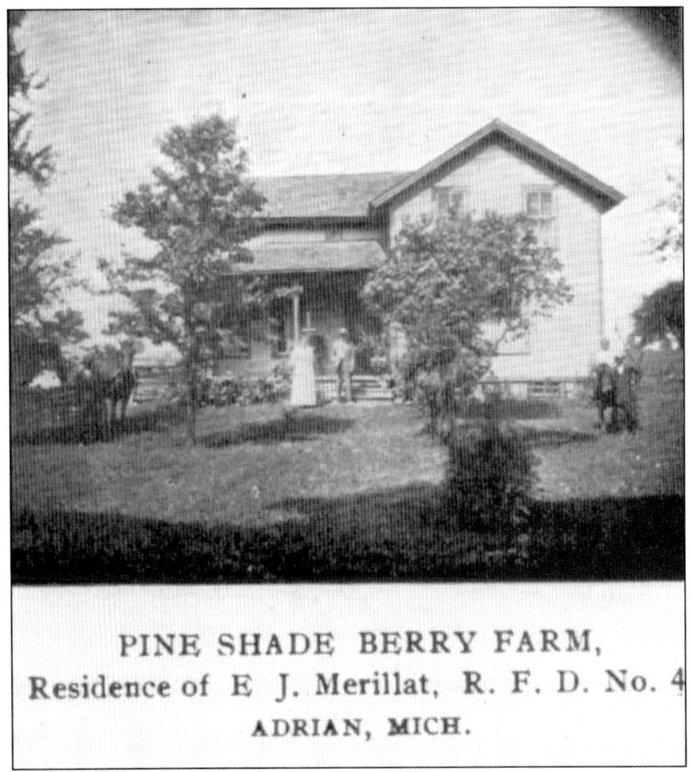

PINE SHADE BERRY FARM. Providing berry crops for local markets as well as canning companies became a very valuable industry. Although many families still made their own preserves, mass production was reaching this market, creating a need for many crops, even berries. Pine Shade Berry Farm, also the residence of E.J. Merrilatt, was located in Adrian.

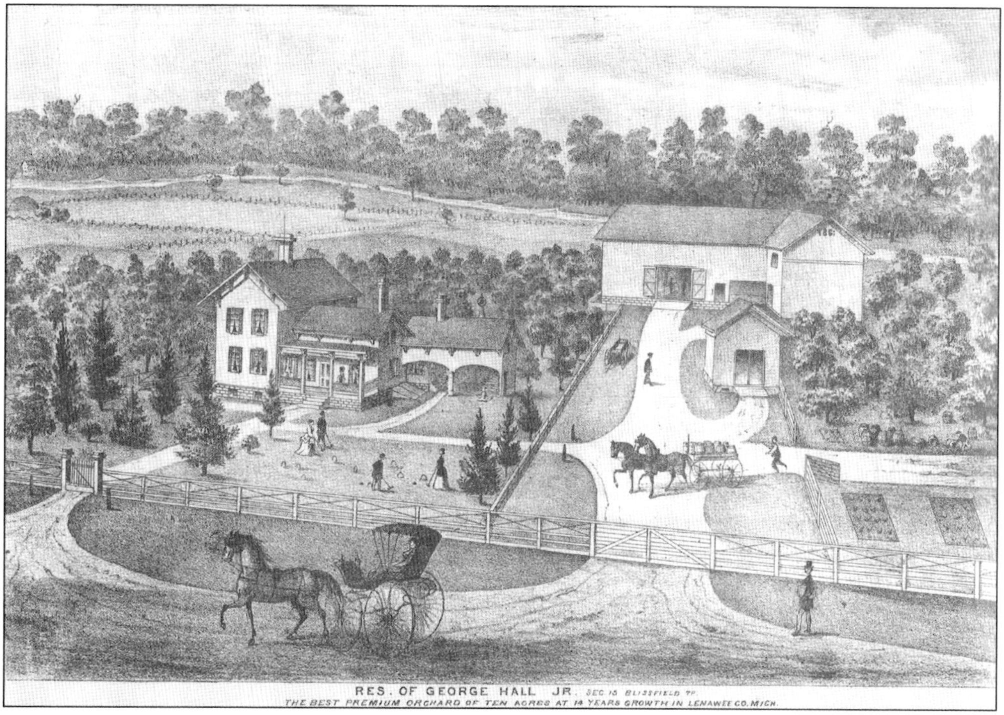

BEST PREMIUM ORCHARD. Advertising 14 years of quality orchard products, the Best Premium Orchard in Blissfield provided a plentiful variety of fruits to the market.

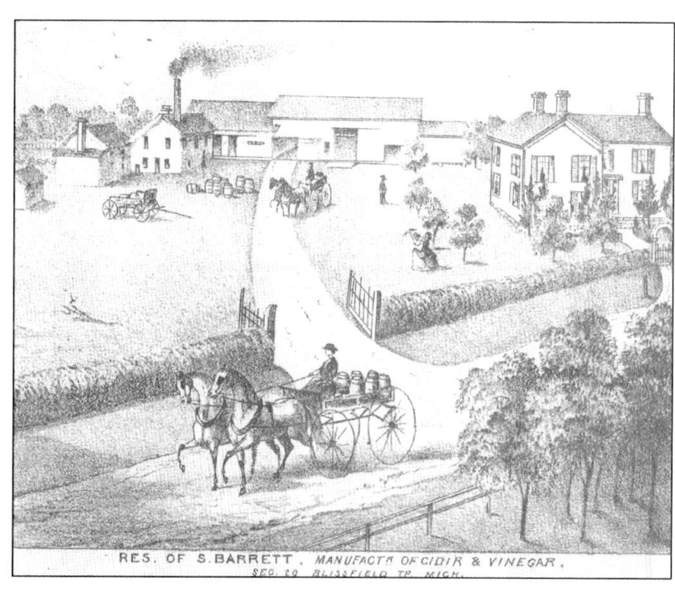

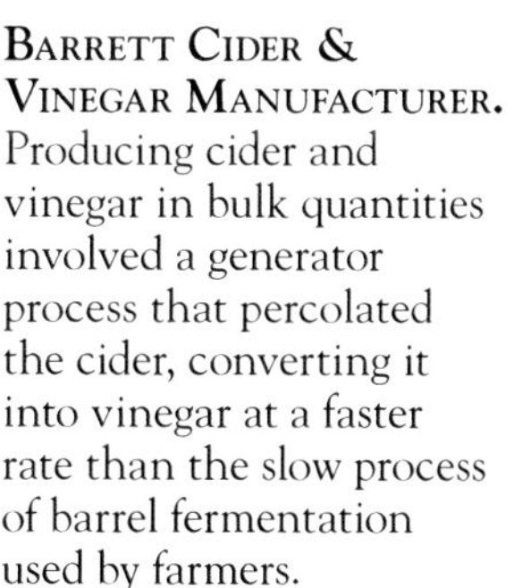

BARRETT CIDER & VINEGAR MANUFACTURER. Producing cider and vinegar in bulk quantities involved a generator process that percolated the cider, converting it into vinegar at a faster rate than the slow process of barrel fermentation used by farmers.

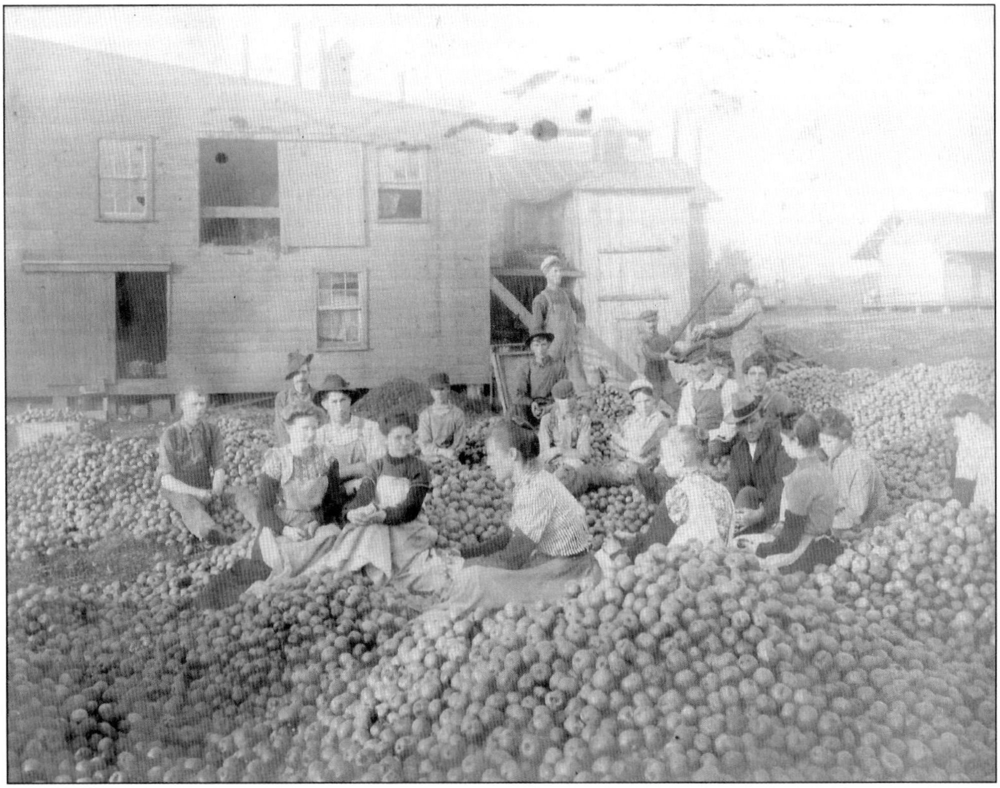

Addison Canning Company. Workers pose in the apples outside of the Addison Canning Company. Tomatoes and apples were processed at this facility, which was located on the northwest shore of the Addison Mill Pond.

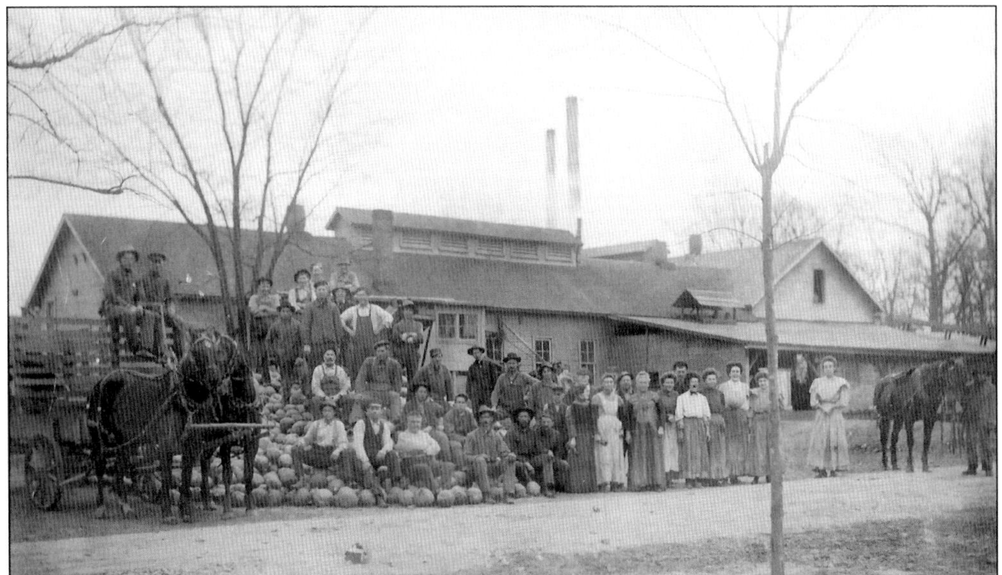

Blissfield Dryer House. Unlike tomatoes and other soft produce, which required gentler care, pumpkins were merely dumped outside the dryer house for workers to sort through. Posing with the pumpkins is the staff of the dryer house.

Six

LOCAL FARMS

Pioneers arrived with the intention of creating a future for themselves and their families. A family tradition was established for many, as is shown by the number of Centennial Farms in Lenawee County. After 100 years of continued agricultural usage through the same family, a property owner may apply to the Michigan Centennial Farm Association. With such devotion to family tradition, Lenawee has held a higher number of Centennial Farms than any other county in the state for many years. Even when a property comes under new ownership, renovation of the buildings or the home and improvements in the fields can often be seen.

Lenawee emerged from acres of untouched land to become a county consisting of three cities, eight villages, and twenty-two townships. Memories and artifacts of the frontier settlements and pioneering traditions are held close to many hearts. Many of the pioneers were farmers or were raised on farms, yet migrating west meant learning how to be a frontier farmer, starting with untouched ground. Most began with a log cabin and a garden patch to sustain them through their first year, eventually expanding to a field of plentiful crops. Later, they would have a cow, chickens, a sheep, or pigs, and even bees to pollinate the fruit trees and vegetables as well as provide honey. With a small orchard and a garden to provide food for themselves, they could run a self-sufficient farm.

The ways to trade apples for oranges and many other swap-meet methods developed quickly as the population grew. Then came the time when the farmers had to become businessmen. Money was a necessity, as civilization developed around them. Methods of crop improvement began in the 1800s, and with the development of the Dairy and Food Commission, inspections were made to grade the quality of produce and ensure healthy standards. As standards and regulations were created throughout the years, the Lenawee farmers worked harder. Many farms have shut down, as later generations lost interest in carrying on the tradition, yet many substantial farms continue to operate.

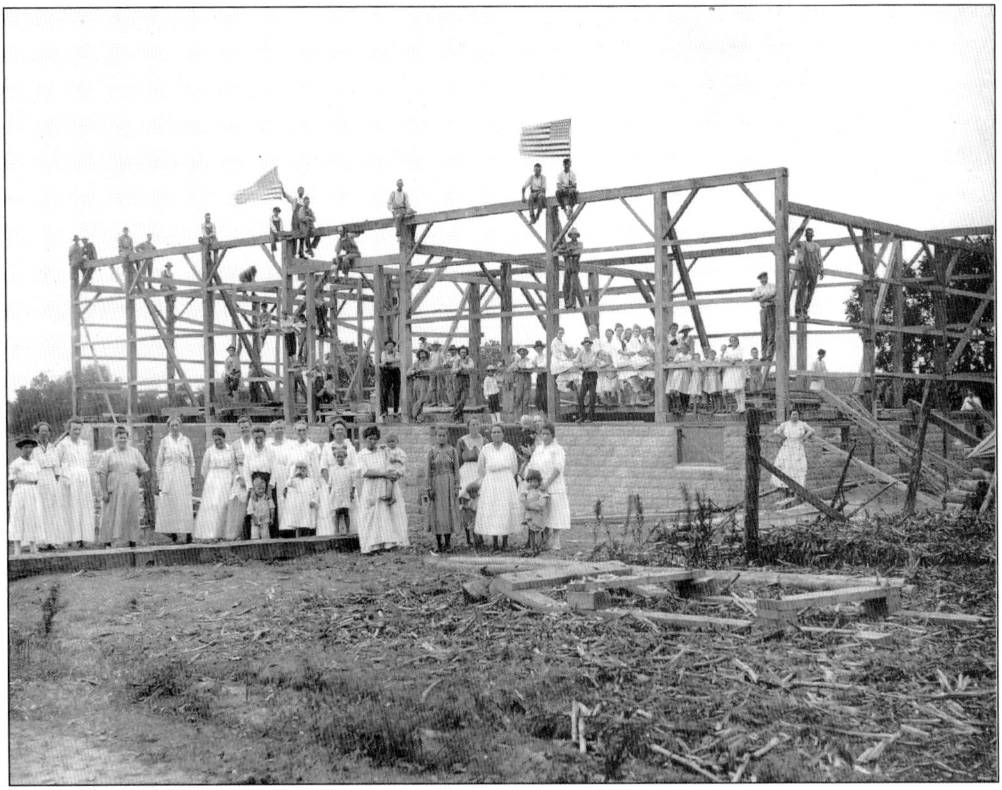

McClenethen Family Barn Raising, c. 1910. At the end of another hard day's work, the McClenethen family is shown in front of the frame of their new barn on East Horton Road in Ogden Township. This building was known as Dwelling No. 233 at the time of this photograph. James G. McClenethen married Jane E. Richey in 1856. (Courtesy of the Winzeler family.)

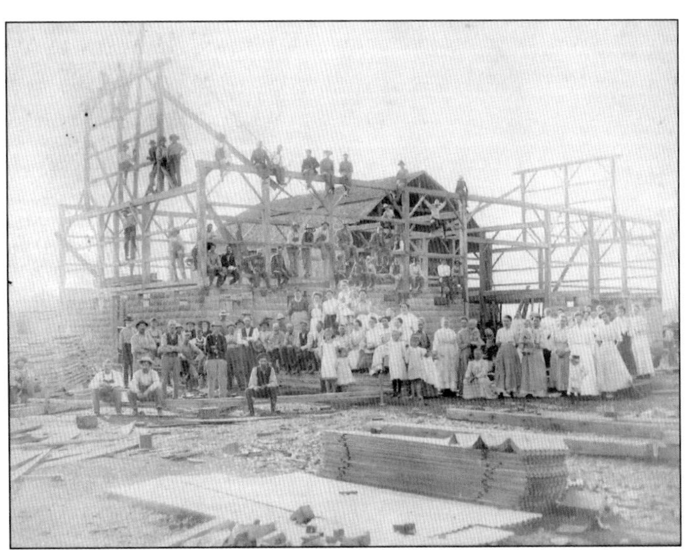

McClenethen Family Barn. The McClenethens owned a parcel of 40 acres on East Horton Road in Ogden Township. Although the property has changed hands throughout the years, the barn shown in this photograph is still standing and has been a part of yet another family farm on the same 40 acres for over 50 years. (Courtesy of the Winzeler family.)

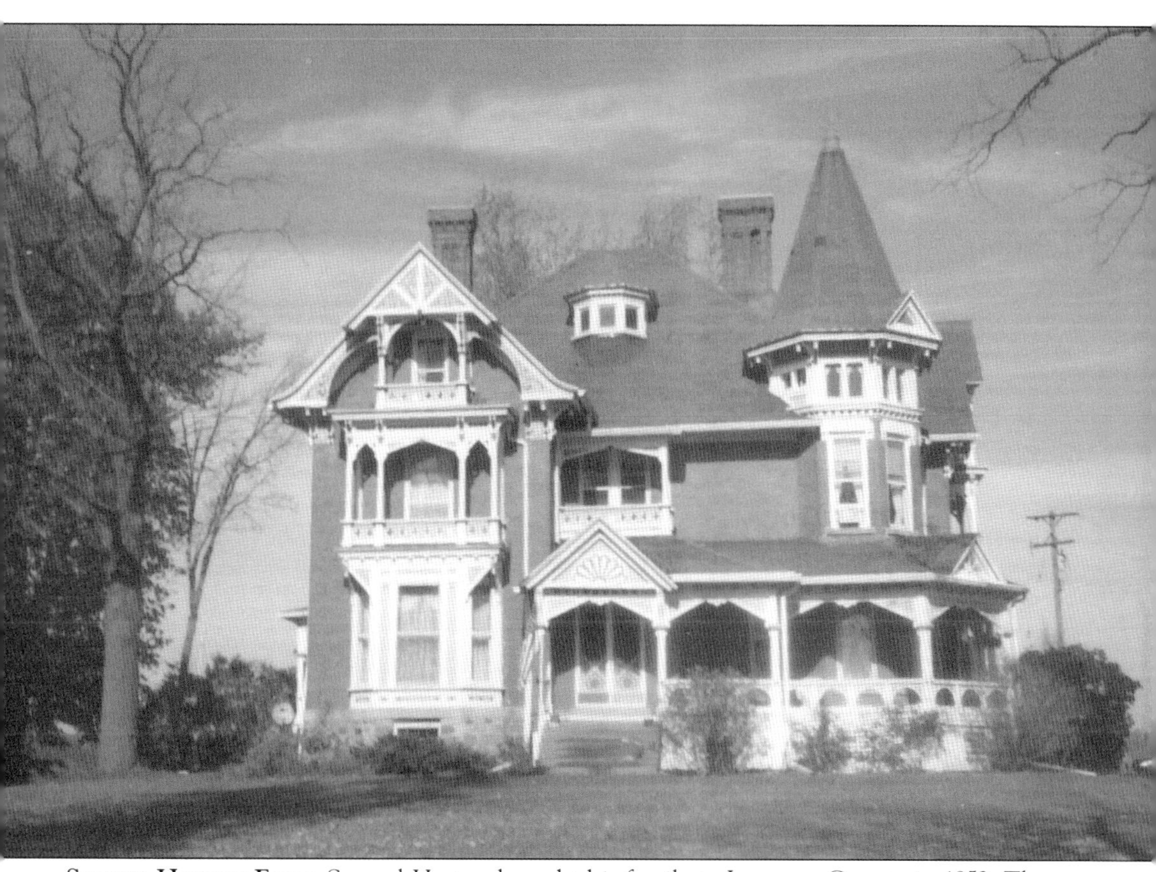

Samuel Horton Farm. Samuel Horton brought his family to Lenawee County in 1852. They purchased a farm in Fairfield Township and began manufacturing cheese by 1853. They were the first family to establish cheese manufacturing in Lenawee. Samuel's wife, Lucinda, was the cheesemaker, implementing a unique recipe for New York–style soft cheese. In 1866, Samuel established the second cheese factory in Lenawee County. He and Lucinda had three children: Alice, George B., and Harriett. They began with 10 cows on their farm, and due to their success, they owned 469 acres of land and 50 cows and operated two cheese factories at the time Samuel passed away on April 25, 1872. George B. took over the business after his father's passing.

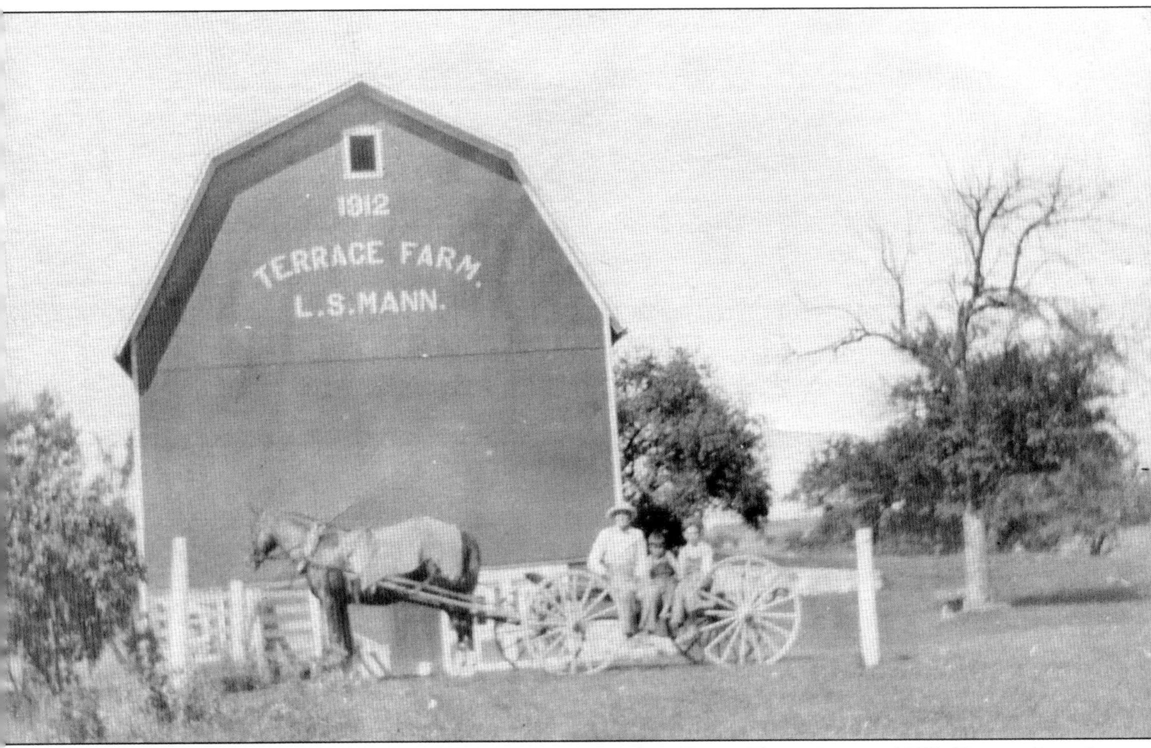

LEONARD S. MANN FARM. Daniel Mann Sr. arrived in Rome Township in 1835. He purchased property, cleared the land, and prepared it for farming by himself. In 1839, he married Anna Stoddard, and together they raised six children: Loretta, Charles, Daniel, George, Phillip, and Leonard.

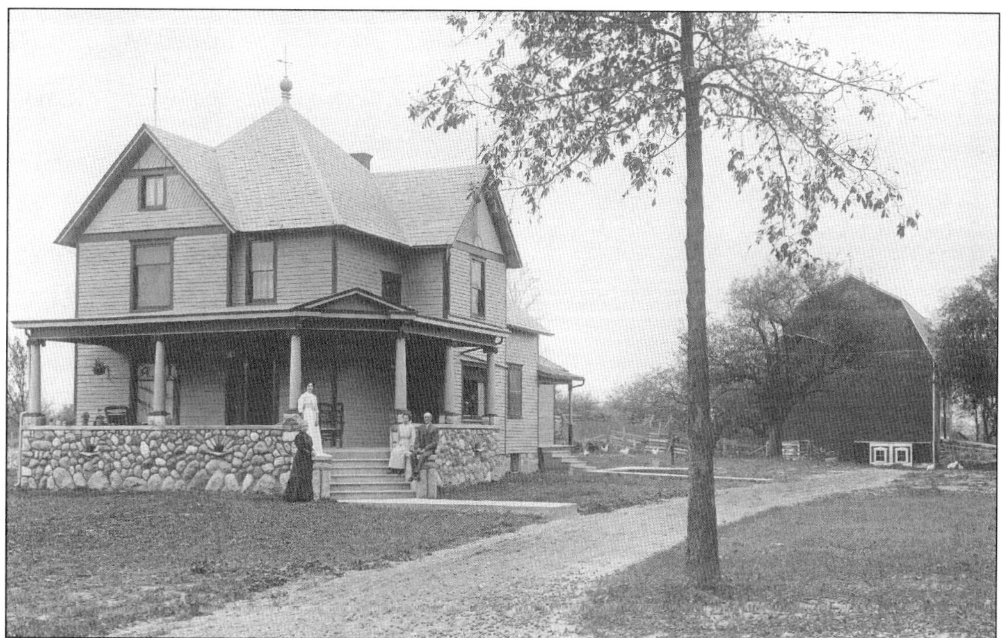

Leonard and Carrie Mann Farm. This is a front view of the home built by Daniel Mann on Brooks Highway in Rome Township. Mann expanded his farm to include 275 acres. Several outbuildings were placed on the land, as well as the fine frame house shown here. Leonard—the youngest son of Daniel and his wife, Lucinda—and his wife, Carrie, had inherited the farm by the time this photograph was taken.

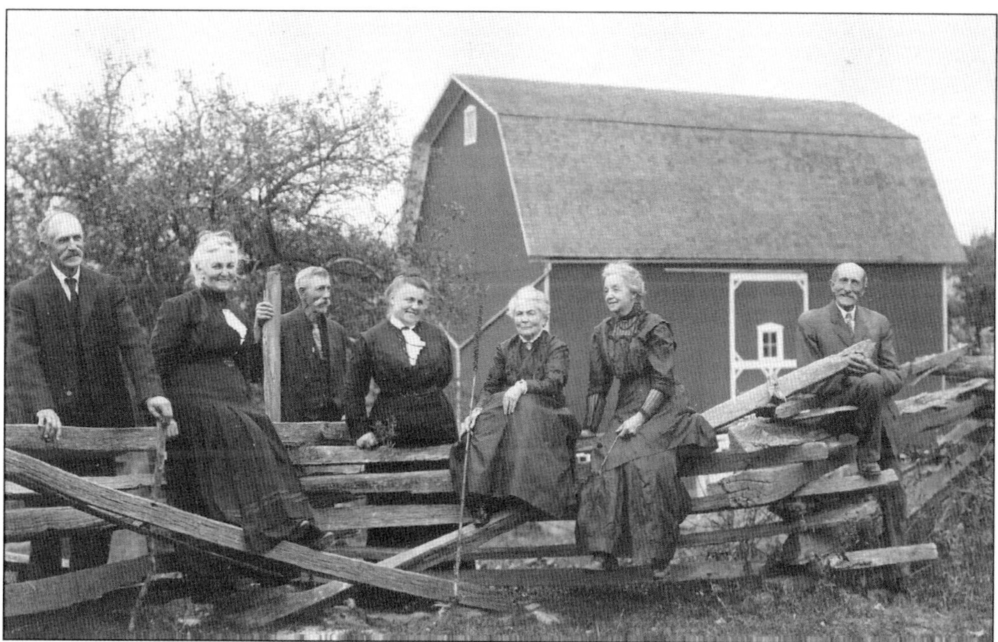

Mann Family. Leonard and Carrie Mann are on the far right in this family photograph taken on the Mann Farm.

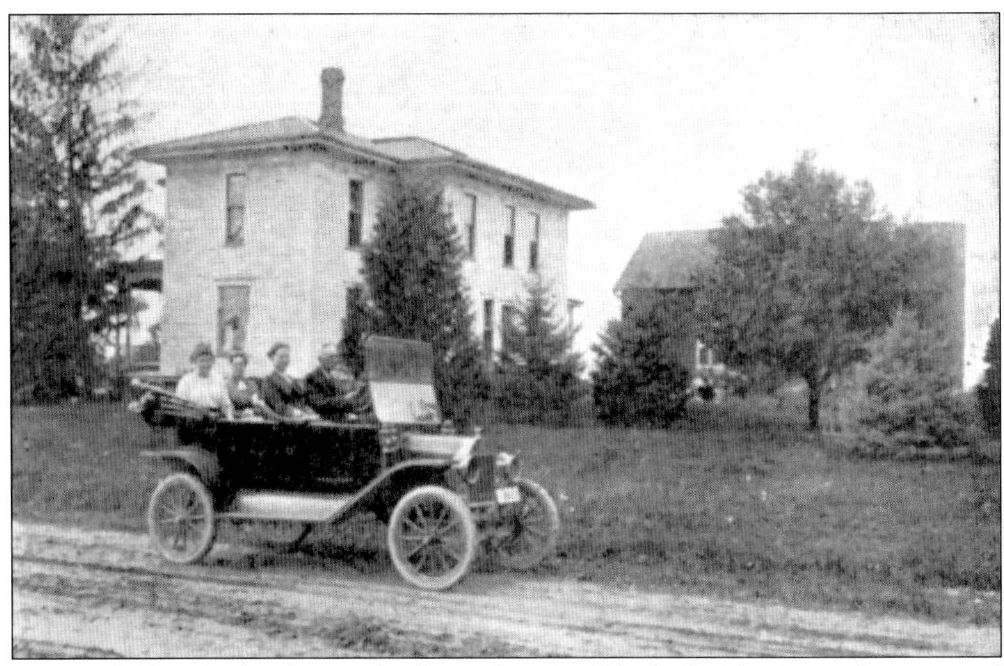

LUCRETIA L. BEAL. In this photograph taken in the early 1900s, the Beal family is in their motorized vehicle in front of their home on the 400 block of Townsley Road. The Beal family, which extends back to the pioneer days of Lenawee County, has played a significant role in local history.

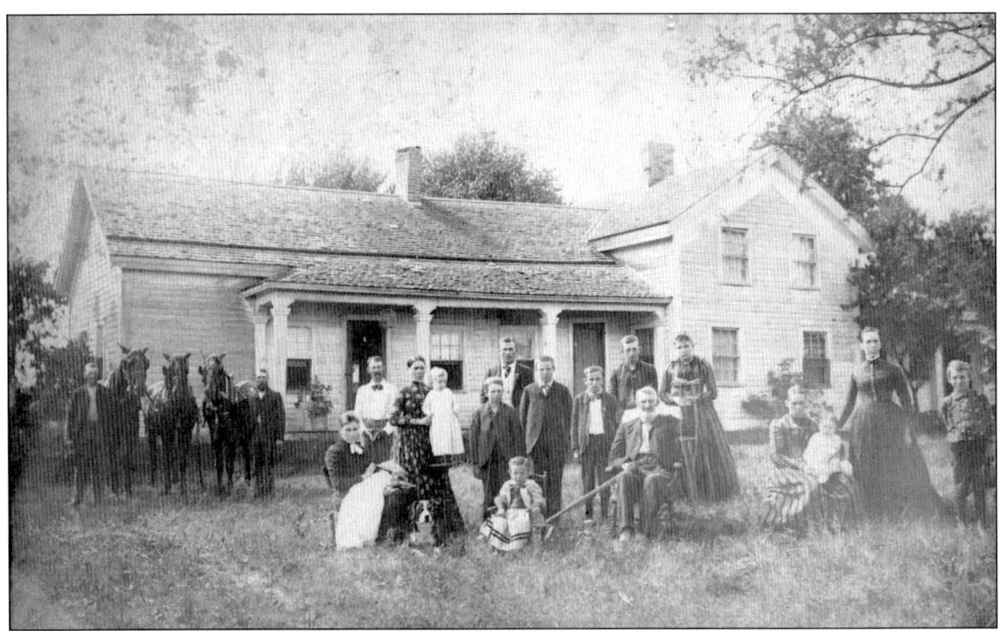

JUDSON FAMILY FARM. This photograph shows the Judson family reunion in 1899 at the Frank V. Judson farm. The property adjoined the Raisin Center Church.

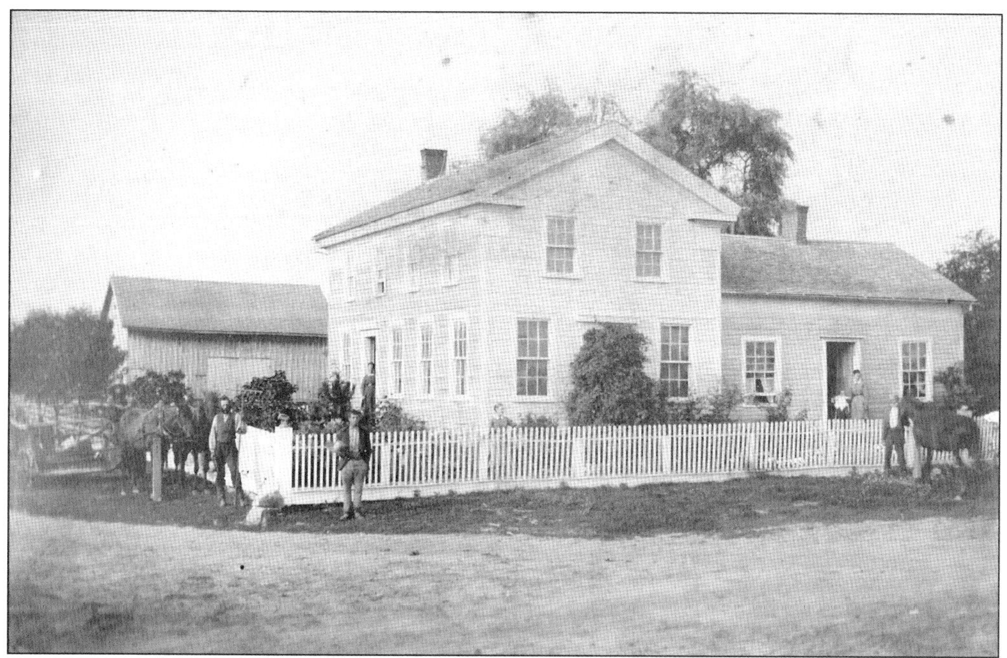

Charles A. Murphy Residence. Serving as a home to the Murphy family throughout the late 1800s, this property in Rollin Township was destroyed during the Palm Sunday tornado on April 11, 1965. It was a horrific day filled with devastation and death from the many tornados that moved from Indiana into Michigan.

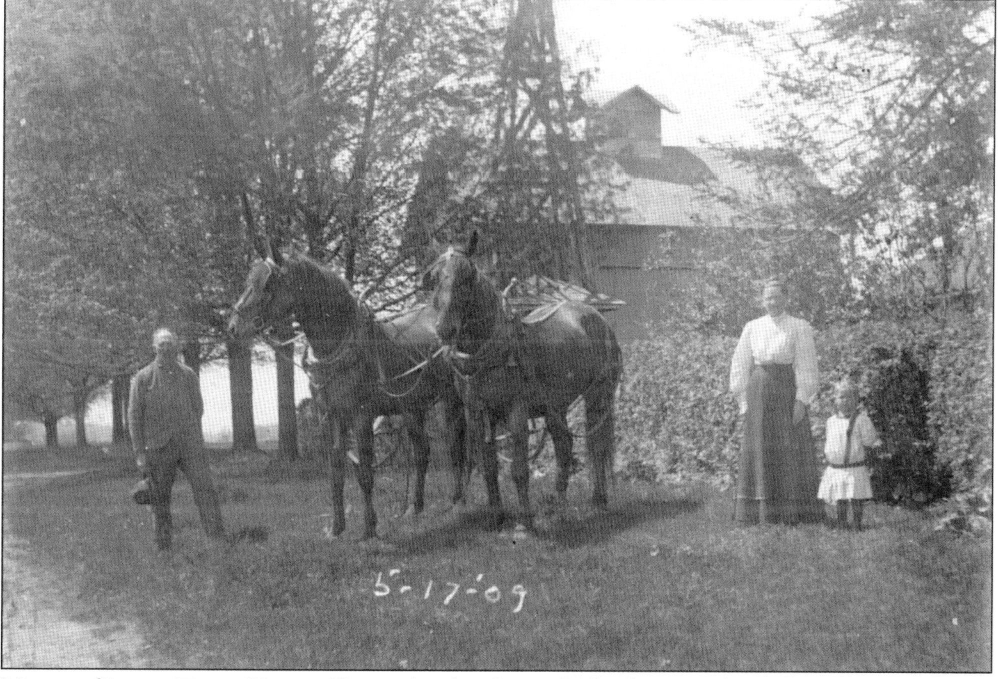

Murphy/Sloan Farm. Emma Sloan, the daughter of Charles Murphy, and her husband, L.L. Sloan, are shown in their rock garden on the family farm. Young Geraldine Rhoads stands next to Emma.

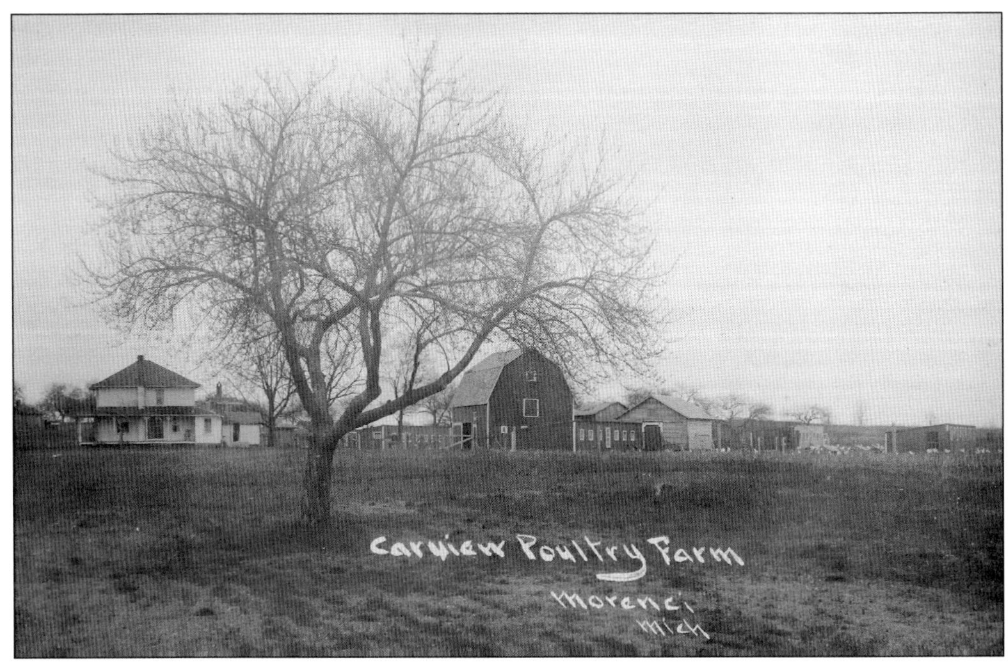

Carview Poultry Farm, Seneca Township. The Carview Farm was a breeder of fine poultry on Weston Road near Morenci. Pictured below is a happy flock of chickens—obviously cage-free—on the Carview Farm.

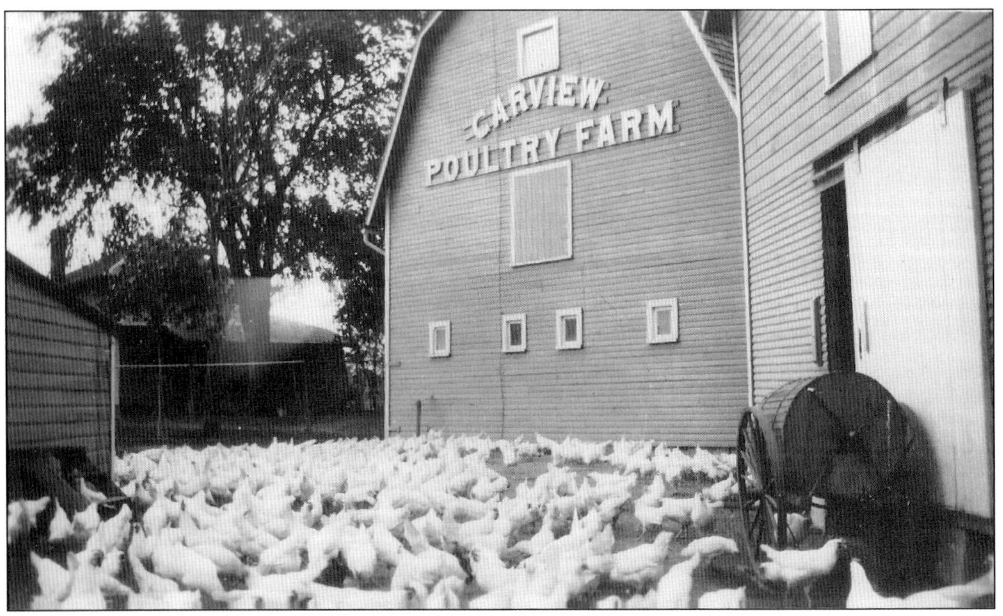

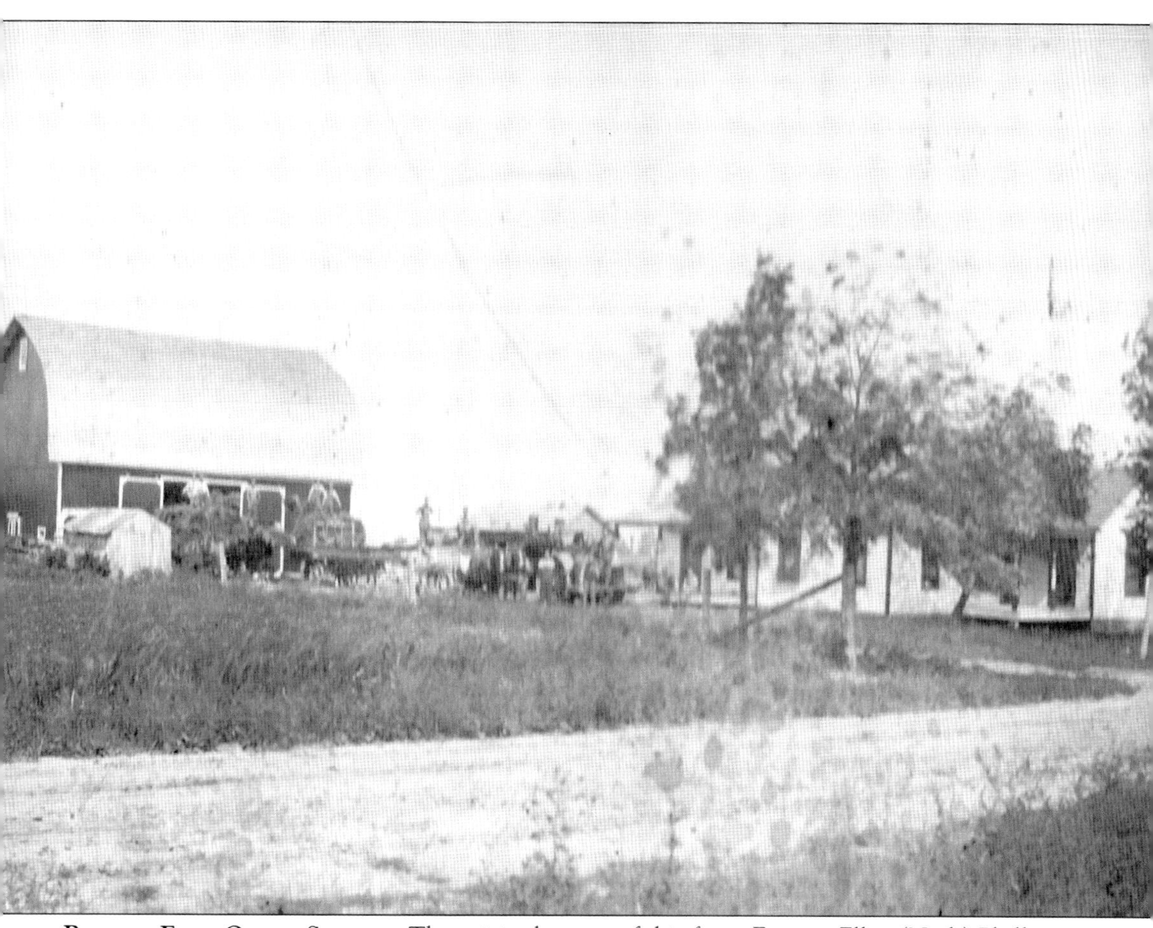

Phillips Farm Ogden Station. The original owner of this farm, Frances Ellen (Nash) Phillips purchased acreage in 1884. In combination with property owned by her husband, Franklin Seymour Phillips, they owned 90 acres in Ogden Township. As a pharmacist, Franklin operated his business from his home, which eventually included a general store and drugstore, post office, railroad ticket and grain agency, telegraph office, the F.S. Telephone line, Bank of F.S. Phillips, and even a funeral parlor. After Franklin Phillips's death in 1906, many of the ventures were closed; however, his daughter Susan Hicks (Phillips) Whittaker ran the general store, post office, and telegraph service while renting out the farmland. Upon her death, the land was divided, leaving 30 acres to Franklin Albert Phillips, who farmed the land with his son-in law Jerry Marlatt; they were the first true farmers of the property. In 2001, Jerry and Lisa Marlatt inherited the property. Renovation was completed in 2003. A daylily business is operated on one acre of the farm, which is recognized as a Michigan Centennial Farm.

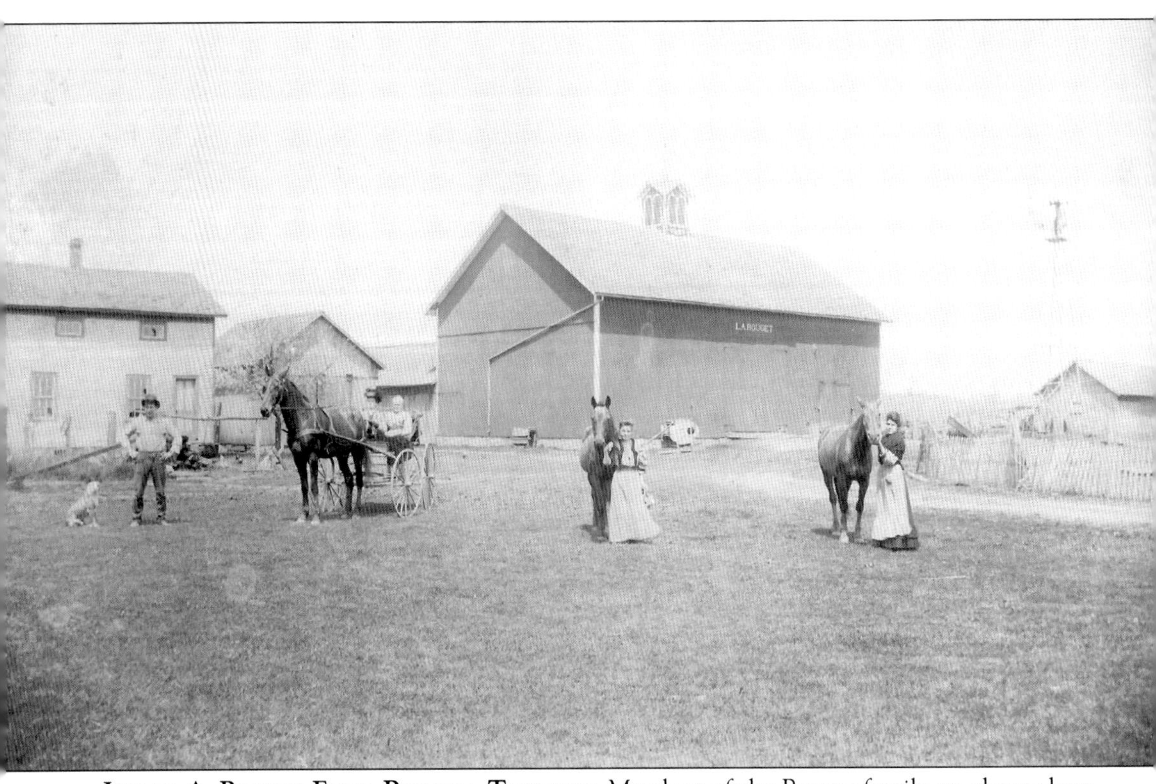

Lester A. Rouget Farm, Palmyra Township. Members of the Rouget family are shown here with their horses in front of the barn. Throughout the late 1800s, Lester and Martha Rouget maintained a farm on Rouget Road east of South Grosvenor Highway in Palmyra Township with their children, William L., Rosa A., and Margaret K.

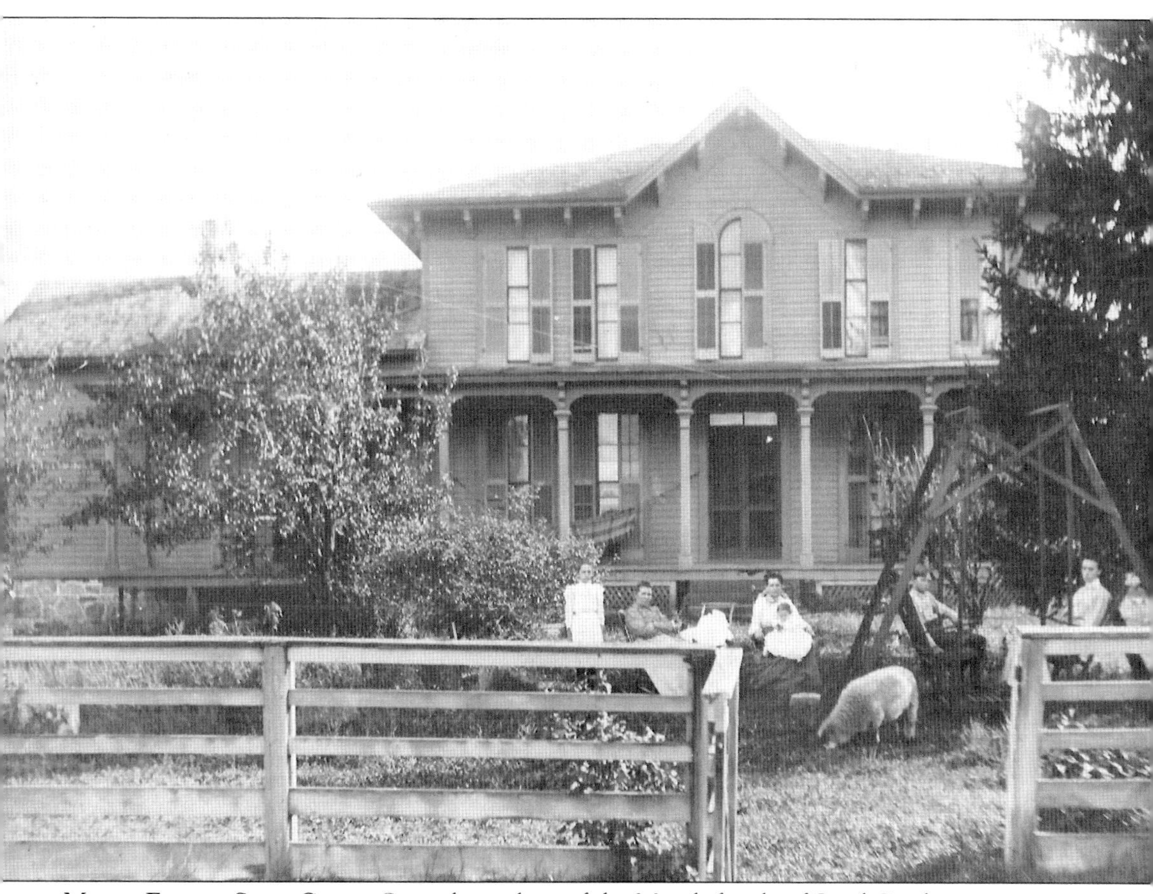

Meech Family, Sand Creek. Several members of the Meech family of Sand Creek are present in this photograph. Even the family sheep is present in the front yard.

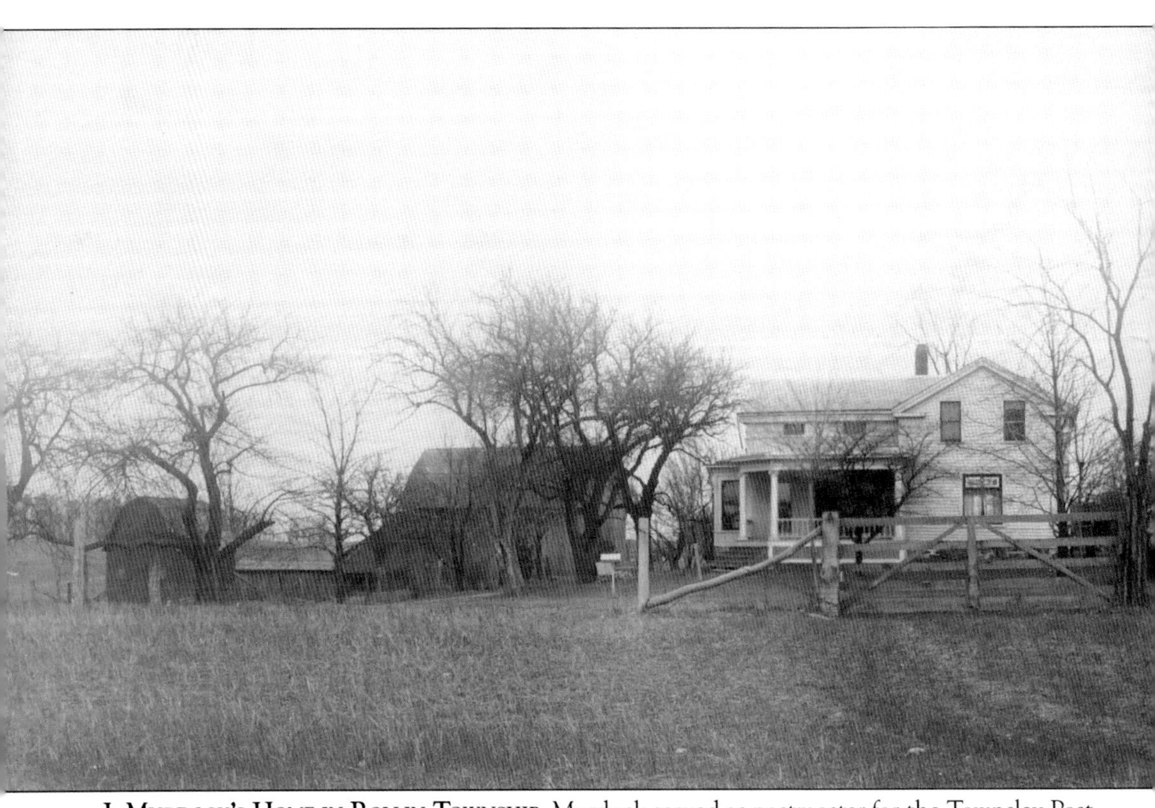

J. Murdock's Home in Rollin Township. Murdock served as postmaster for the Townsley Post Office, which he ran from his home.

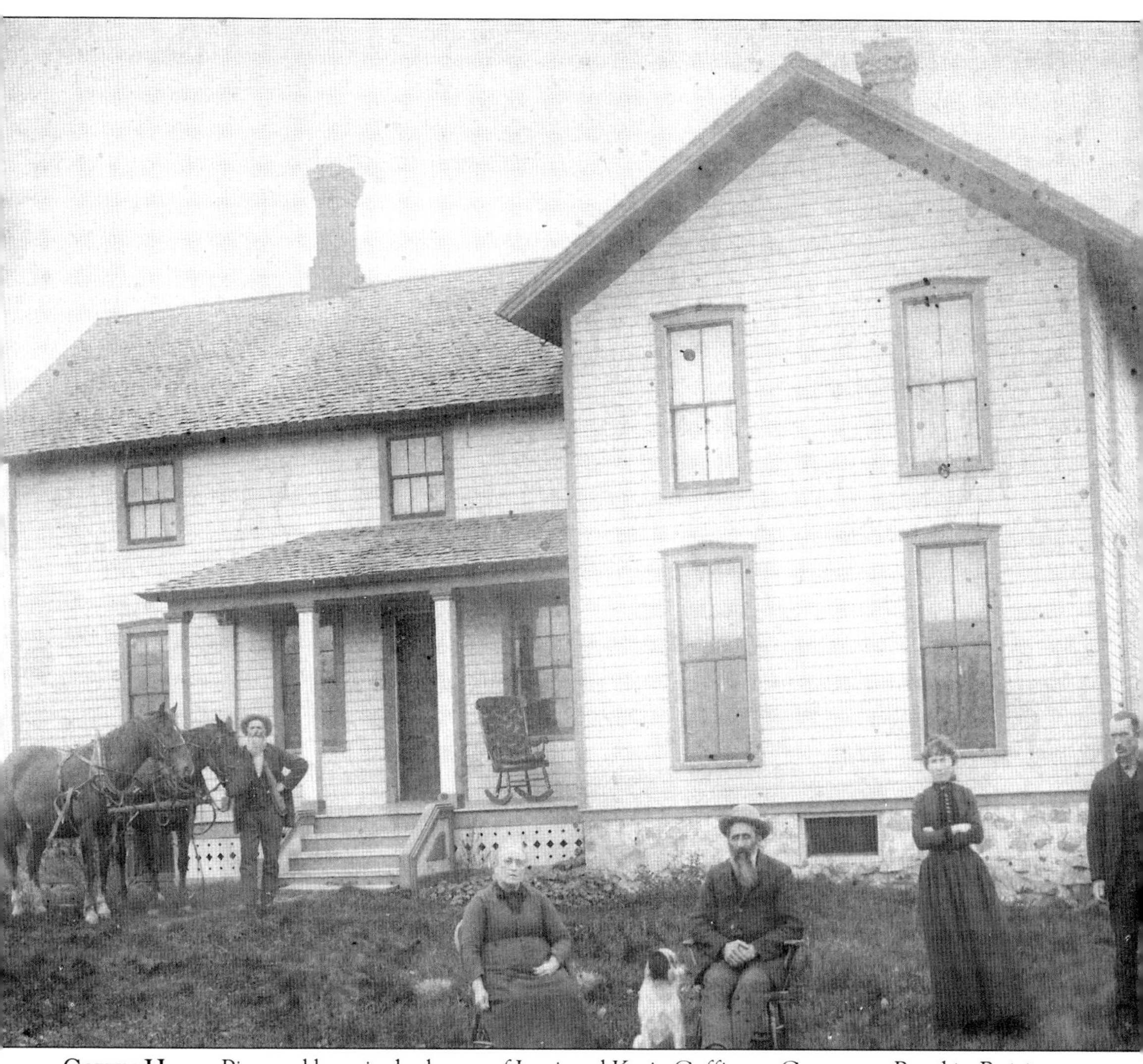

COFFIN HOME. Pictured here is the home of Levi and Katie Coffin on Grosvenor Road in Raisin Township.

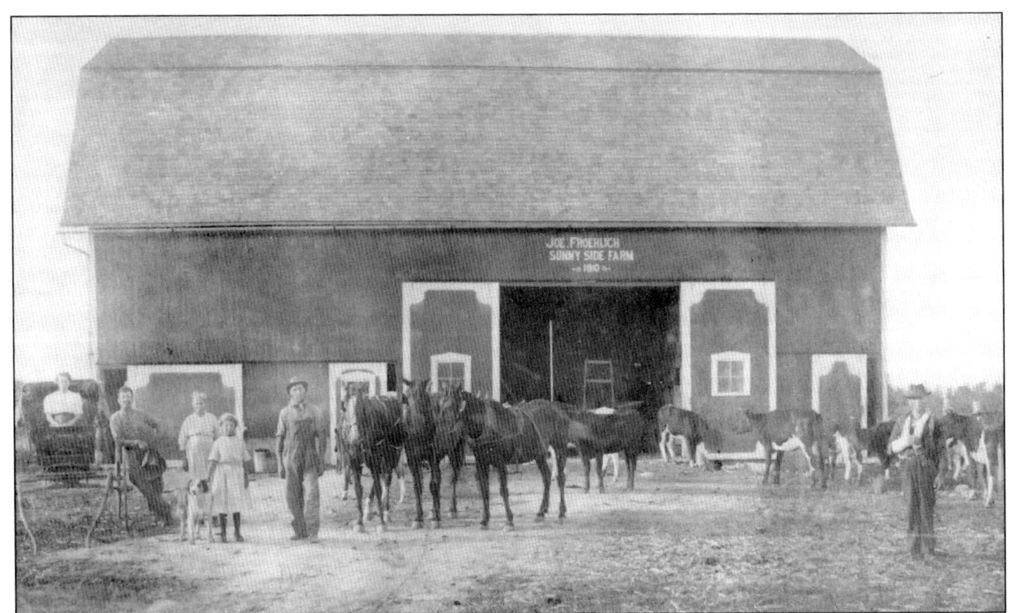

Froehlich Farm. Established in 1910, the Sunny Side Farm, owned by Joe Froehlich, is shown in this photograph.

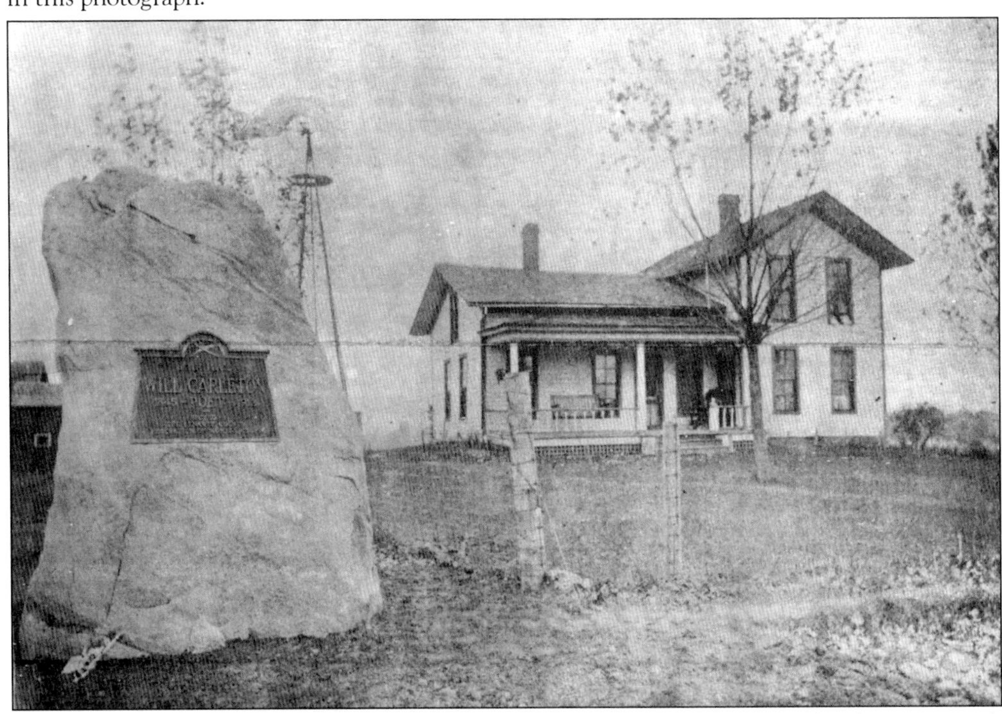

Will Carleton Home, Hudson. This world-famous poet was born to John and Celeste Hancock in 1845 and raised in Hudson. A plaque was placed on a boulder marking the location of their family home on Carleton Road. Will attended a one-room school and graduated from Hillsdale College in 1869. Although poetry was always his primary interest, his first occupation was as a journalist. He wrote about small-town America, county fairs, fields, and farmyards. Locally, October 21 is celebrated as Will Carleton Day in memory of the pioneer poet.

Seven

Grange

The National Grange was created on December 4, 1867, by the US Department of Agriculture with the objective of serving American farmers. Through the creation of a fellowship, the organization strives to improve the socioeconomic structure of communities. Functioning at a national, state, county, and often a more localized level, efforts are made to find the best approach to farming in each region. Sponsoring social activities such as picnics, ball games, and county fairs is a tradition for the organization. Educational projects hold the same level of importance. This organization is recognized as being the first to allow membership by men, women, and children.

In 1873, George Horton introduced the Grange to Lenawee County, with the first being established in Tipton. The Fruit Ridge Grange, originally known as Weston Grange No. 276, was organized on February 10, 1874, through the assistance of George Horton. A Grange hall was built and dedicated in January 1881; at this time, the name was changed to the Fruit Ridge Grange. Sadly, this building was engulfed in flames and destroyed during a Farmer's Institute meeting. By 1889, this subordinate grange held the largest membership in the nation. Horton provided his service as the subordinate master for more than 20 years.

Thirty-four granges had been established in Lenawee County by 1900, with 26 owning their own halls. A history of the Hudson Grange states that it was the center of community livelihood. Following a discussion of good farming technique, there was a supper, followed by square dances, card parties, and entertainment provided by the children. A Grange fair would be held each year for fundraising. Women would dress up in gingham, and exhibits of embroidery, grain, and canned goods were presented. In 1948, the 4 Towns Grange was noted in the local newspaper as celebrating 50 years. Although membership had dwindled, those who remained stated that faith, hope, and perseverance kept them going. The Madison Grange states that members are "called upon to help our community wherever need arises dovetailing our efforts with our customary Grange attitude."

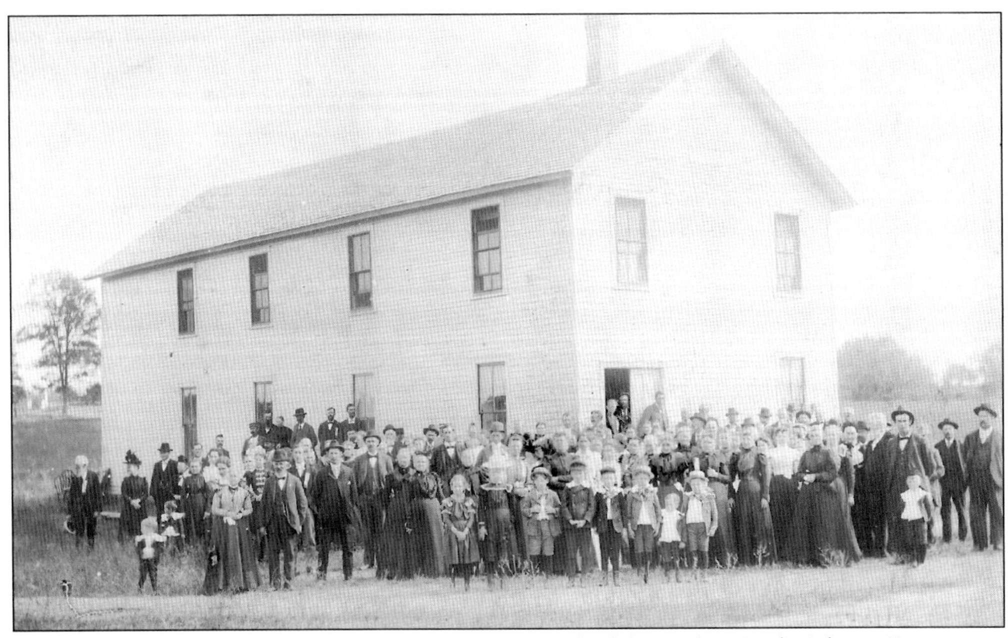

North Adrian Grange. A gathering to dedicate and celebrate the North Adrian Grange was held in the new hall. Obtaining enough members to fund their own hall was always a major accomplishment. Many subordinate Granges held meetings in homes or a business if they did not have their own hall.

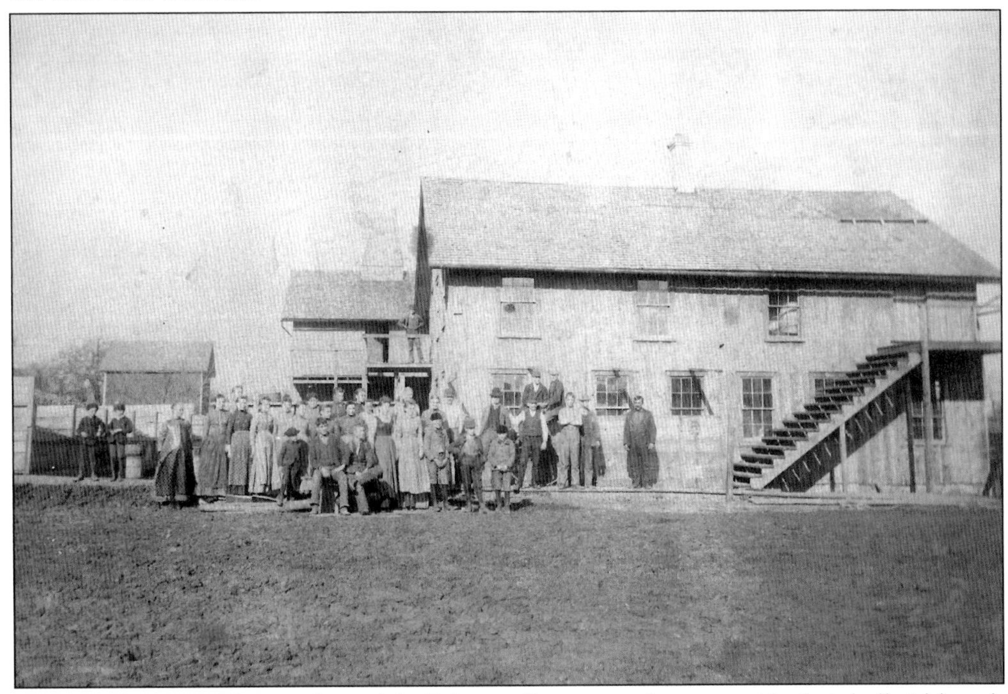

Palmyra Grange. The members of the Palmyra Grange are shown outside their hall. Although the Grange was formed as a fraternal organization, the Order of Patrons of Husbandry, it was among the first organizations to admit women as members. They have always held a vote equal to that of the men.

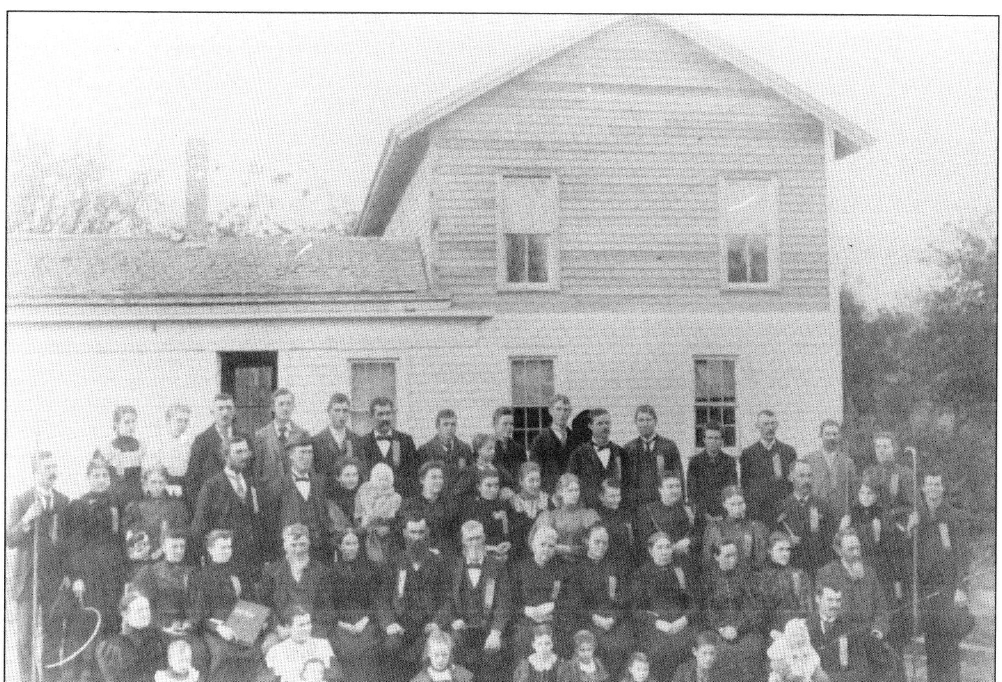

Rome Grange. In 1896, members of all ages are shown in front of the Grange hall in Rome Township. Providing service to others upon the foundation of loyalty and democratic ideals is what the fraternity was based upon. The Rome Grange was organized in 1874.

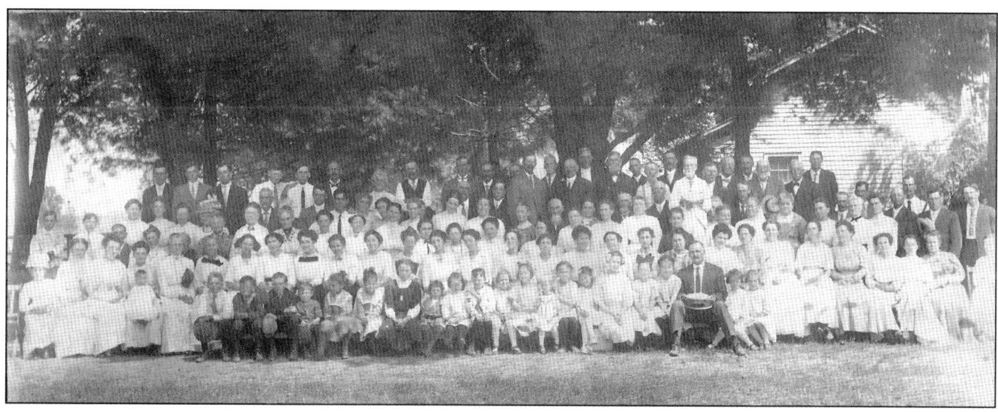

Tecumseh Grange. Members of all ages enjoyed the picnic celebration in 1911 at Devil's Lake. The local Granges were built around the community, allowing men, women, and children of all ages to join. At the age of 14, they were even eligible to vote. Social activities such as picnics allowed the families to be active on a more casual level.

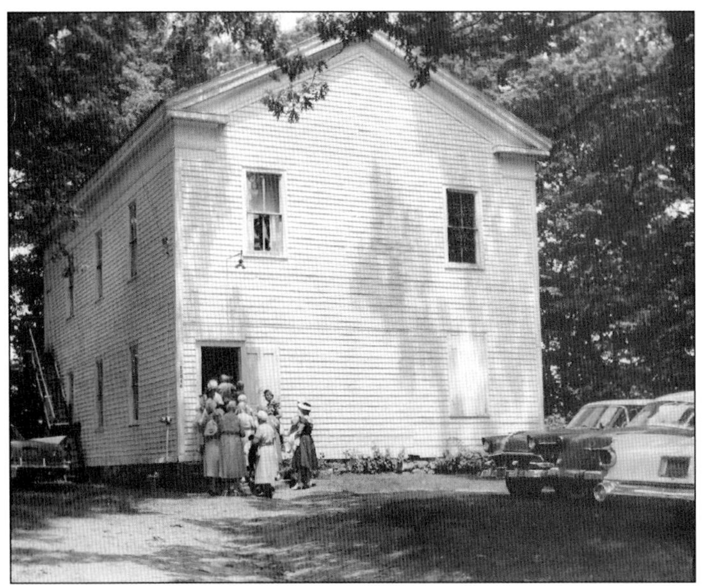

MEDINA GRANGE HALL. With use of the former Medina Academy as a meeting place, members are shown entering the hall for a meeting in 1960. Meetings were for members only; however, educational programs and social activities were often open to the public. The main objectives of the organization—developing leadership, improving community life, and expanding opportunities for all people—were always the focal point.

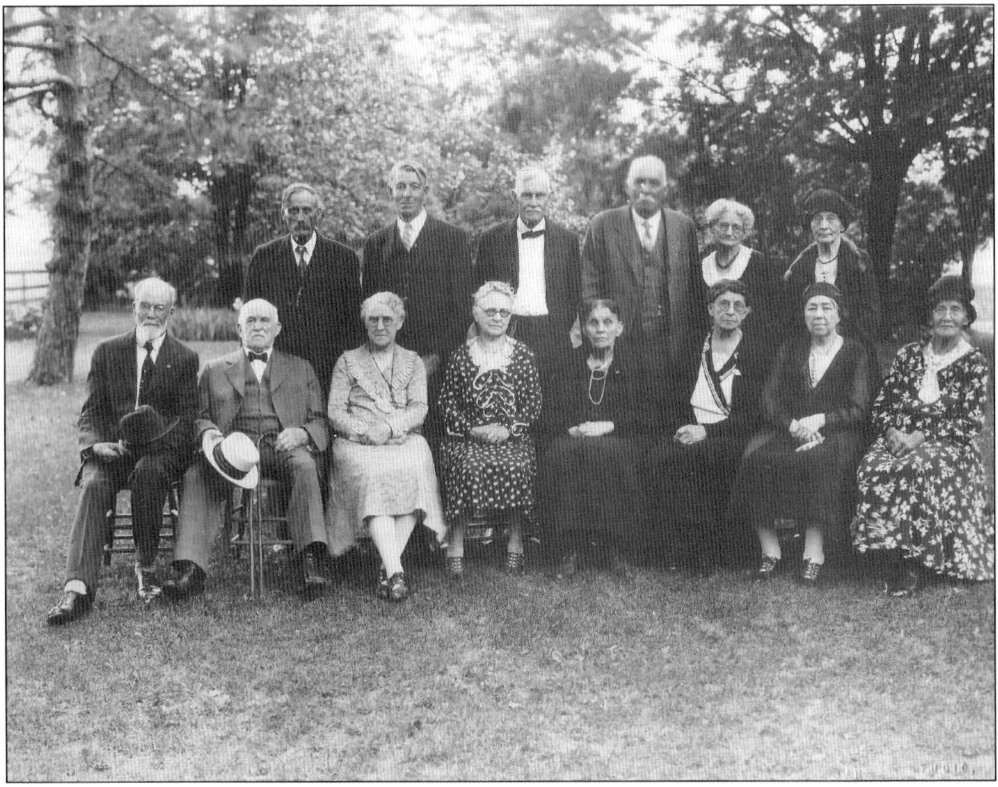

GOLDEN SHEAF CLUB. Taken on Horton Day in 1931 at the George B. Horton home in Fairfield Township, this photograph shows members of the Golden Sheaf Club. These are members who had served the longest with the Grange. Pictured are Adelbert Ward, Chas Cone, E.C. Cook William Knox, Mrs. William Knox, William Howell, Mrs. Chas Case, Mrs. Mary Beal, Mrs. Emily Wimple, Mrs. George B. Horton, and Mrs. Nellie Smith.

Eight

Railroad

By the mid-19th century, many pioneers had increased their farming operations from a matter of survival to one of mass production. Transporting their crops to the mills or to market by wagon and cart was becoming a tedious and time consuming process. On October 3, 1836, mass transportation came to Lenawee with a private corporation establishing the Erie & Kalamazoo Railroad. This was the first train west of Schenectady, New York. The complete route was to extend from Toledo to the headwaters of the Kalamazoo River; however, the tracks were never laid past Adrian. Initially drawn by horses along thin iron rails supported by oak stringers, the train hauled passengers in a pleasure car, as well as open cars for bulk transport of merchandise. In January 1837, locomotive No. 1 was on the tracks. Stockholders who owned property along the track were allowed to use the rails for personal transport. Several railroads were created over the years, passing through different corners of Lenawee County, changing ownership as well as merging with different railroads. The Michigan Southern Railroad completed its route from Monroe to Hillsdale in 1844, with stops at Adrian and Hudson, hauling freight and passengers. Also known as the Wabash, the Detroit, Butler & St. Louis Railroad entered Adrian from Detroit on May 12, 1881.

The railroad not only connected some of the frontier towns, but created new growth where depots were built. Many communities developed around the railroad, then, as the railroad died in some areas, sadly, so did the communities. Feeder roads, equivalent to plank roads, were built from the tracks to mills or farms along the routes to enable loading without the cost of laying tracks directly to the site. Some plank roads were actual routes running deep into the woods where it was not feasible to run tracks at that time.

Tales of the steam locomotive include sometimes having to stop along the route while the crew and passengers gathered wood to burn. There were also times when the passengers had to help push the train. In spite of these tedious tasks, the train was appreciated, bringing faster postal service and marketing, and even providing transportation for children to and from the high school in Adrian.

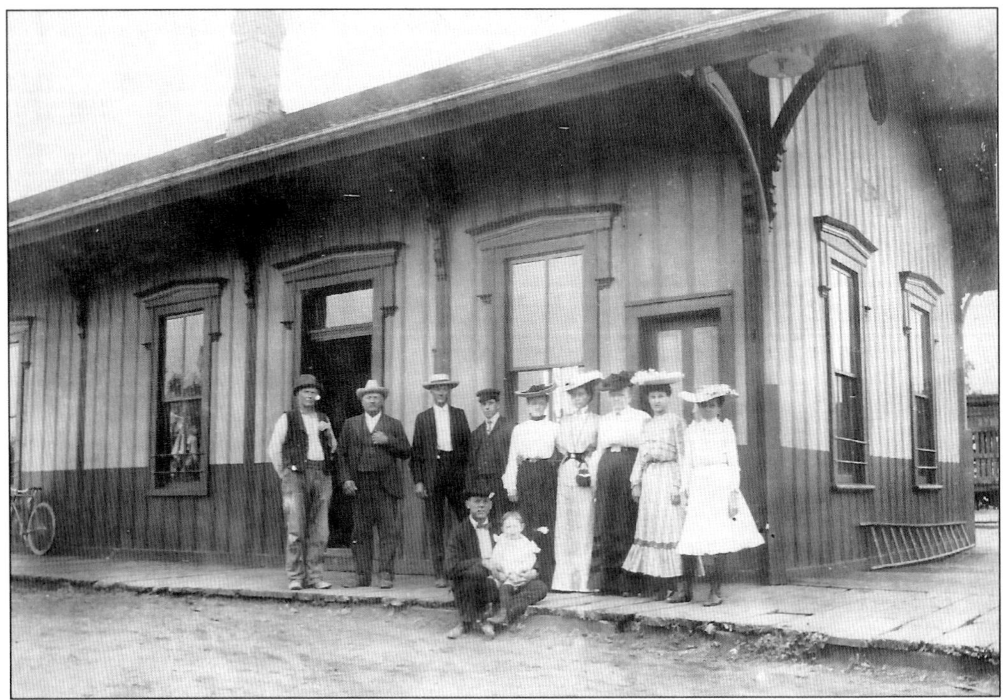

Adrian Depot. The first depot built in Lenawee County was in Adrian on the Erie & Kalamazoo Railroad. A connection was made by rail to Toledo, or Port Lawrence, Ohio, as it was known then. On November 2, 1836, the first railroad car left the Port Lawrence depot headed for Adrian. This train used pure horsepower, with the horses changed every four miles. The first steam locomotive arrived in January 1837.

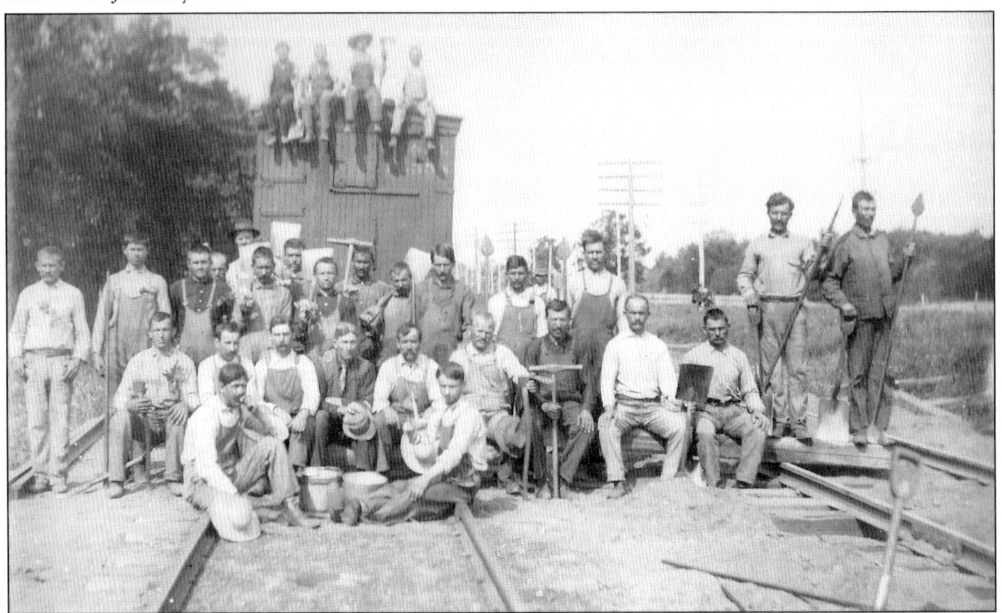

Adrian Lake Shore Crew Laying the Tracks. With tools in hand, railroad men pose while in the midst of laying the tracks. The Lake Shore & Michigan Southern Railroad ran from Chicago to Buffalo, New York, with plenty of line to be laid in between.

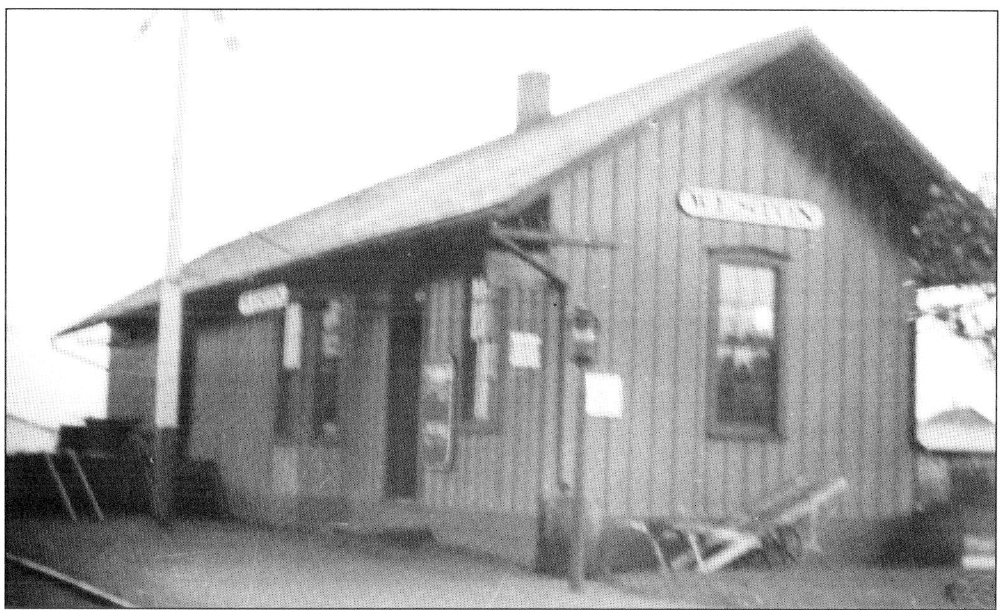

WESTON DEPOT. In the spring of 1872, the Canada Central Railroad, later owned by the New York Central Railroad, came through Weston, shipping freight and bringing supplies to the local businesses in this isolated hamlet of Fairfield Township. Industry came and left this little community, taking the railroad tracks with it during the 20th century. (Courtesy of the Fairfield Fire Department.)

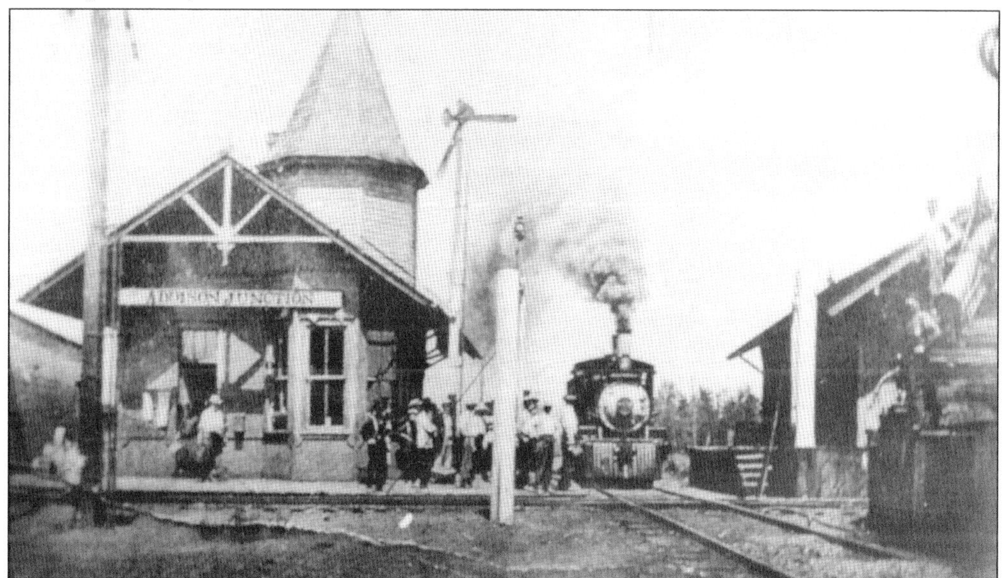

ADDISON JUNCTION. Completed in 1896, Addison Junction was considered the crossroads for the east-west Lake Shore Line, with the rails from the junction to Jackson complete, and the oncoming north-south Cincinnati Northern Railroad. The train provided the convenience of short distance rides to the neighboring lakes, as well as long-distance freight or mail delivery. Sadly, on May 11, 1915, embers from a passing train set the depot on fire. The depot and freight building collapsed. The building was replaced with a smaller, less elaborate structure. All train service ended in 1932.

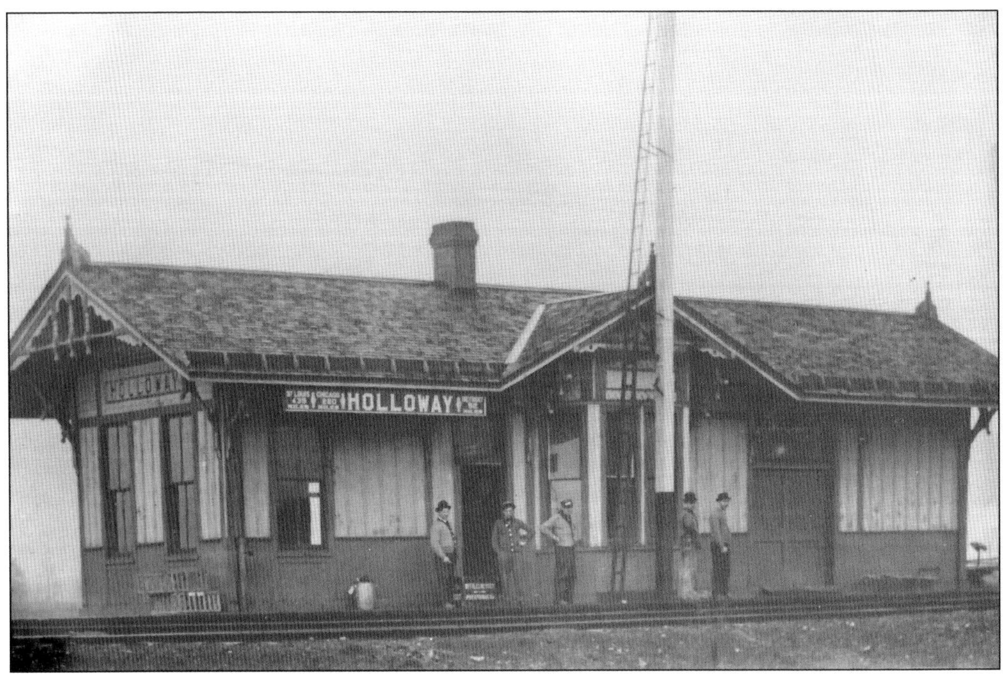

Holloway Depot. Just north of Lenawee Junction, the unincorporated village of Holloway stands in Raisin Township. The Wabash Railroad used this stop primarily for the shipping of stock and produce.

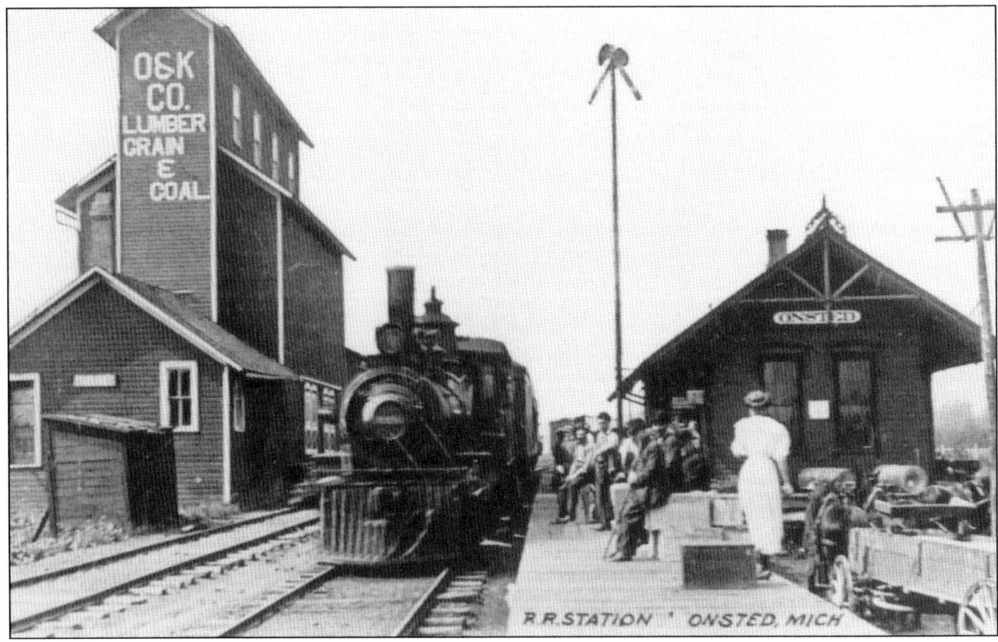

Onsted Depot. Originally known as Union Corners, this fragment of Cambridge Township blossomed into a village named Onsted with the arrival of the railroad in 1884. The right-of-way for the railroad was given by landowners John Onsted and James E. Gibbs. Freight cars and passenger trains arrived twice a day. The depot was built by the Michigan & Ohio Railroad, later becoming a branch of the Lake Shore & Michigan Southern Railway.

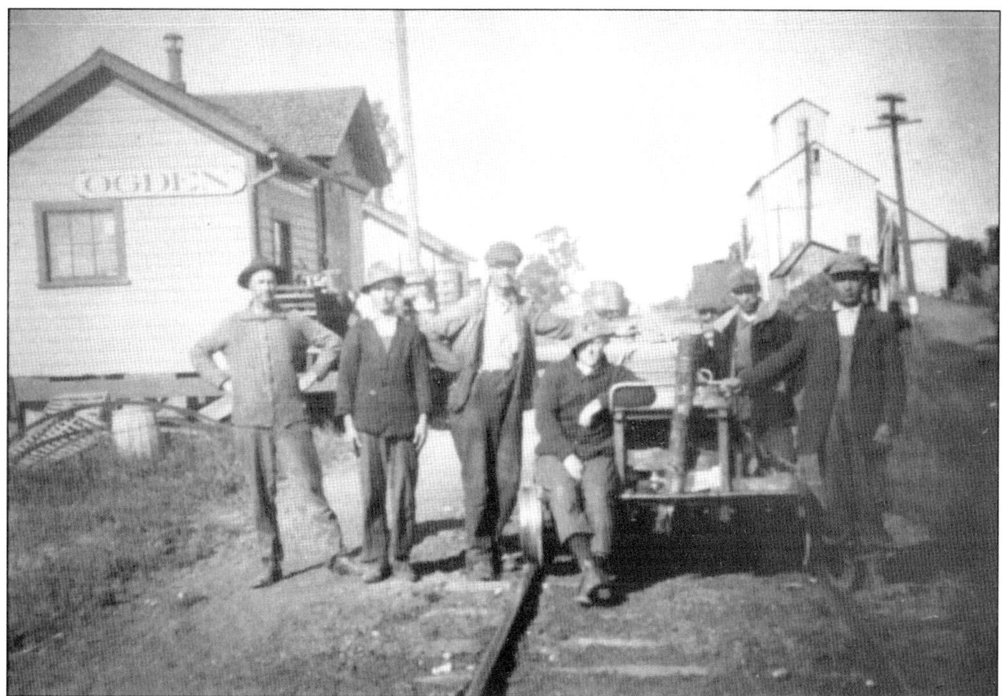

OGDEN CENTER. The Ogden station can be seen at left in this photograph of several men pausing with a roller cart on the tracks. The grain elevator is on the right. Those whose property bordered the tracks were given rights to use the rails for carts.

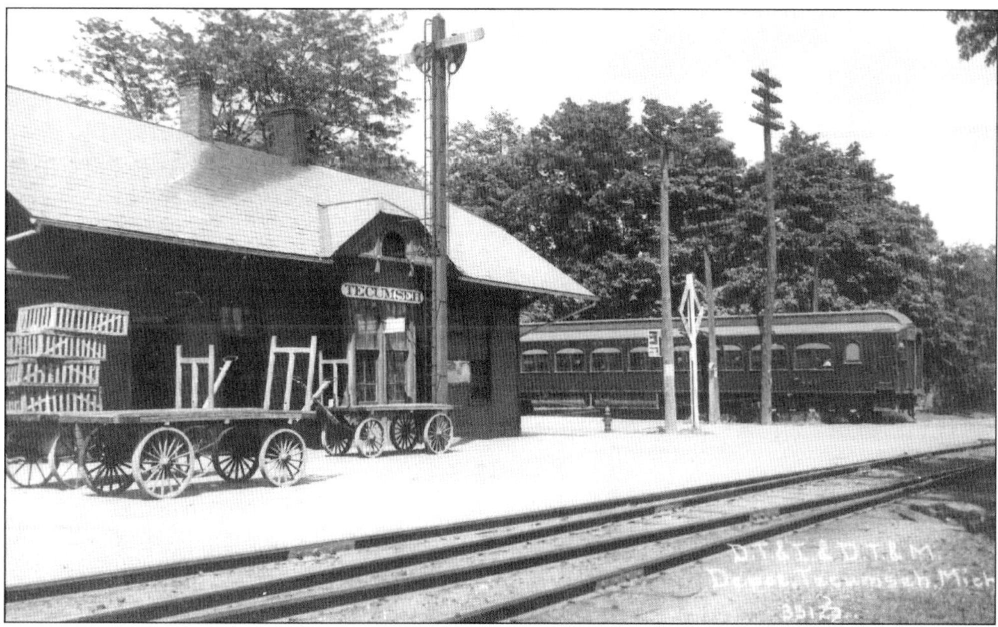

TECUMSEH DEPOT. Tecumseh was a part of the Michigan & Ohio Road, the line that ran through the northern edge of Lenawee. This depot was built in 1884 at Cummins and Evans Streets. Trunk lines from the railroads ran into the celery farms to make shipping more convenient. Other farms along the way also enjoyed this service.

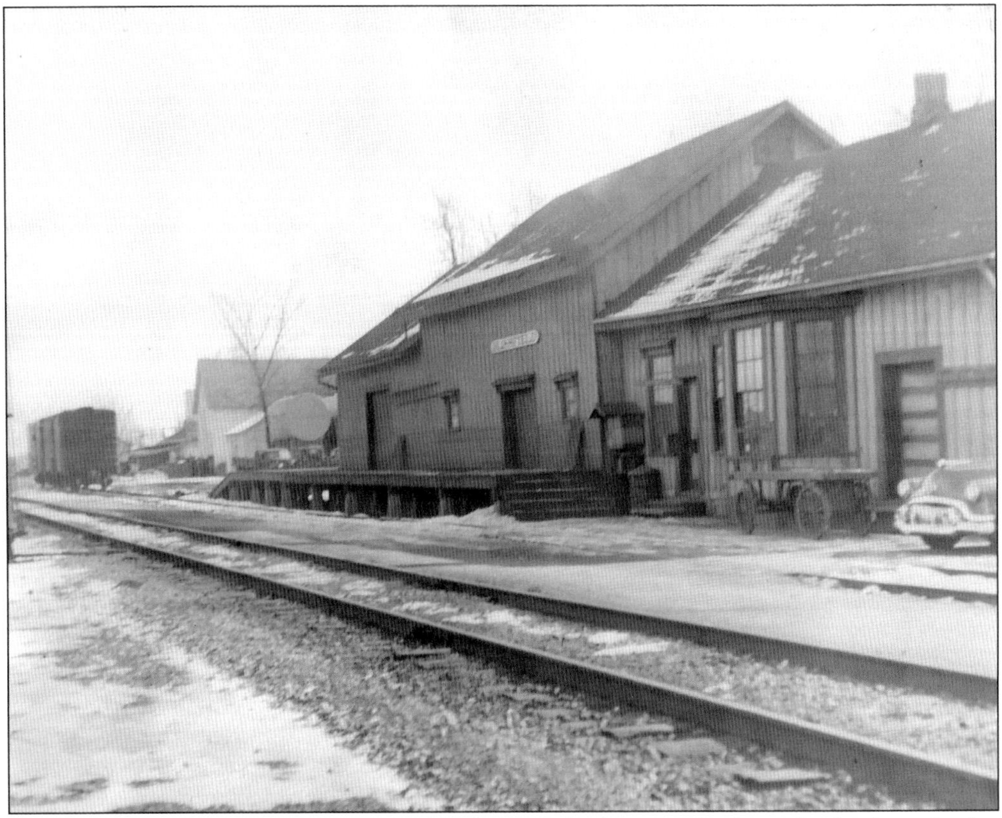

Blissfield New York Central Depot. This photograph taken in 1904 shows the freight and ticket depot on Russell Street in the village of Blissfield. Known as the largest shipping point for fattened livestock between Chicago and Toledo, Blissfield was a major trading point for farmers.

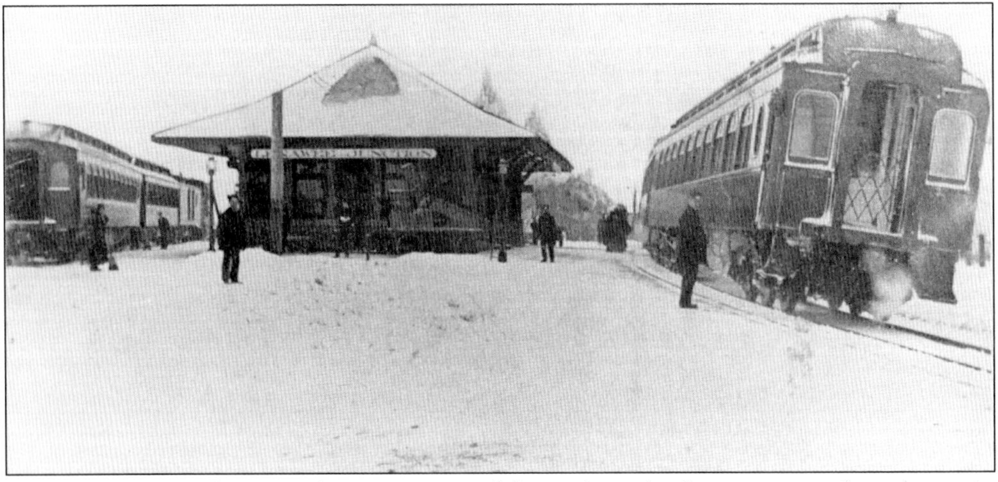

Lenawee Junction Station. An intersection of the tracks at this location created another main stopping point for freight and passengers to switch directions.

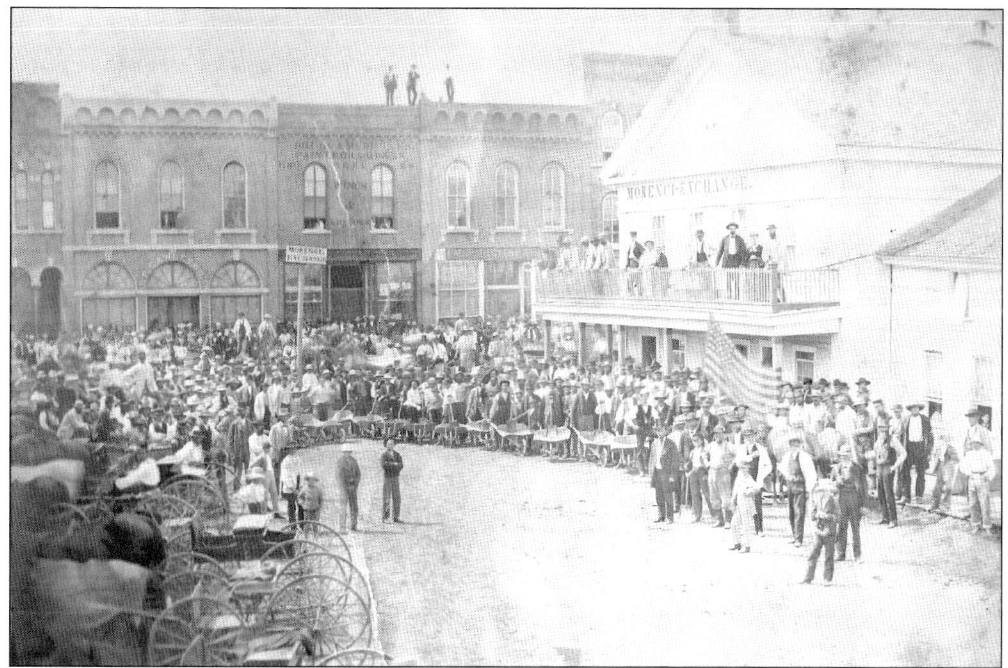

Morenci Railroad Inauguration. On July 27, 1871, the celebration for the inauguration of the Chicago & Canada Southern Railroad took place. A large crowd gathered to break ground for the railroad bed. Excitement for the railroad and the business that it would bring to Morenci and surrounding communities was felt by many.

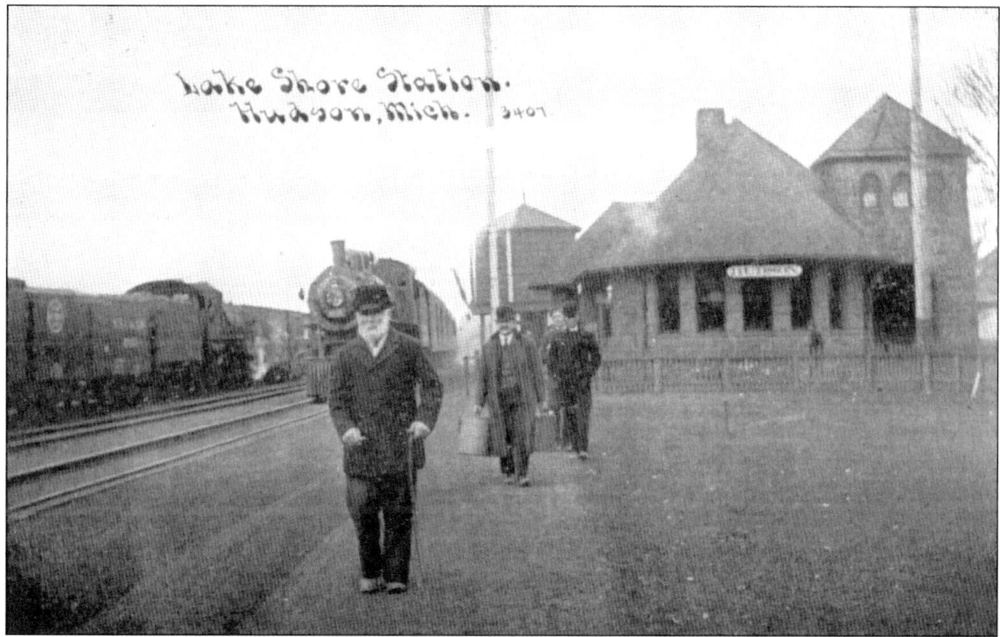

Hudson Lake Shore Station. Passengers leave the station of the Lake Shore Railroad. Large quantities of farm products were shipped from this location. With the Lake Shore & Michigan, New York Central, and the Cincinnati Northern Railroads passing through Hudson, it became a very influential part of the agricultural market.

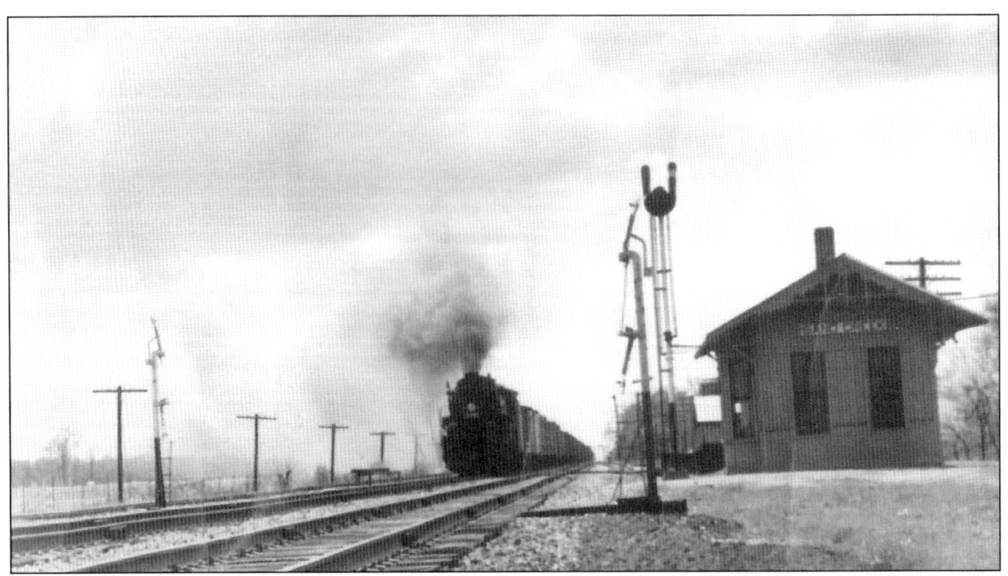

Sand Creek Depot. As a part of the Wabash Railroad, a shipping and trading point was created in Sand Creek for the farmers. This also provided an opportunity for people to commute. In the early 1900s, many children had to take the train to go to high school in Adrian. This depot was razed in 1960.

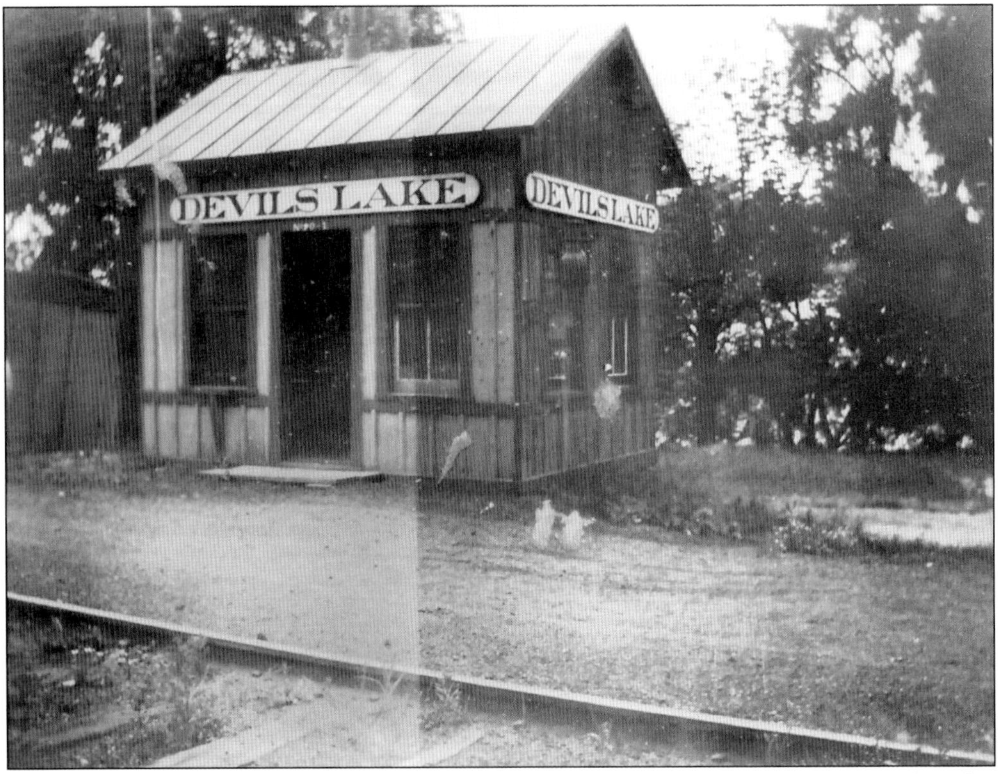

Devil's Lake Depot. This little depot was built next to the Club House Hotel on Devil's Lake. The railroad was a major convenience for visitors to Devil's Lake. With the addition of the depot, the Club House would no longer have to provide depot services to the passengers.

Nine

Community Development

As the migration continued westward throughout the 1800s, settlers arrived with the desire to be entrepreneurs. With the local availability of dairy, produce, and livestock, it was time for small business to evolve in Lenawee County. From markets to bakeries and even daily delivery of dairy products, individuals found ways to turn the products of local farmers into profit while meeting the needs of those who lived in the cities. Retail businesses developed, and right before their eyes, the downtowns emerged.

The market for equipment and implements for farming also opened up as farming continued to prosper throughout the region. Several machine shops existed throughout the region as horse, oxen, and even man himself pushed or pulled the farm equipment. Samuel W. Raymond, the owner of a Ford dealership in Adrian, created the Raymond tractor with the intention of reducing cost of labor and farm equipment. Raymond used a Ford Model T engine with his own innovation to create the turning power and an adjustable hitch that would allow more depth with turning the three-wheeled tractor around at the end of each row. He produced 150 tractors prior to selling his patents to John Deere and Oliver in 1925. In 1973, Raymond's son Harold F. Raymond sent one of the original Raymond tractors to Greenfield Village in Dearborn, Michigan.

Many industries emerged, yet it was one man, J. Wallace Page, in a blacksmith shop in 1885, who made Adrian the "home of the wire fence." With as many as eight fence factories listed in Adrian by 1907 and Page Fence known internationally, Adrian then became the "fence capital of the world." Allowing livestock to roam freely was acceptable as settlement began. As decades passed, more land patents were sold, and neighbors appeared—in some cases, creating boundary and trespassing disputes. Fencing became a necessity to keep livestock within their own pastures, as well as a way to discourage predatory animals from entering. Page Fence created door mats, fences, and cages used by zoos, circuses, and fairs worldwide.

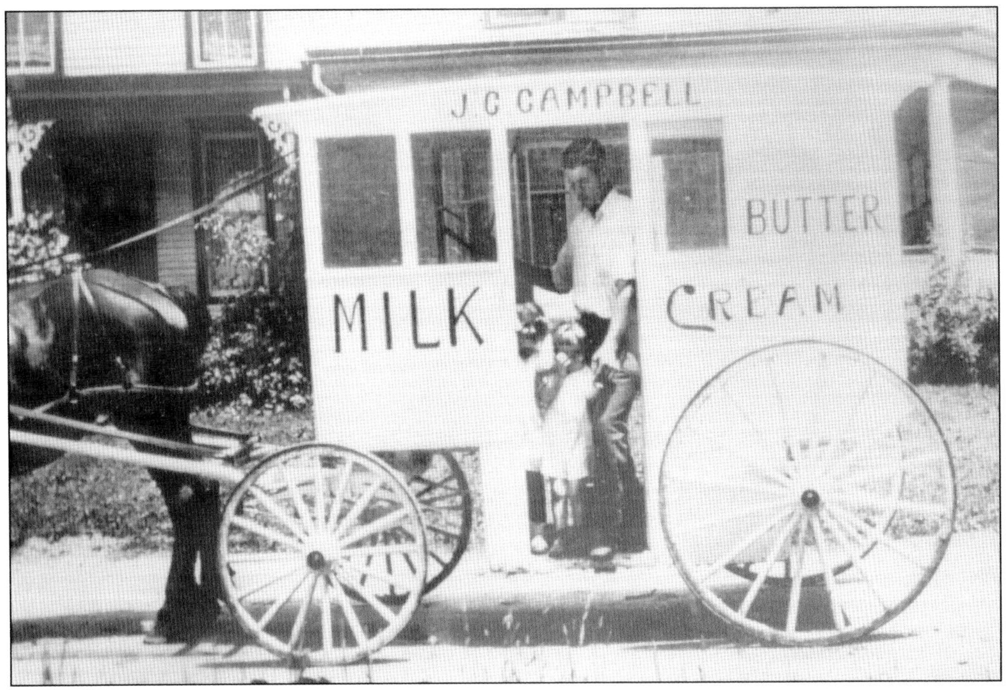

J.C. Campbell Delivers Milk in Clinton. It was common for J.C. Campbell to have his young son with him in 1930 while delivering milk in Clinton.

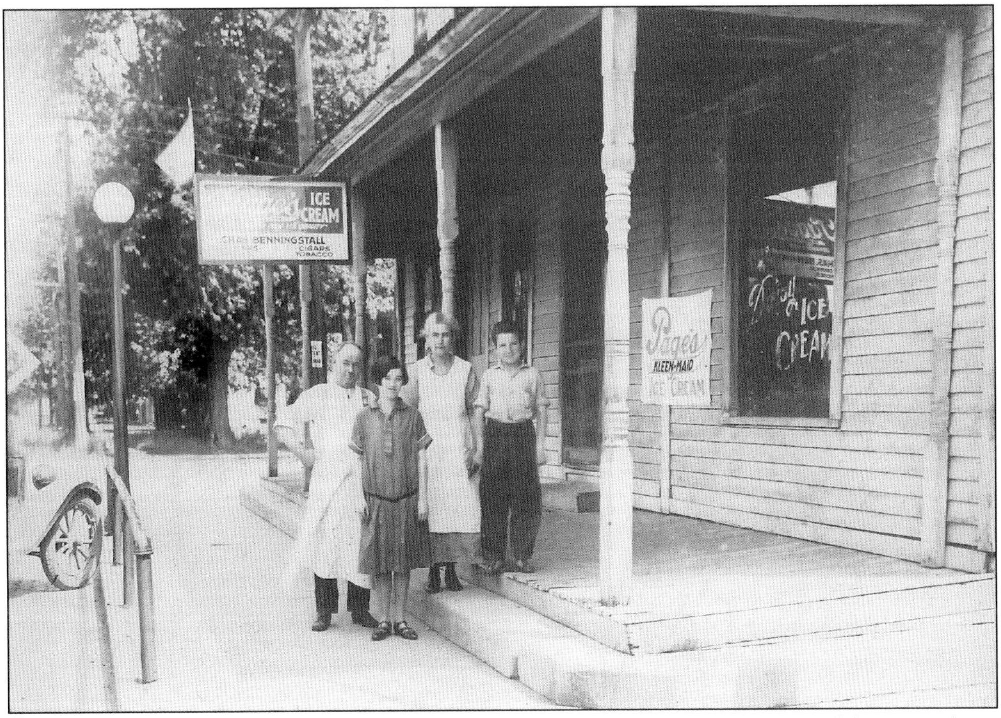

Page's Ice Cream, Deerfield. Mr. and Mrs. Carpenter shared the pleasure of dairy products through their ice cream shop in Deerfield. They also used the shop to keep the kids out of trouble by occupying them with billiards and other games in their hall.

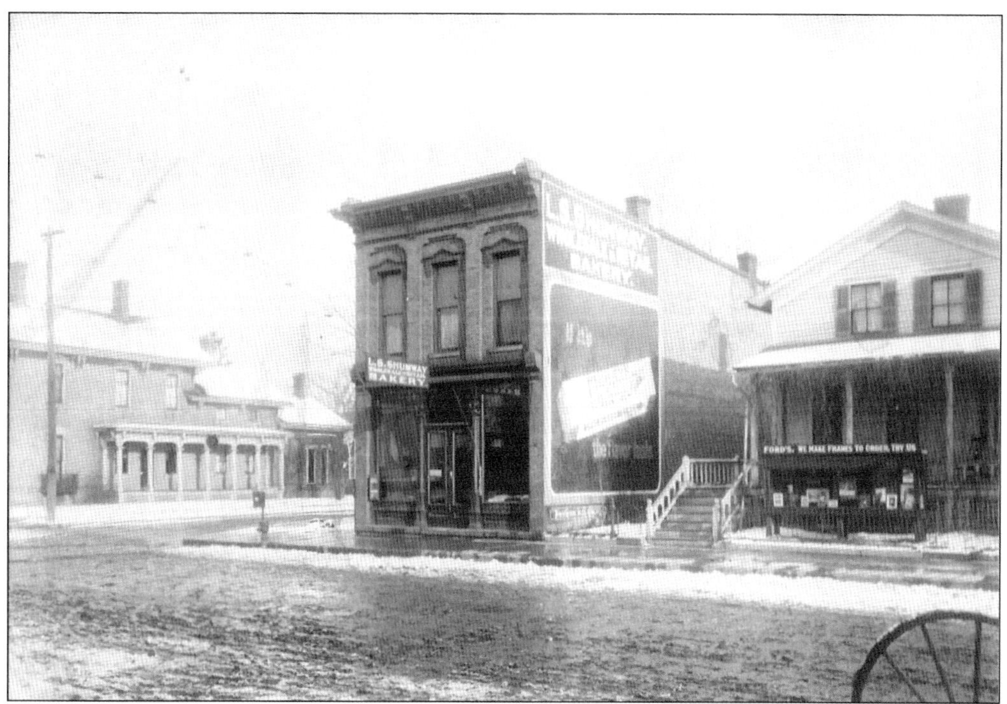

L.S. SHUMWAY BAKERY, ADRIAN. Located on Main Street in downtown Adrian, the L.S. Shumway Bakery sold baked goods to both wholesale and retail customers.

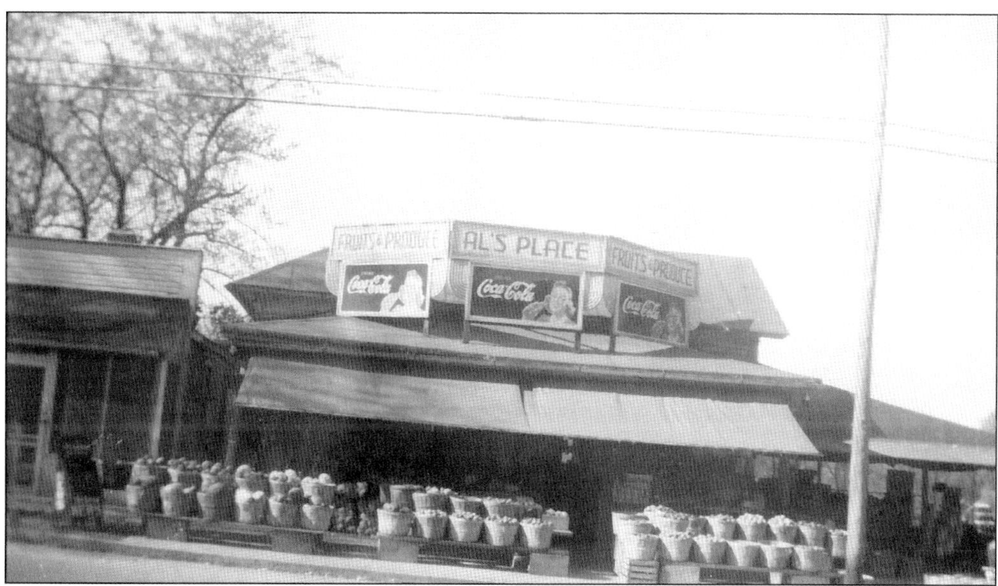

AL'S PLACE, ADRIAN. A well-known market for many years, Al's Place was located in downtown Adrian. Serving the farmers by providing a market for their produce and the public by providing the convenience of an in-town location to shop, this business was an asset to the community.

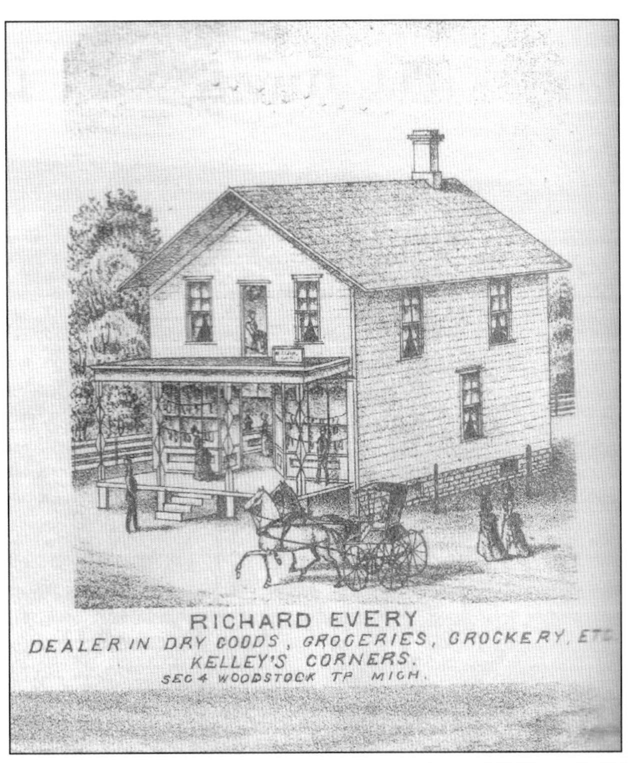

KELLEY'S CORNERS. Though it was just a small market in Woodstock Township that supplied groceries and merchandise in the 1800s, Kelley's Corners eliminated days of travel for those who had settled nearby.

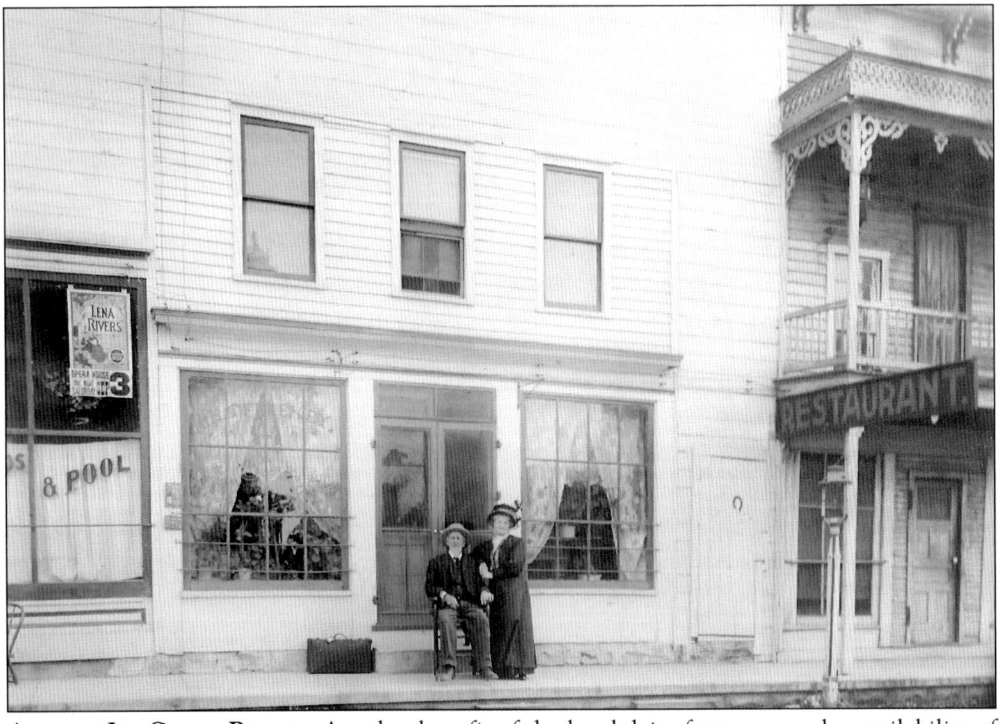

ADDISON ICE CREAM PARLOR. Another benefit of the local dairy farmers was the availability of milk to make ice cream, turning it into a commercial venture. This ice cream parlor was owned by B.E. Colwell.

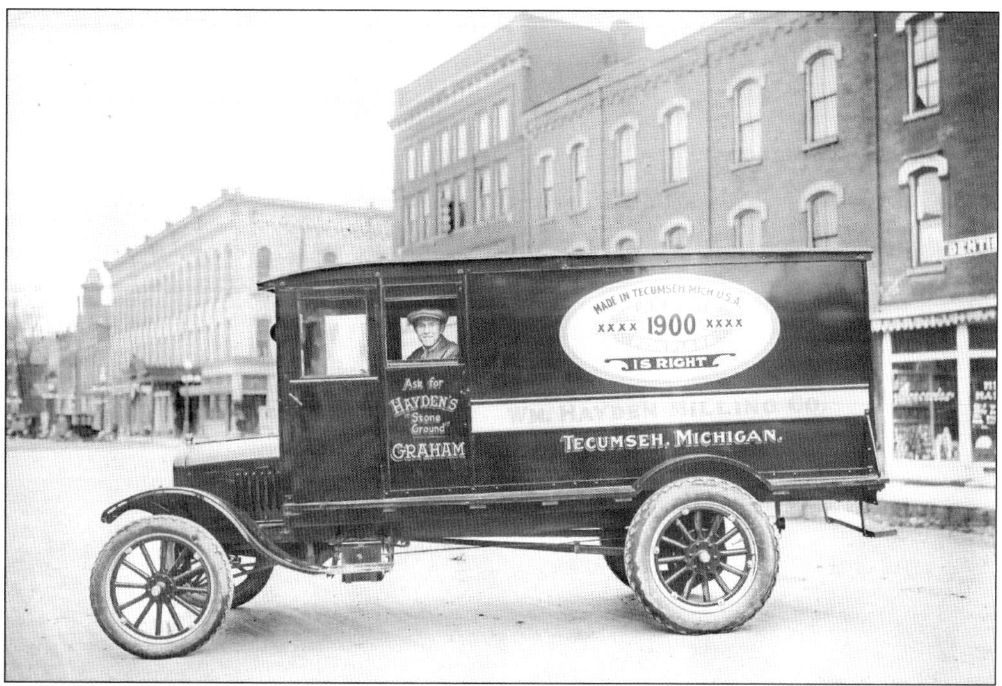

HAYDEN'S GRAHAM FLOUR DELIVERY. Pictured here is a delivery vehicle for the pure 1900 stone-ground graham flour made in Tecumseh at the Hayden mill. William Hayden advertised that through the process of a water-powered mill and the use of the choicest variety of local virgin wheat, the highest quality of flour was provided.

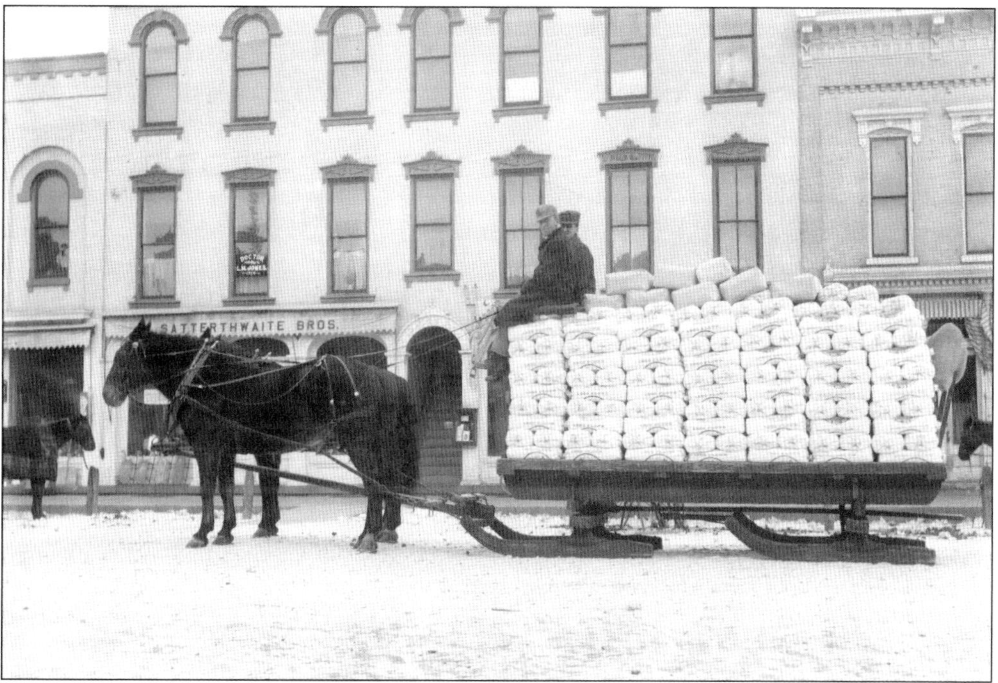

HAYDEN'S DELIVERY IN WINTER. Taking advantage of the horse-drawn sleigh during the winter months in 1919, Hayden's continued delivery to customers throughout the area.

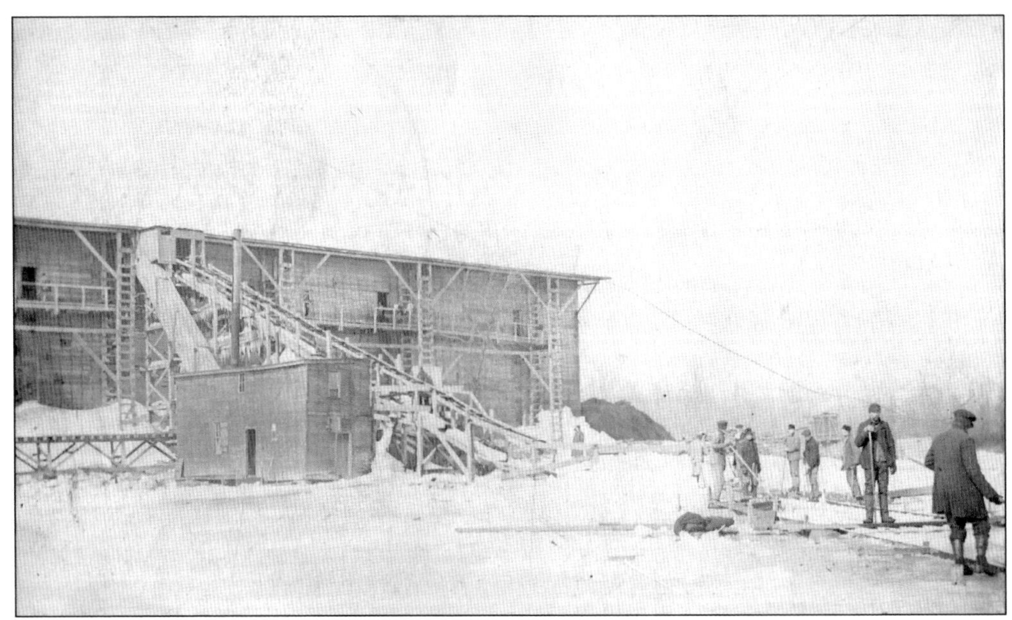

Michigan Lake Ice Company's Icehouse at Devil's Lake. Harvesting ice on the lakes was a tedious and dangerous job. After removing the snow from the frozen lake, an ice saw was used to cut through the surface. Blocks of ice were cut and scraped to present a smooth, clear surface for market. The blocks were then hauled to the icehouse for storage. Most of the blocks were moved by train from the Manitou Beach location. Several smaller icehouses stood around the lakes, serving those who owned cottages as well as the local markets.

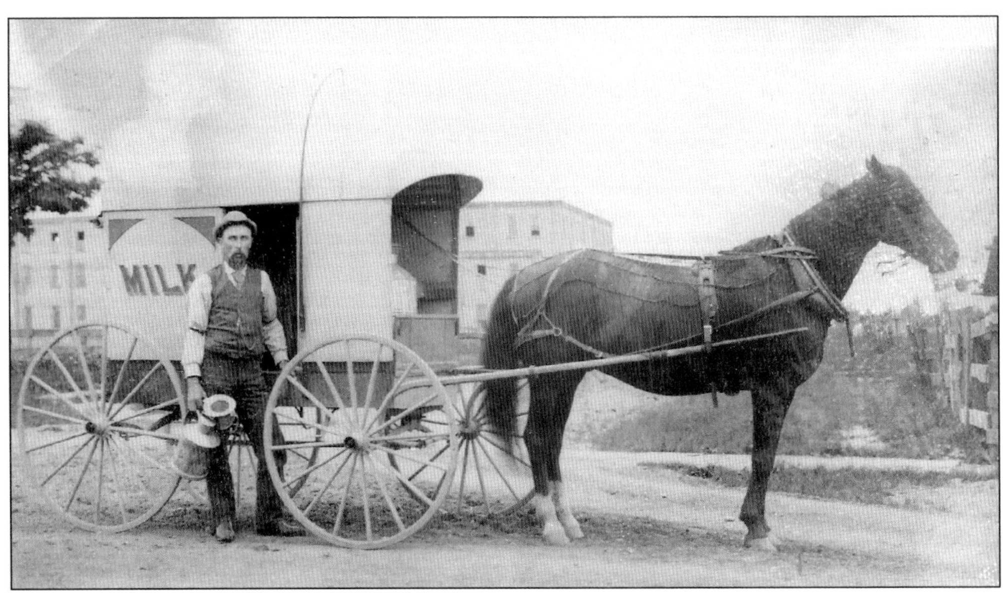

Milk Man in Palmyra. In 1895, milk delivery throughout Palmyra Township was done by Nathan Augustus.

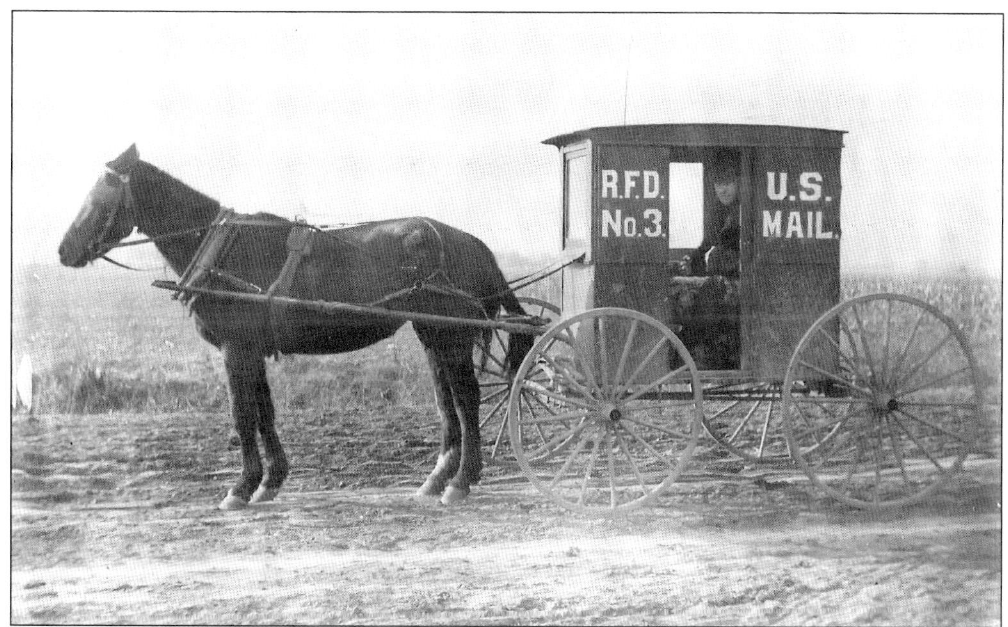

MAIL DELIVERY. The horse-drawn Rural Free Delivery No. 3 wagon is pictured in Blissfield with postal worker Art Stearns in 1912. The federal Rural Free Delivery program began in 1896.

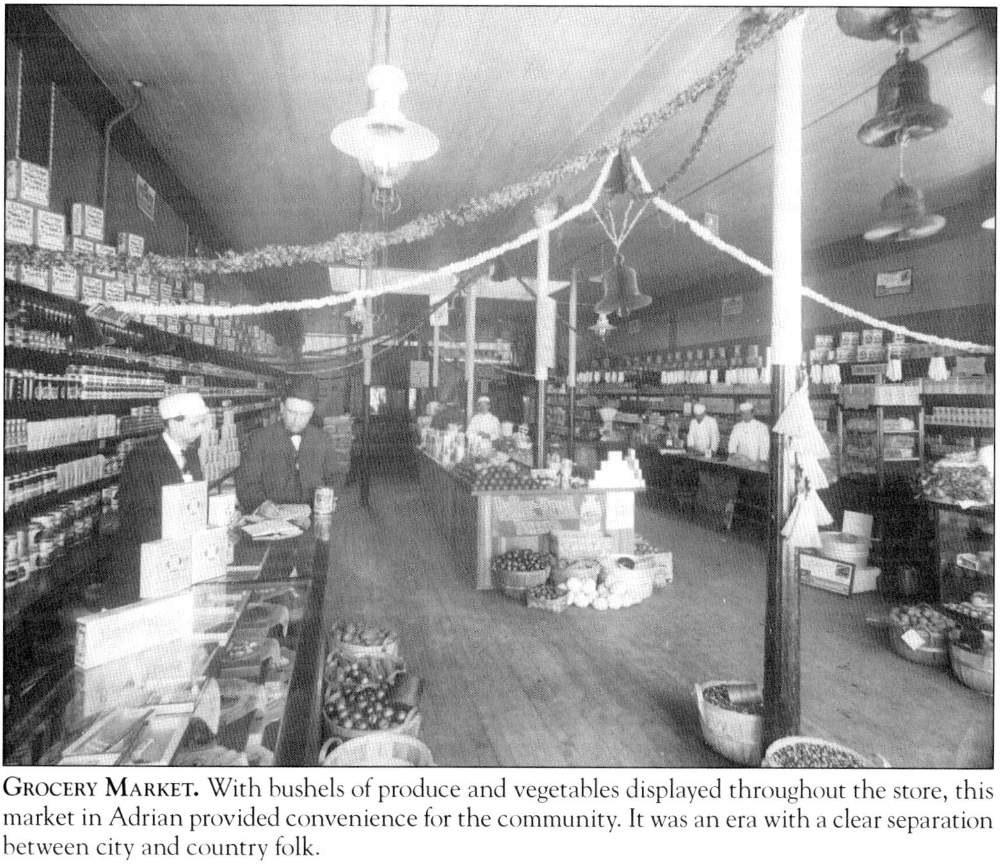

GROCERY MARKET. With bushels of produce and vegetables displayed throughout the store, this market in Adrian provided convenience for the community. It was an era with a clear separation between city and country folk.

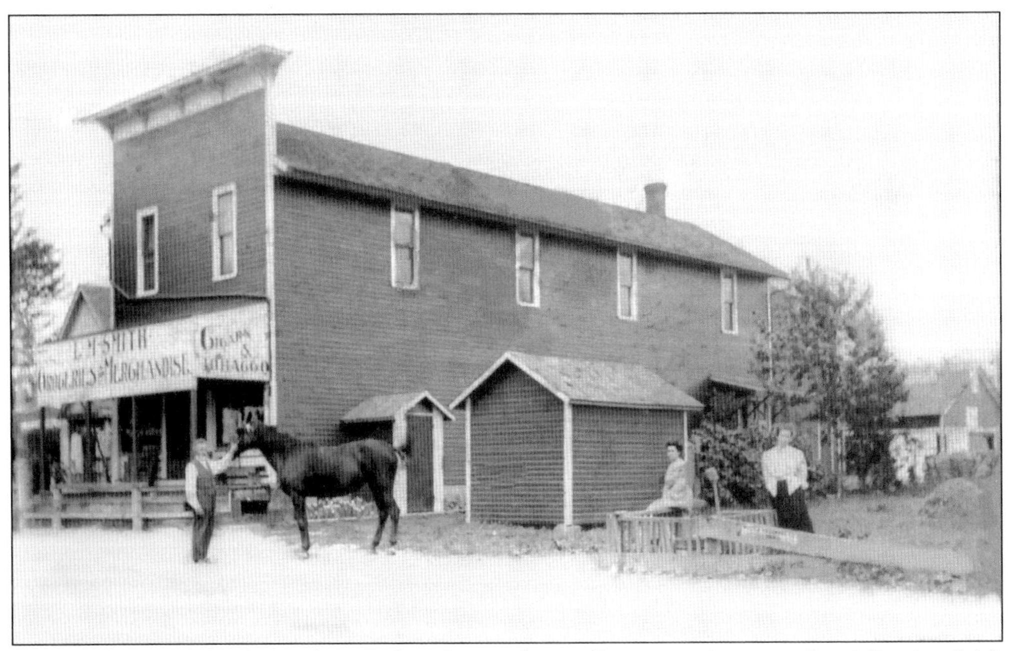

L.M. Smith Market, Sand Creek. Standing in front of his general store in Sand Creek is L.M. Smith, holding his horse. Providing goods and merchandise for the locals was very much needed in each settled area.

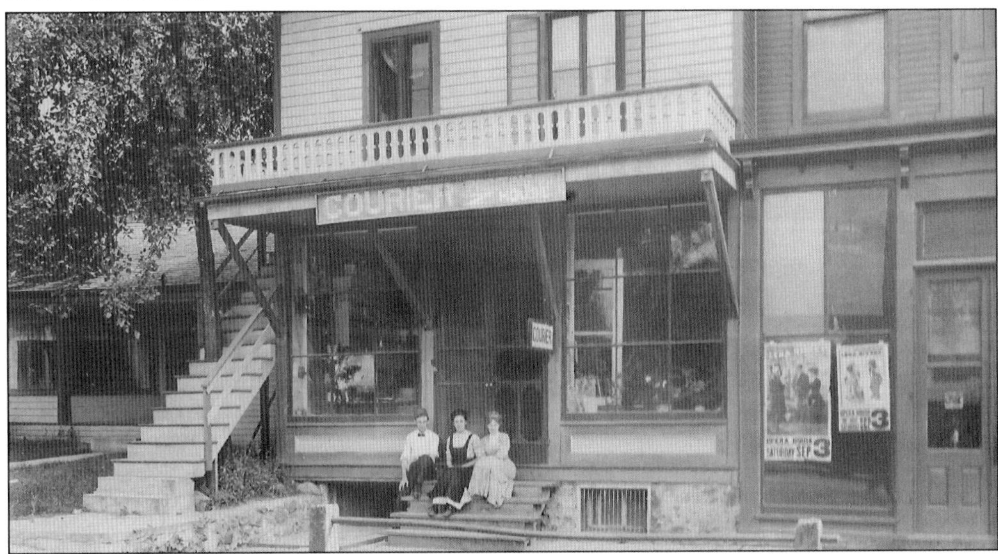

Courier Printing House, Addison. This 1910 photograph shows the Courier Printing House in downtown Addison. At this time, L.W. Stephenson was in charge of the business. The creating and printing of the local newspaper, the *Addison Courier*, was one of many services provided by the printing house. The first issue of the *Courier* was printed on June 27, 1884. For many years, local news was actually printed in Tecumseh. When ownership of the newspaper passed to previous editor Aaron Kempton in 1888, a facility was established in Addison to print the *Courier* in town. J.B. Stephenson obtained ownership of the paper in 1904 and transferred it to his son L.W. shortly thereafter. The last issue of the *Courier* was printed in January 1960. After having many owners, the printing shop finally closed in 1990.

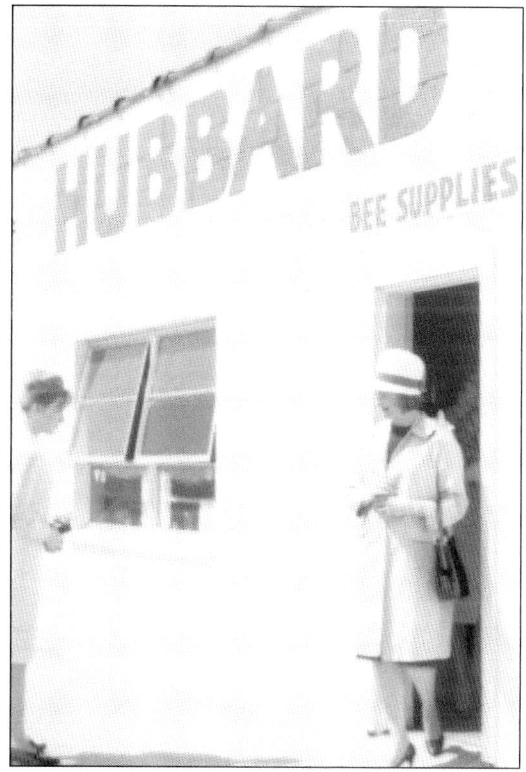

HUBBARD BEE SUPPLIES. Thelma Little is shown in the doorway of Hubbard Bee Supplies in Cambridge Township. Many kept their own bee colonies to produce honey for their own use or to sell.

KELLS FOUNDRY & MACHINE COMPANY. Phillip Kells and his three sons manufactured iron, brass, and aluminum castings at their business in Adrian. Brick and tile machines were also produced at this site from 1882 to 1906. The business was sold in 1906 to Walter Cook.

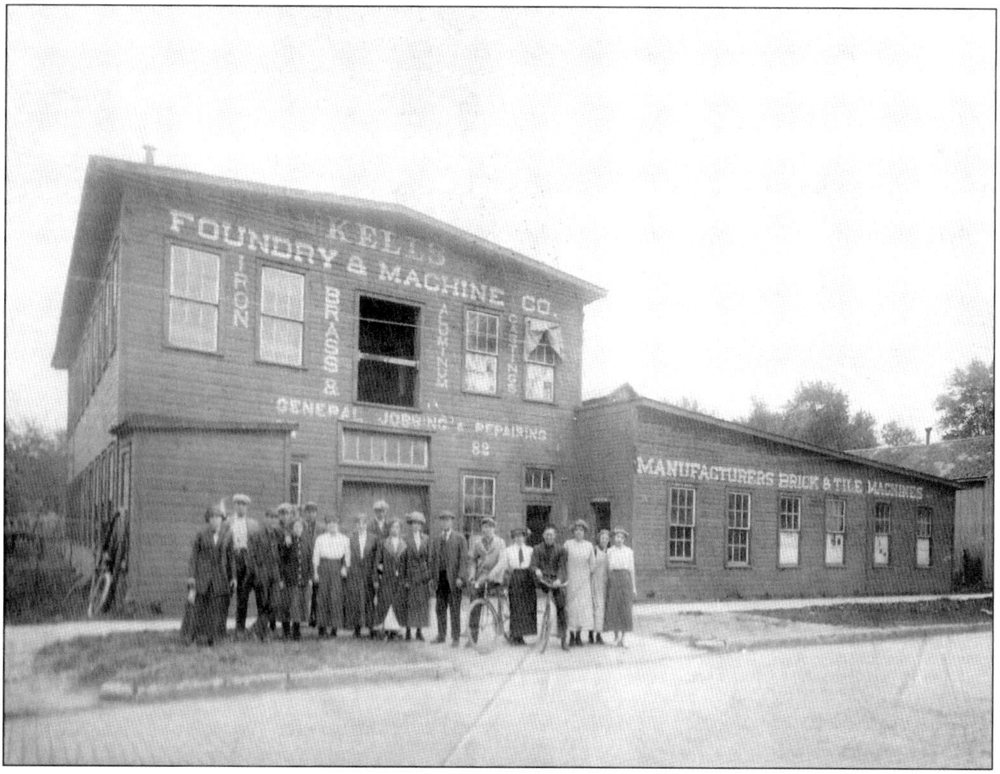

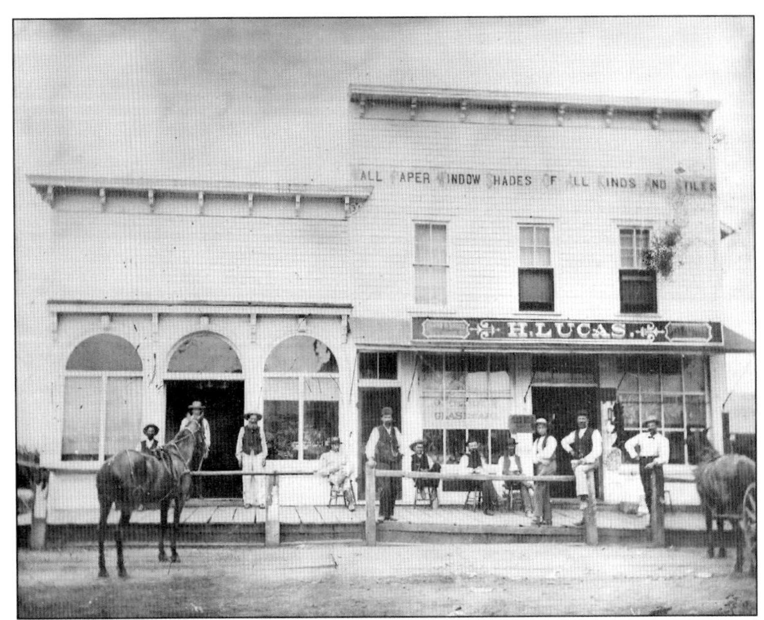

H. Lucas Store, Weston. In the hamlet of Weston, located in Fairfield Township, the H. Lucas Store served as another general store for the local residents throughout the area. (Courtesy of the Fairfield Fire Department.)

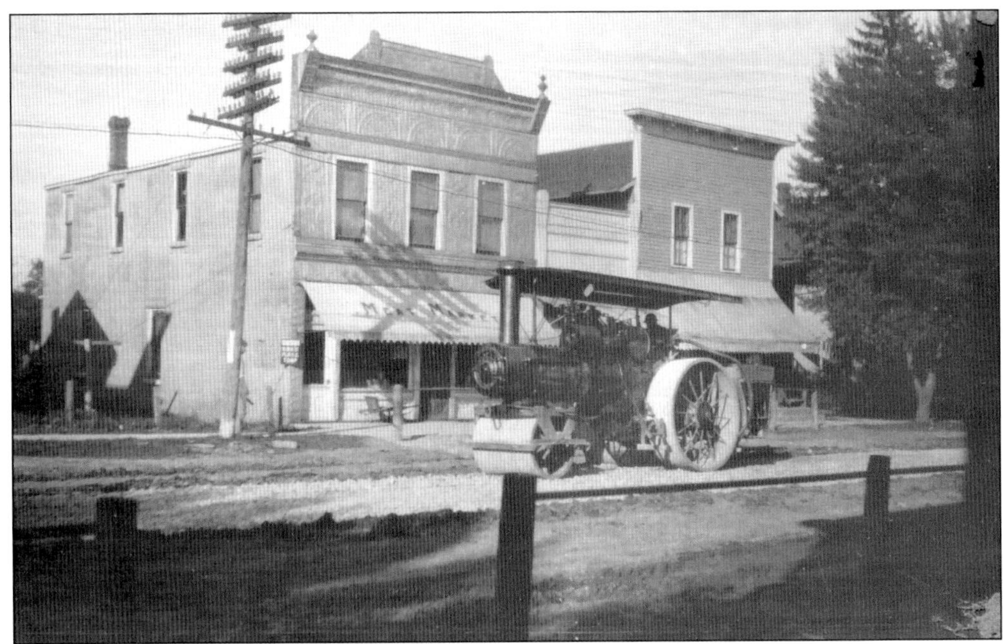

Steamrolling the Road, Weston. With the steam roller pressing gravel into Main Street in Weston, the hamlet took the first step toward eliminating muddy roads. (Courtesy of the Weston Fire Department.)

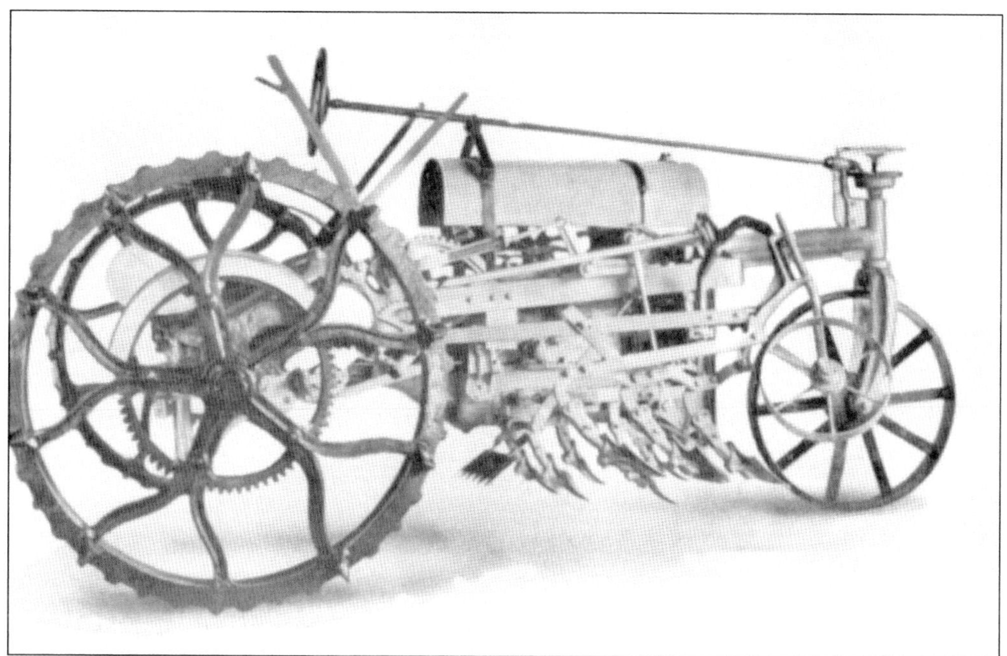

Raymond Tractor. The Raymond tractor was built with components of the Ford Model T, using the engine, transmission, and differential. The three-wheel design was the first of its kind. Raymond continued to develop accessories. Creating machinery that was simple and durable was his goal.

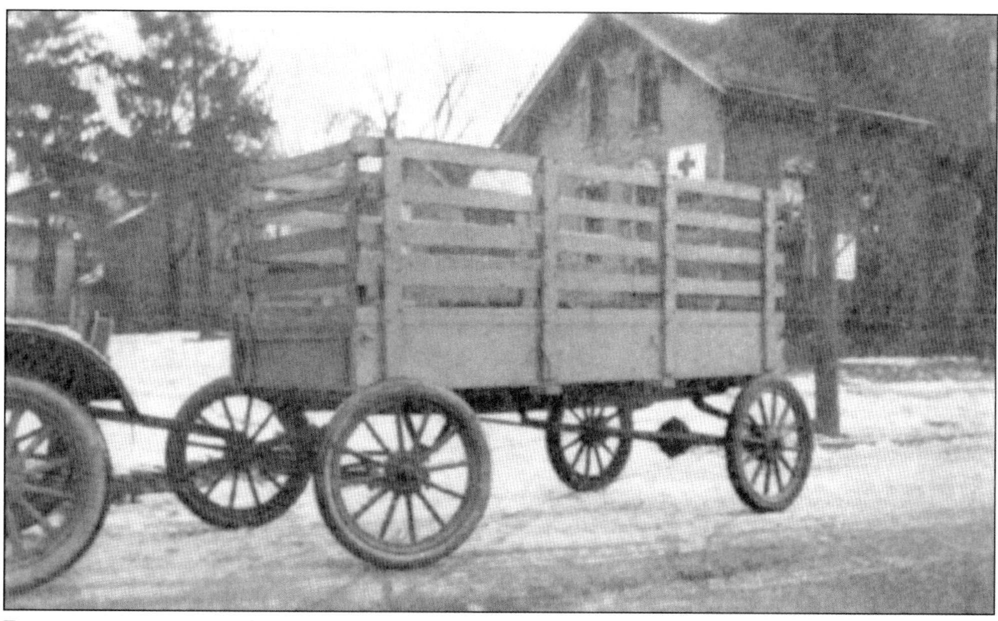

Raymond Wagon. With parts of the Model T that were not put to use for the tractor, Raymond created a wagon convenient to tow with the Raymond tractor. An adjustable hitch was created, allowing motion to the left or right, so that the farmer could turn around faster and easier in the field.

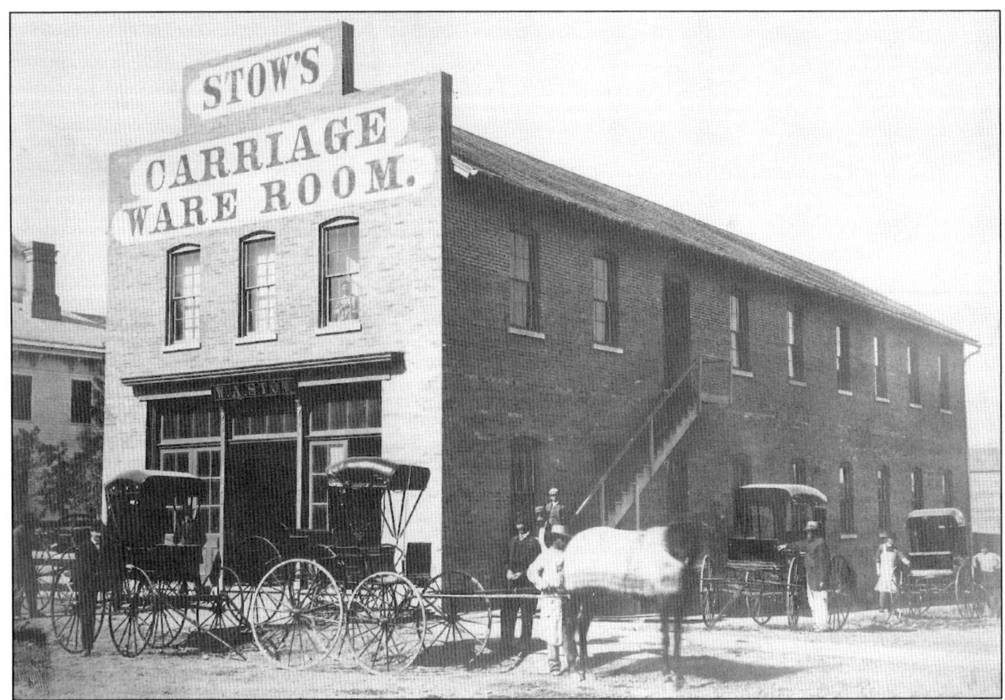

STOW'S CARRIAGE WARE ROOM. This business, located in Adrian, provided the luxury of high-quality carriages to the community. Maintenance and custom work on carriages and buggies was also provided by Mr. Stow.

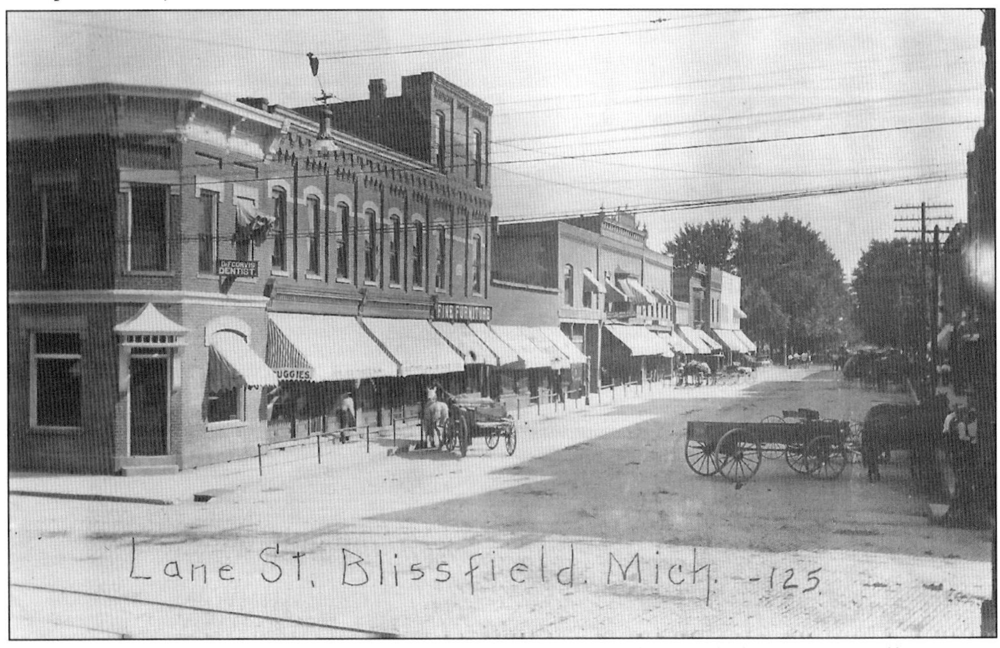

DOWNTOWN BLISSFIELD. This view of Lane Street in Blissfield shows full development of businesses on both sides of the street. The office of the local dentist, Dr. F. Corvis; purveyors of retail furniture and buggies; and the Rothfuss Piano Company are among the businesses shown in this photograph.

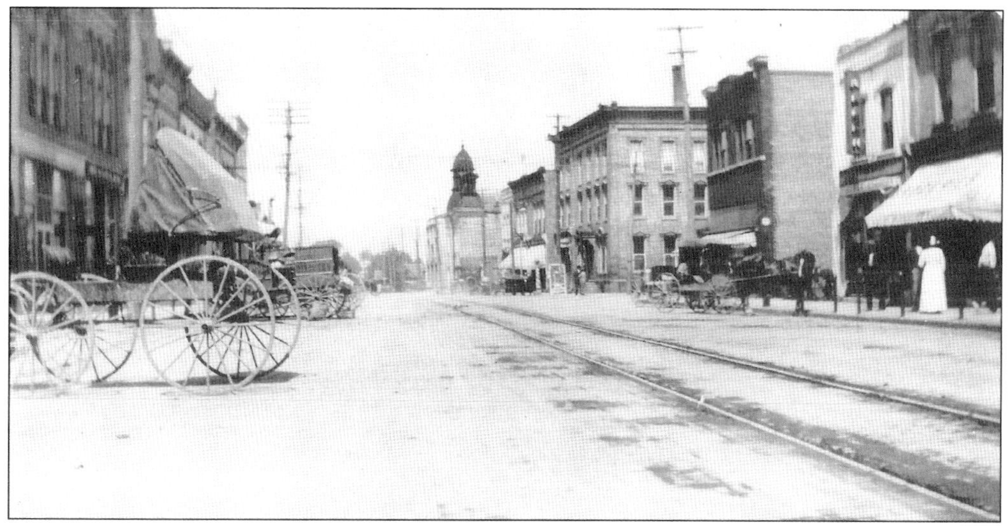

Downtown Morenci. A flourishing city is shown with its classical architecture in this photograph of downtown Morenci in the late 1800s.

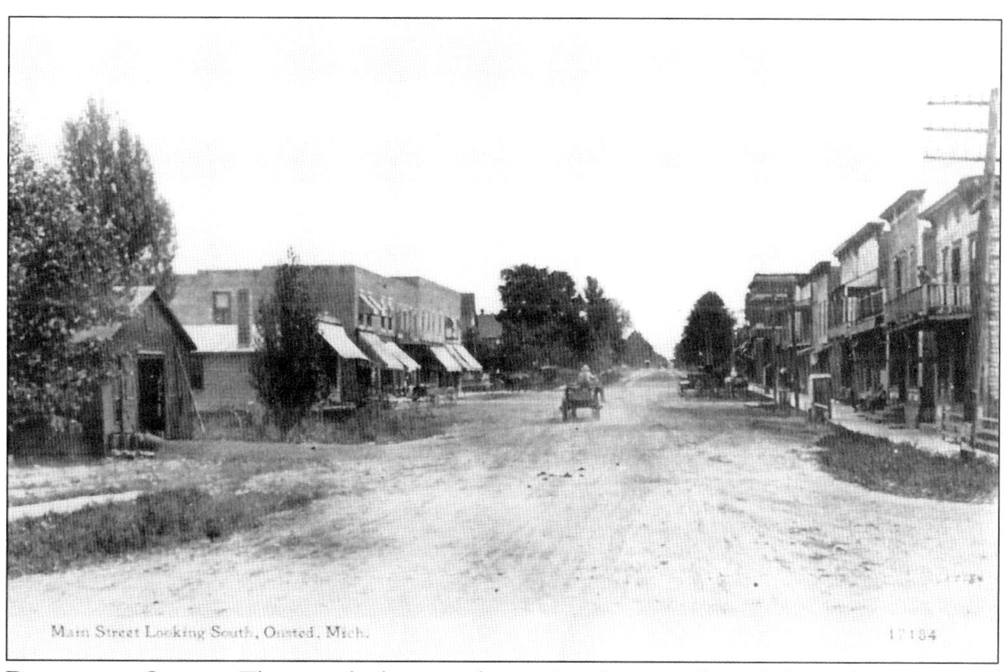

Downtown Onsted. This view looking south on Main Street in Onsted shows the presence of many small businesses in the community.

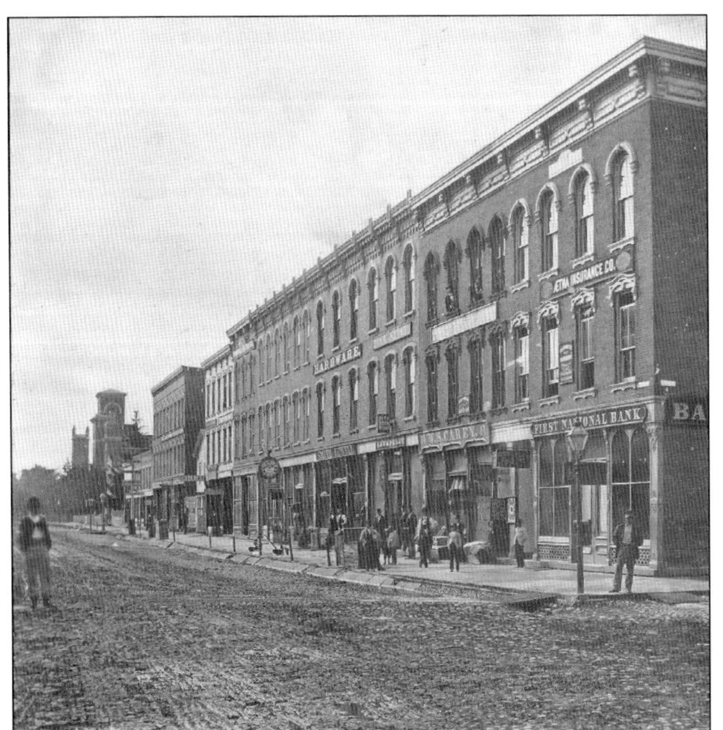

Downtown Adrian. The development of classic architecture in the city of Adrian is visible in this view of downtown. People even posed in a third-story window for this photograph showing the First National Bank, Aetna Insurance Company, Geddes & Miller law office, George L. Bachman law office, City Book Store, Smith Jewell Hardware, Victor Sewing, and several other small businesses.

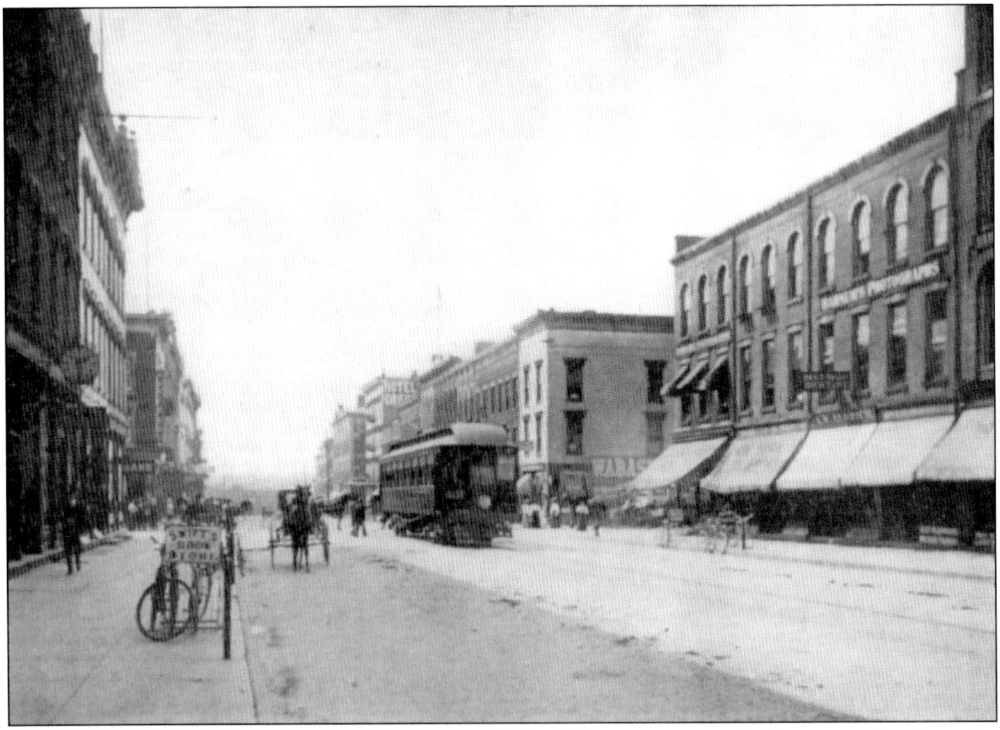

Maumee Street in Downtown Adrian. With awnings accenting the business facades, the development of a prospering city is evident. Shown here are Swift's Book Store, Barnum's Photographs, a hotel in the distance, and a streetcar on Maumee Street.

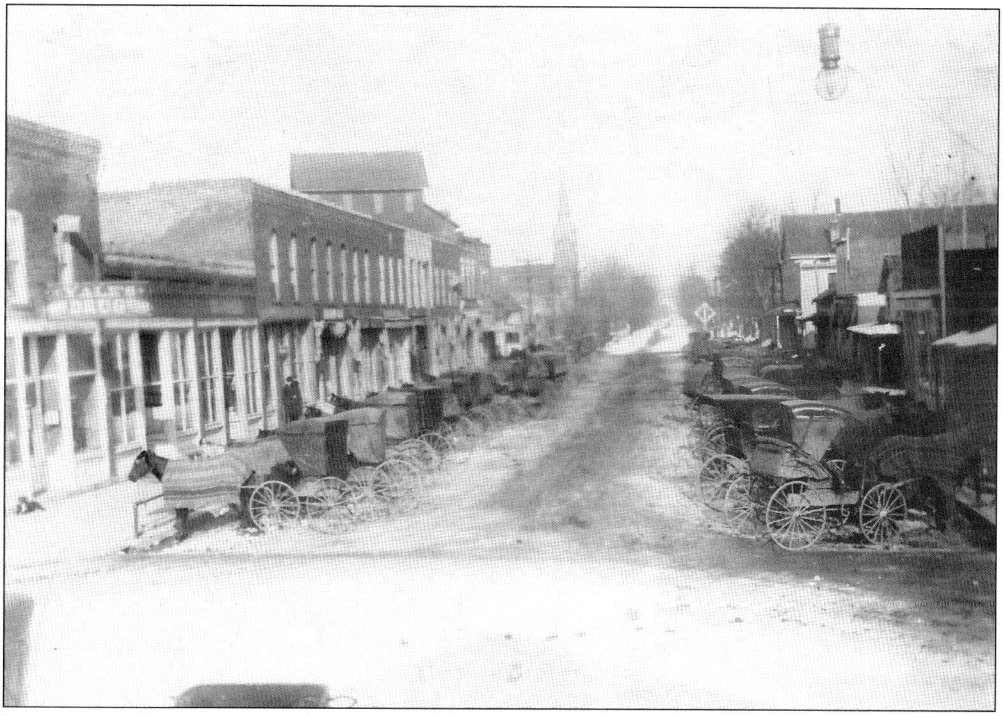

Downtown Deerfield. With horses and buggies on each side of Main Street, the downtown of this small community is busy. Yale's Drugs is on the corner, and a church is visible on the next block.

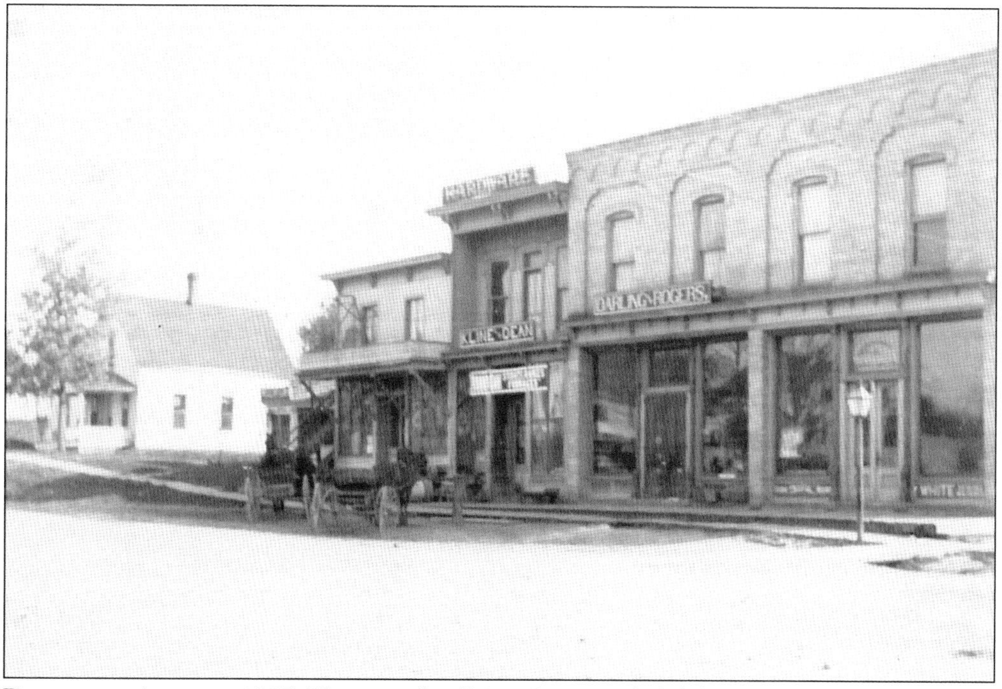

Downtown Addison, 1905. The east side of Main Street included the Kline and Dean Hardware Store; note the advertisement of stoves, ranges, and furnaces in the front window.

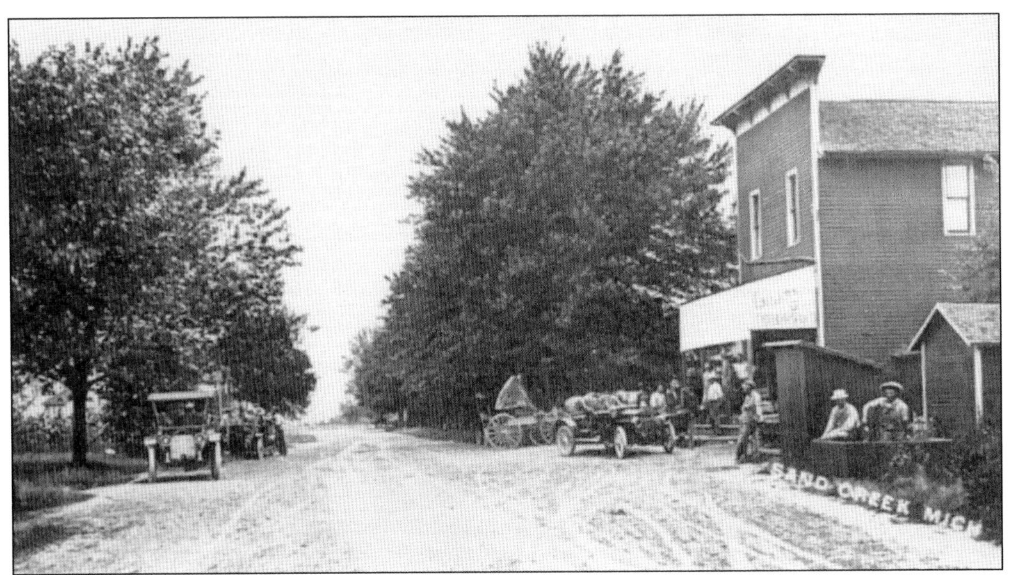

MAIN STREET, SAND CREEK, 1913. This photograph of the main road going through Sand Creek shows one of the more rural communities in Lenawee. The L.M. General Store provided essentials for the residents, although most did their major shopping in Adrian.

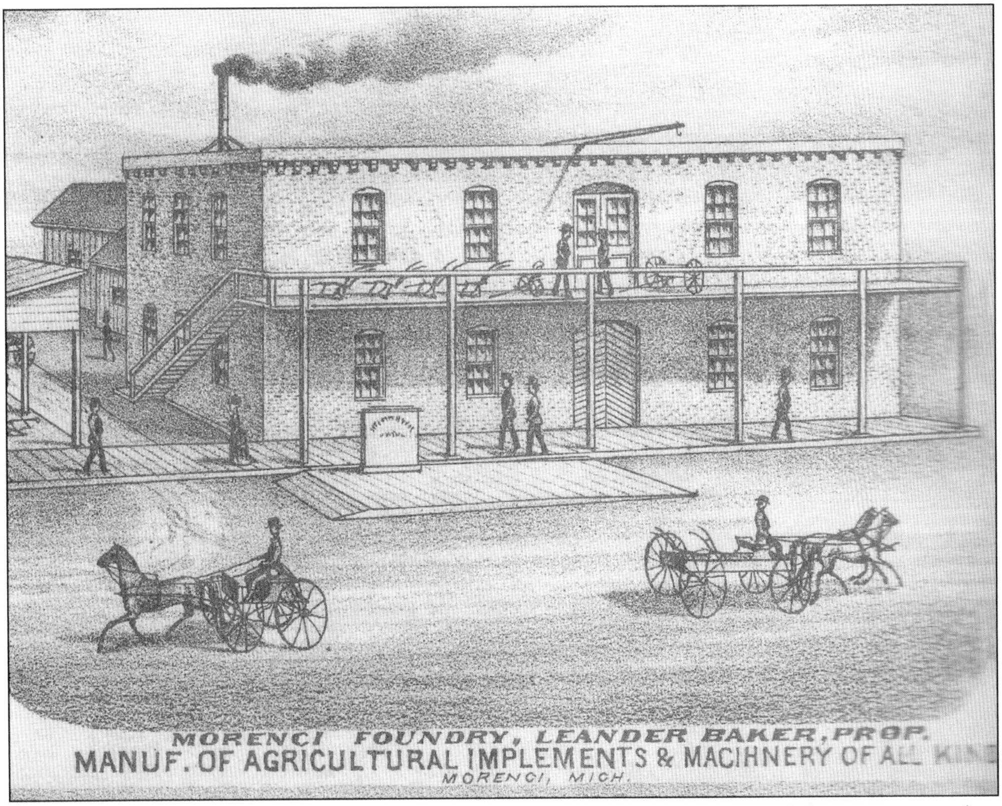

MORENCI FOUNDRY & MACHINERY. Leander Baker was the proprietor of this company that manufactured agricultural tools and machinery. Hand plows, tillers, and rakes were among the types of equipment produced.

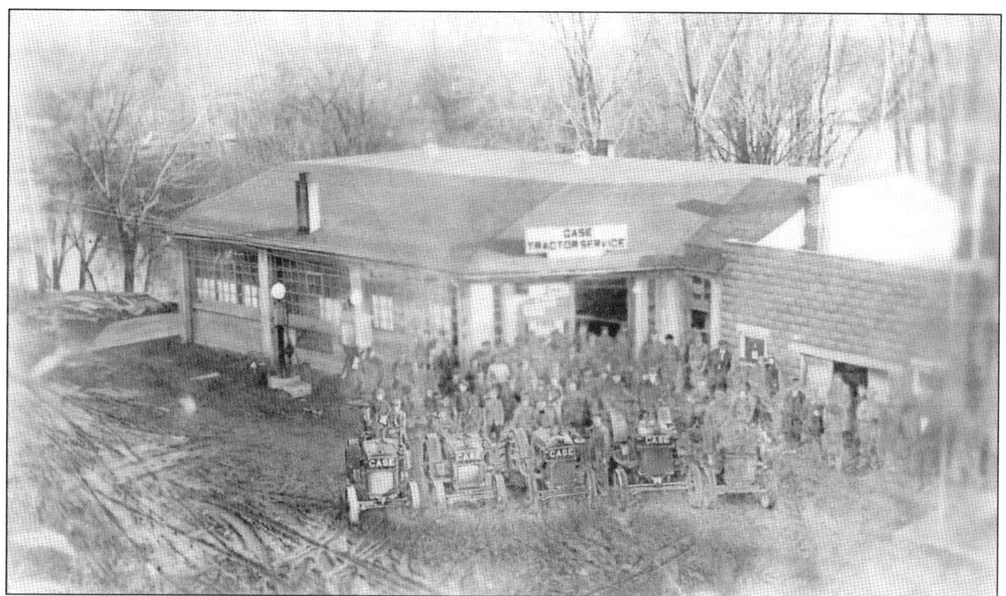

Deerfield Case Tractor Sales. Founded as the J.I. Case Threshing Machine Company in 1844, this company became known simply as "Case" in 1928. It developed into one of the biggest manufacturers of steam engines, traction engines, and steam tractors as well as threshers and other harvesting machinery. The staff at the Case tractor dealership in Deerfield is pictured with a display of their tractors in this photograph.

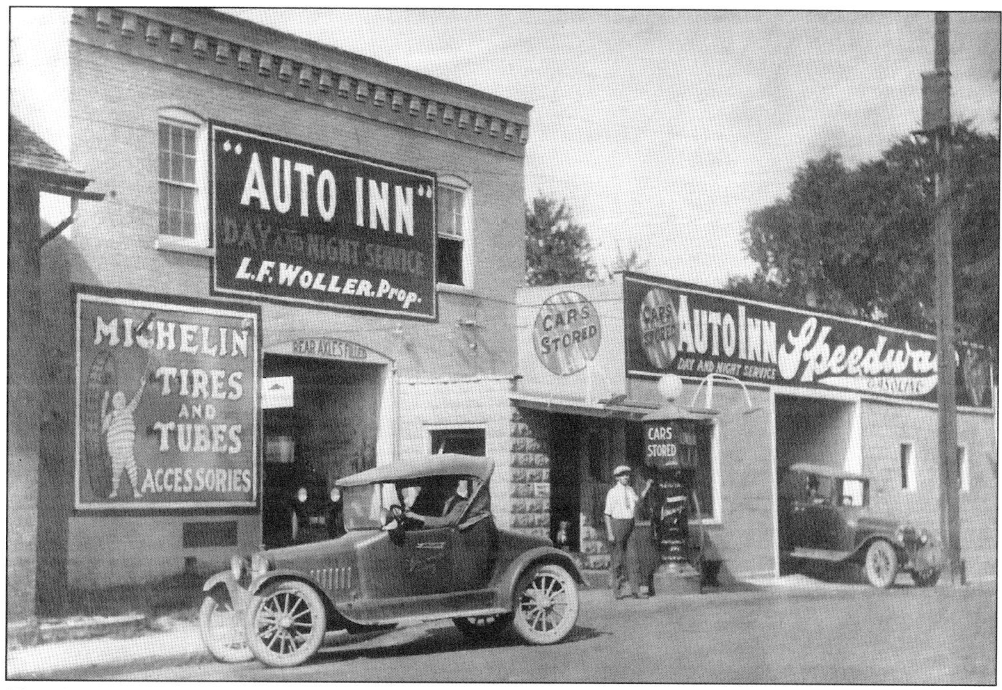

The Auto Inn. Owned by L.F. Waller, the Auto Inn illustrates a change in the times, with day and night service for automobiles instead of wagons or carriages. Located on Washburn Street in Adrian, Waller provided gas, service, and storage for cars. Waller was a successful businessman with several businesses in town, one of them being a taxi service.

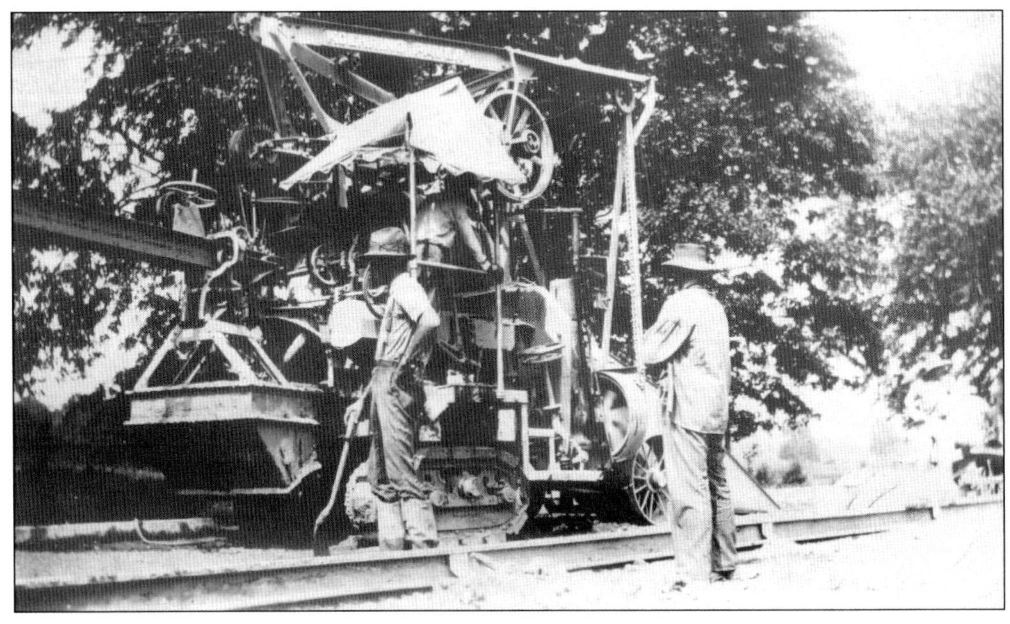

Preparing to Pave M-50. In 1922, the paving preparation for M-50 through Tipton began. A sign of a new age in travel appeared as the state thoroughfares were paved in Lenawee. As workers paved M-50, a smoother ride was on the horizon for the automobile.

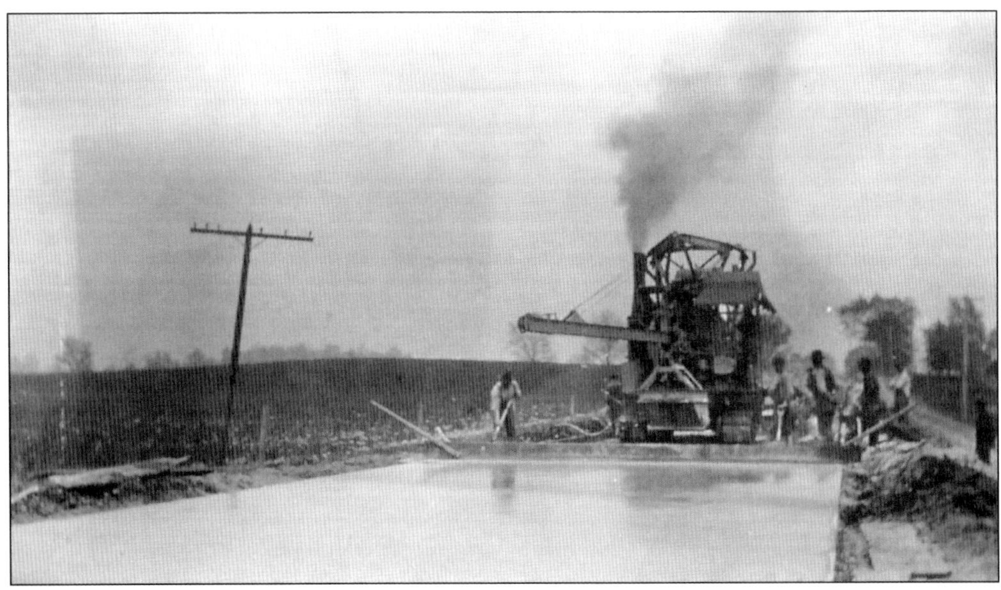

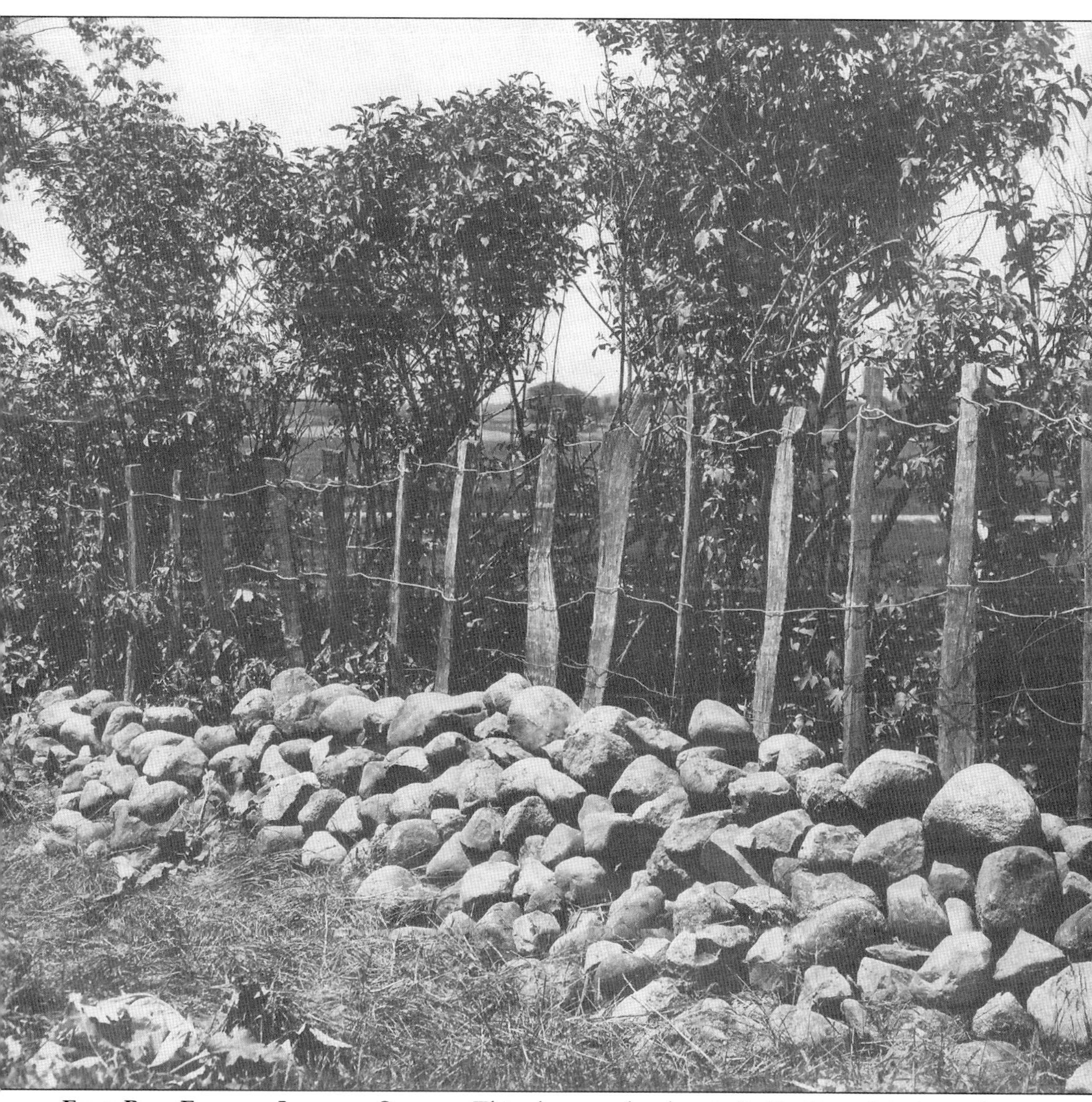

First Page Fence in Lenawee County. This photograph taken in Rollin Township shows the first Page fence woven on a loom. A unique crossover knotted weave gave the fence strength and flexibility.

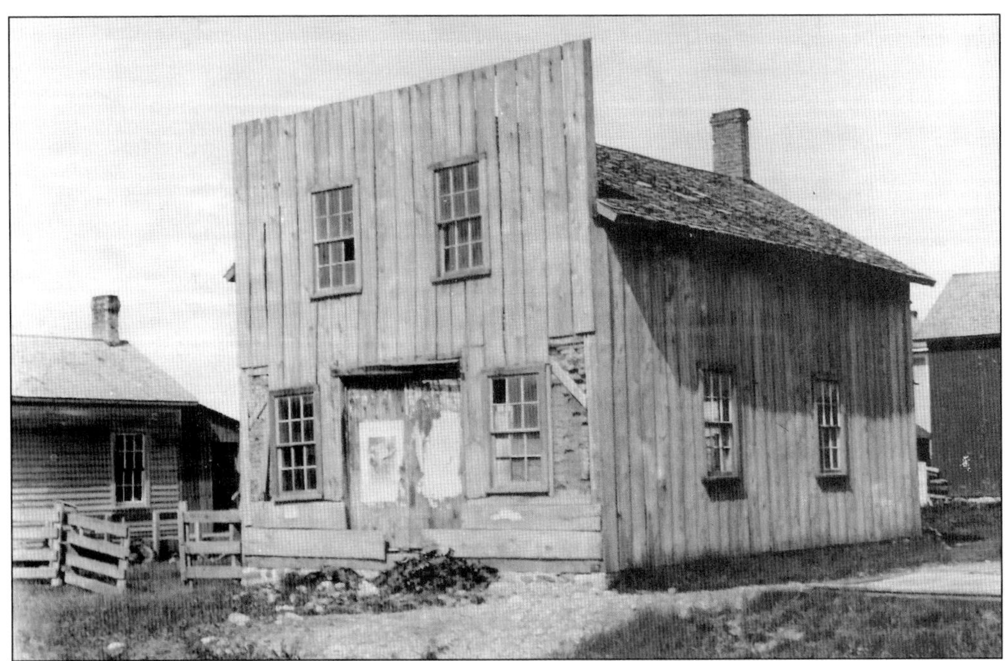

First Page Fence Company in Rollin. This blacksmith shop in Rollin Township is where the ideas began. J. Wallace Page created the loom for his special weave in this building. He experimented with weaving fence wire, trying to create a similarity to the approach used to weave cloth. In 1886, the Page fence was ready for sale.

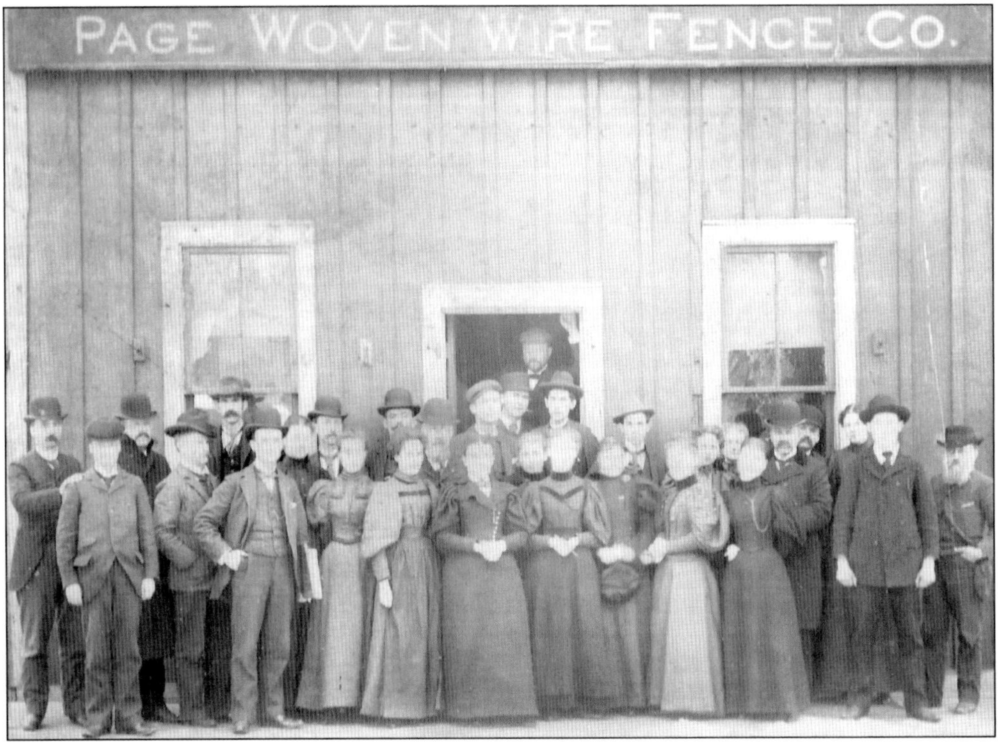

First Page Fence Staff. The staff of the Page Fence Company is pictured here in 1895.

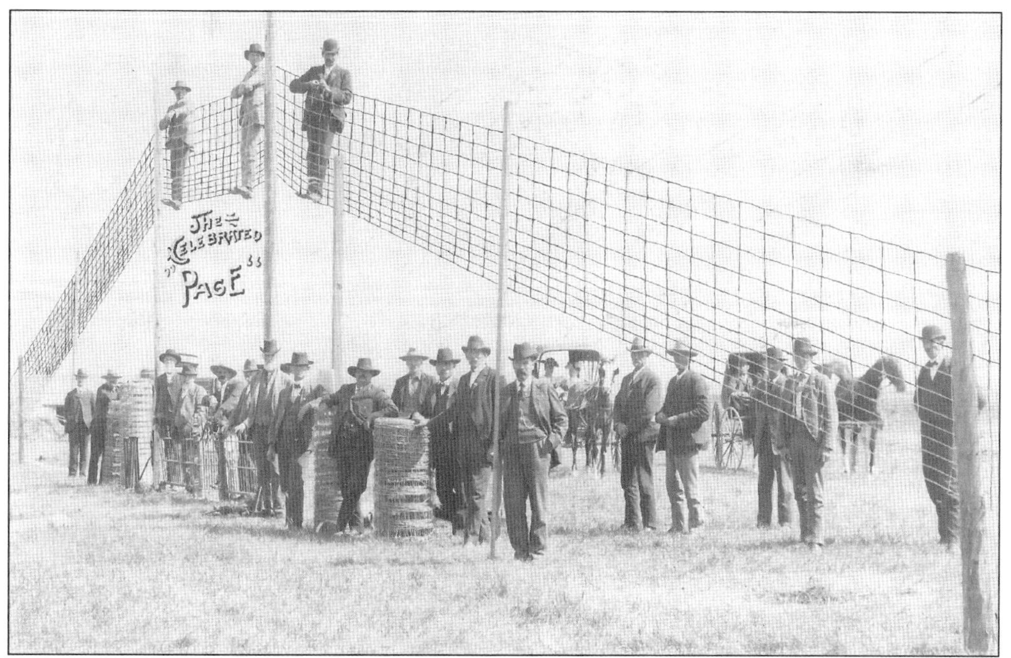

ADRIAN PAGE FENCE AT COUNTY FAIR IN MINNESOTA. Page fences had been used to make bridges, so why not just stand on an upright display? The flexibility and resistance was outstanding, as these men illustrate.

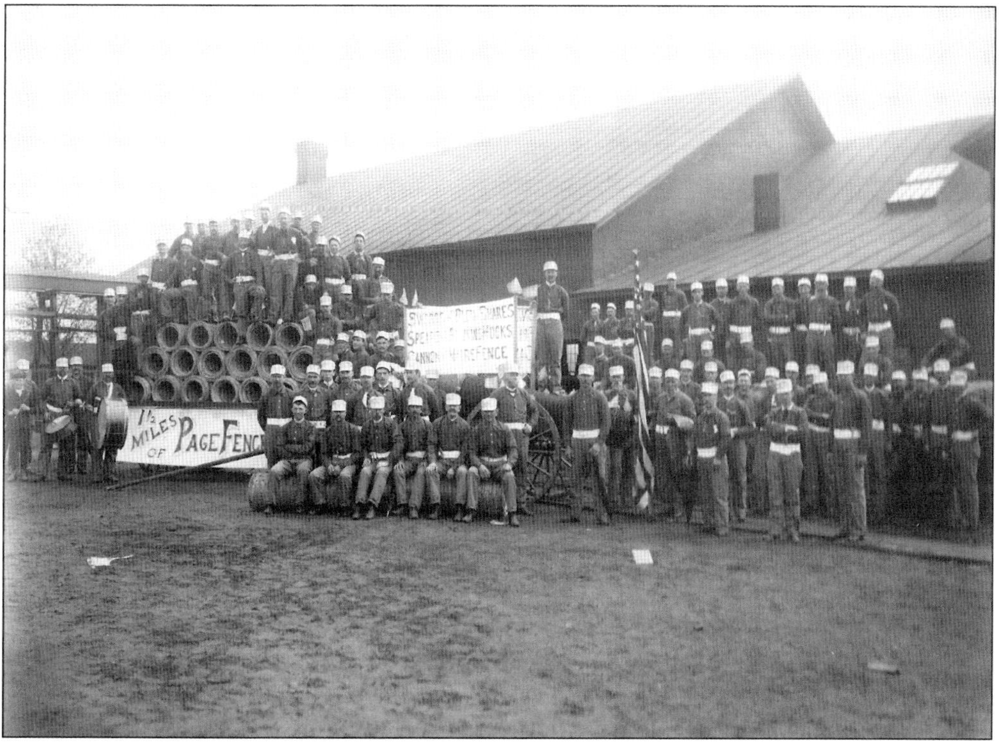

ADRIAN PAGE FENCE. The staff celebrates one-and-a-half miles of woven fence. Many songs and rhymes were written to advertise the company, and were sung at fairs and during parades.

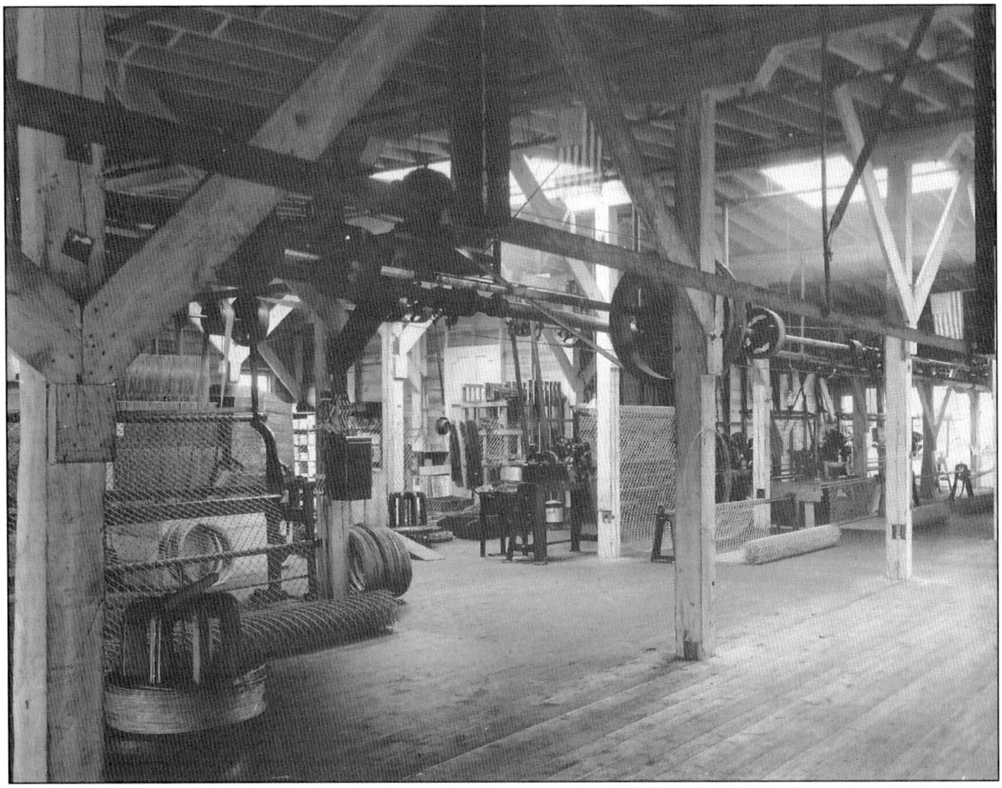

ADRIAN PAGE FENCE INTERIOR. The view shows the interior of the shop, with some woven fence on the looms and a coil of wire waiting to be woven and knotted to perfection.

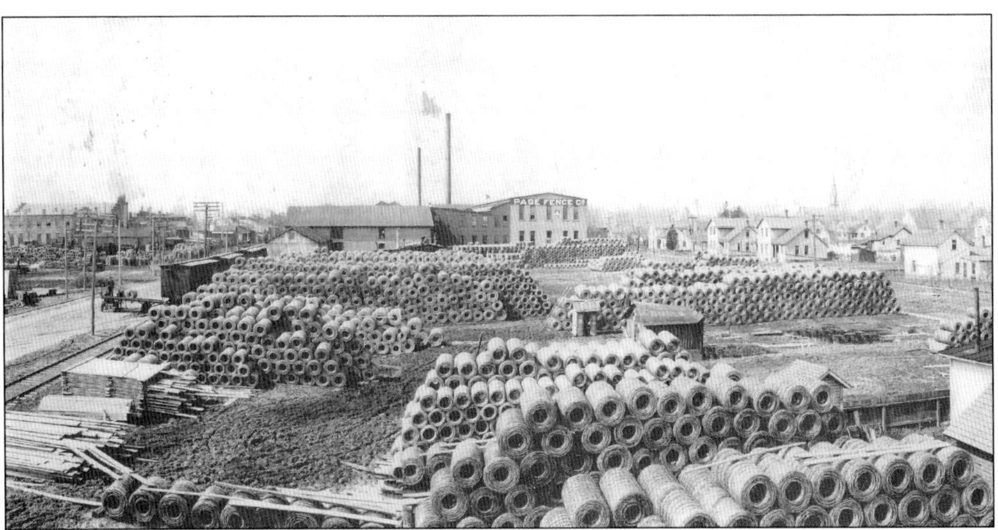

ADRIAN PAGE FENCE YARD. Shown here is the fence yard at the location in Adrian. The business was moved to Adrian in 1887. With the factory in the distance, miles of woven metal twine lie in the foreground.

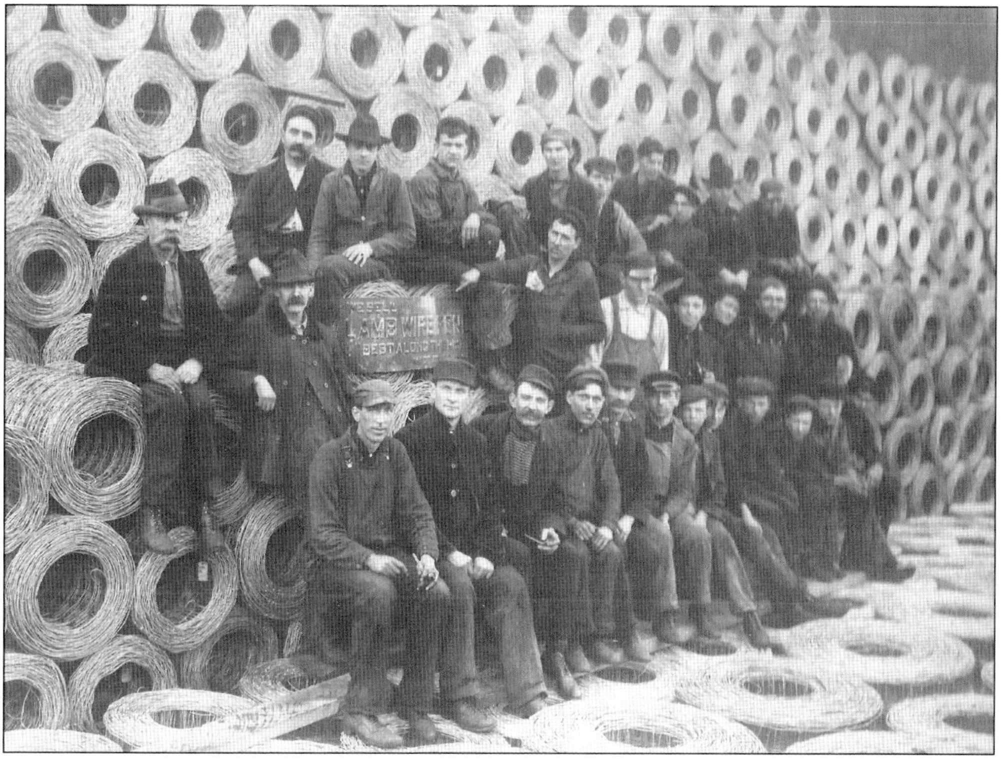

LAMB WIRE FENCE STAFF AT E. MICHIGAN STREET. Although a separate company at one point, the owner of the Lamb Wire Fence Company, C.M. Lamb, worked with Page, providing insight for creating a power-driven loom.

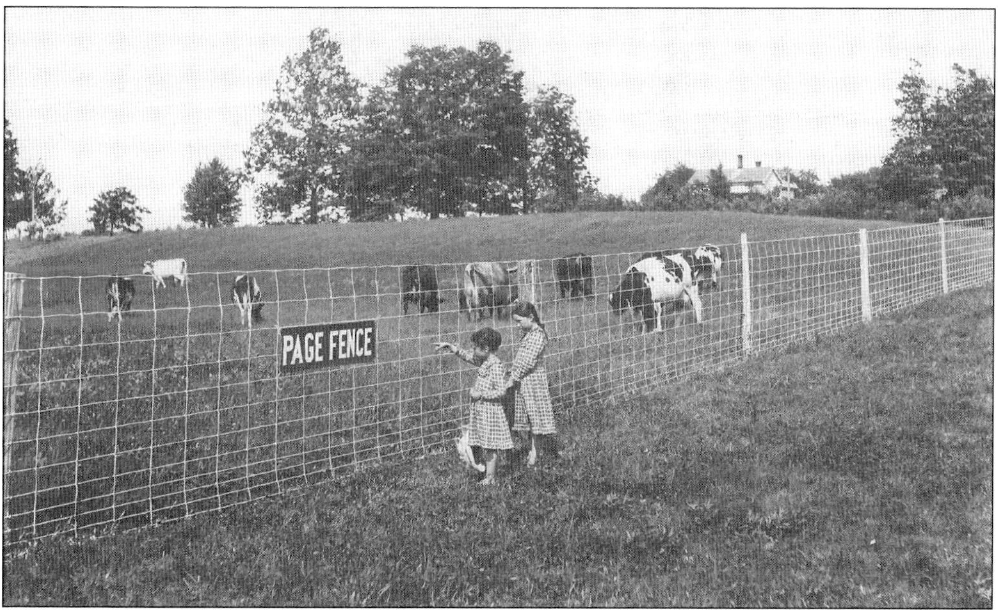

PAGE FENCE AT FARM. With the Page fence installed on this farm near Hudson, Michigan, a strong, flexible boundary line stands between the child and the livestock. The sense of openness still exists with this design, yet it provides a strong barrier.

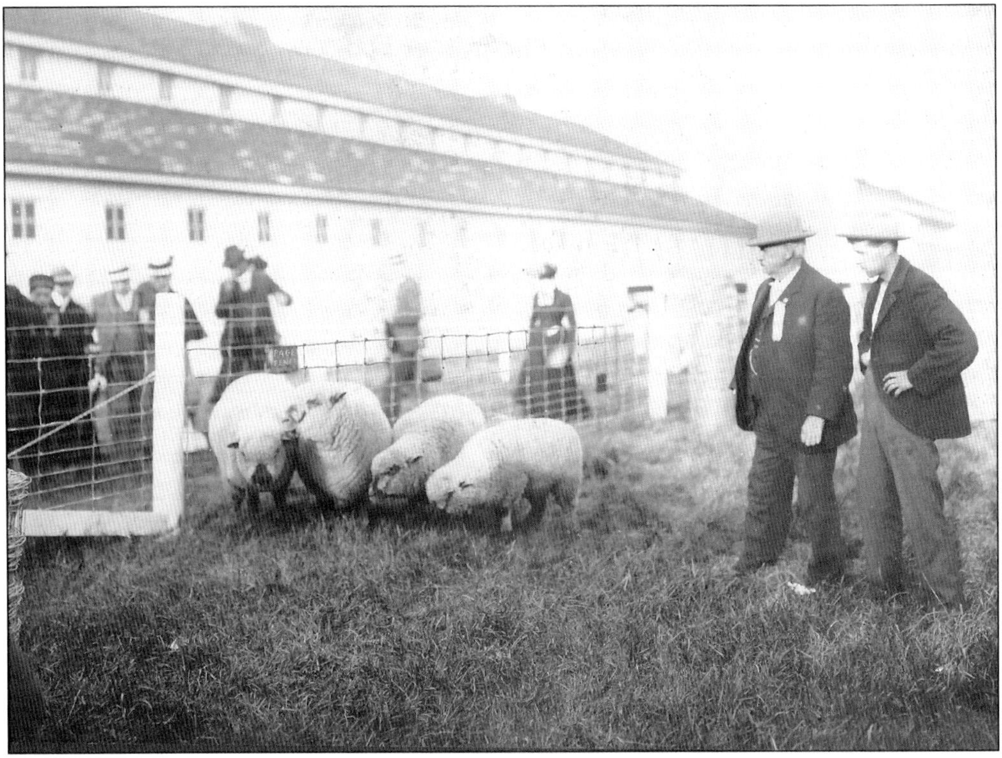

Page Fence at County Fair. Using the fence at county fairs throughout the country was a perfect means of advertising. This photograph was taken at the county fair in Dexter, Minnesota.

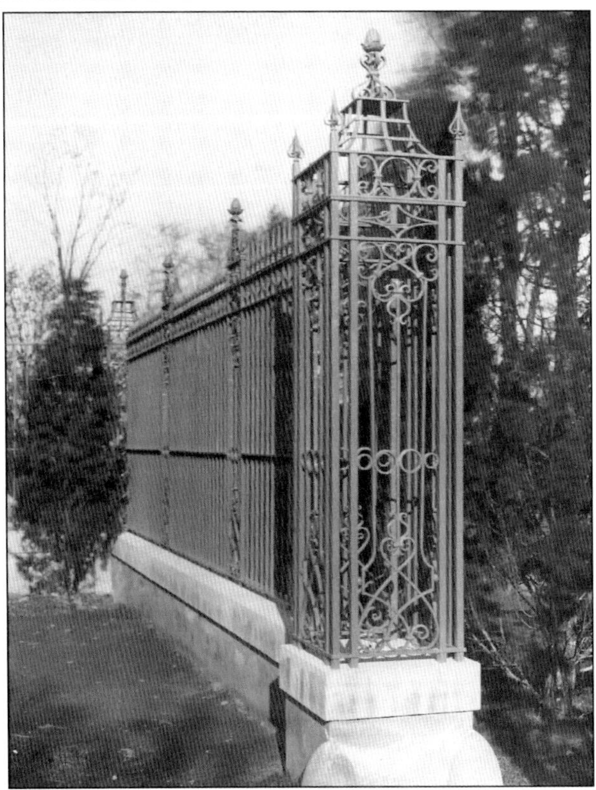

Cast-Iron Page Fence. This photograph illustrates how much the industry has developed, beginning with a simple wide-open weave and progressing to ornate gate posts, as shown here. J. Wallace Page died in 1916. The American Chain and Cable Company purchased the business in 1920, and it closed in 1992 after being purchased by Babcock & Wilcox of England in 1975.

Ten

Agricultural Tourism

From the moment the first settlers got their first view of the masterpiece that nature had created in their new frontier to the present day, all that one has to do is look around, regardless of which corner of Lenawee they may be in, to see the agricultural value that surrounds. Even in the 1800s, many feared that the tranquility would slip away as settlers arrived. Some cottage-lined lake shores were upgraded with modern mansions, yet there is still an aura different from any other place. Campgrounds, modest motels, and diners are still available in every direction, with museums and landmarks in every community. Orchards, vineyards, and wineries add to the charm. The lakes were said to be a fisherman's dream, with a variety of catch such as bass, bluegill, trout, or perch, and today it is the same. An array of historic downtowns still remain throughout Lenawee, bringing a sense of charm. Fun-filled heritage festivals are still a tradition, with the Lenawee County Fair being one of the biggest attractions of the year.

Fortunately, state parks, wildlife sanctuaries, and conservation areas have been created to preserve nature. Many parks can be found within city limits as well. A magnificent example of nature's beauty was created in Tipton by Harvey Fee. Beginning with the attempt to farm after retiring in 1926, he led himself into what he referred to as "a dream-as-you-go development" with the creation of Hidden Lake Gardens. Fee set out to create different scenic transitions for the public to admire along a road that he built through his 200 acres of property. The gardens were planted along the hillsides, bringing immeasurable beauty to the land to this day. After donating the property to Michigan State University in 1945, Fee continued his involvement in the gardens until his death in 1955. The horticultural project grew to 755 acres. Educational programs and exhibits are presented throughout the year.

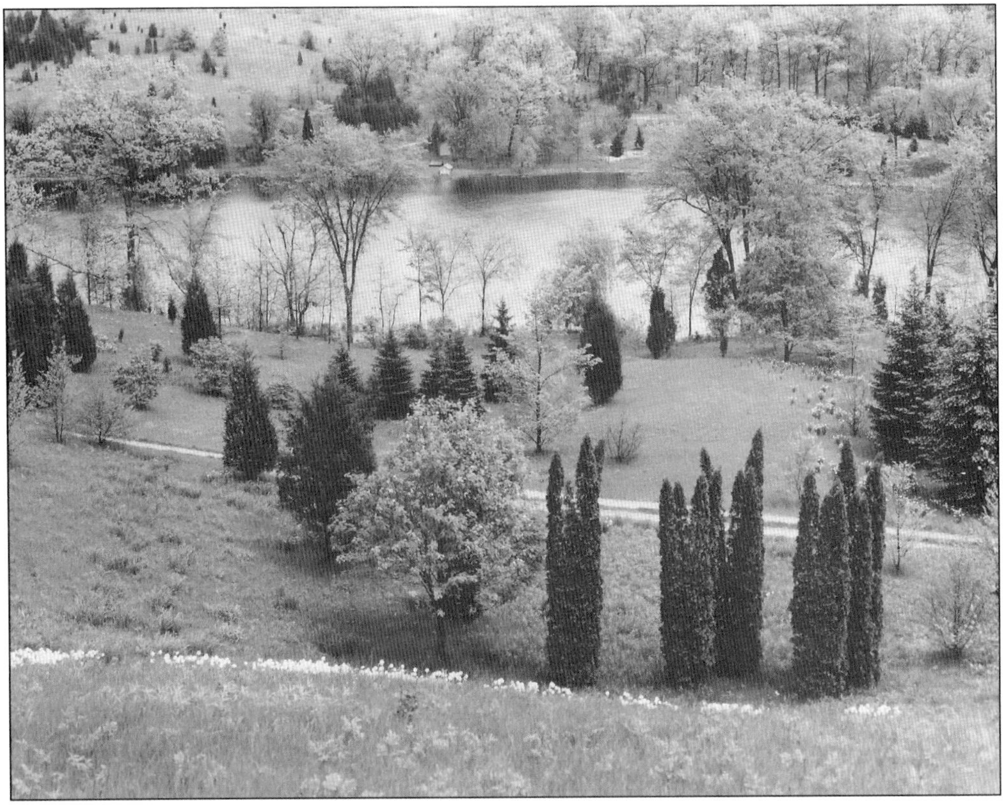

Hidden Lake Gardens' Flowering Hills. Located off M-50 in Franklin Township, Hidden Lake Gardens is full of ever-changing beauty throughout the year. The assortment of trees always brings character to the scenic hillside views. Admiring the beauty of nature while driving along the scenic road or hiking the trails is always refreshing and enlightening. (Courtesy of Hidden Lake Gardens.)

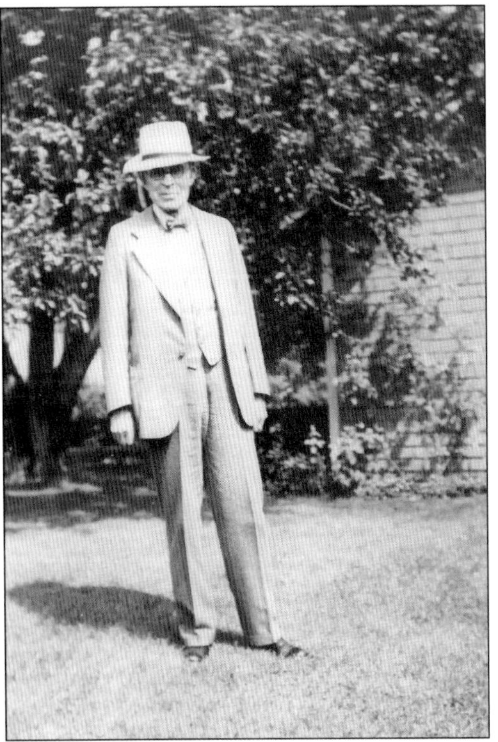

Founder of Hidden Lake Gardens. Harry A. Fee was a modest man. In 1926, he retired from his business as an electrician in Adrian. Fulfilling his own desires, he purchased 200 acres of land, which included Hidden Lake and a farmhouse. After renovating the farmhouse and building a greenhouse, an attempt at farming began. Realizing that the land was not suitable for farming, he began growing nursery stock. He created a small pond and a rock garden and planted a variety of trees and shrubs with an overwhelming assortment of flowers decorating the land. (Courtesy of Hidden Lake Gardens.)

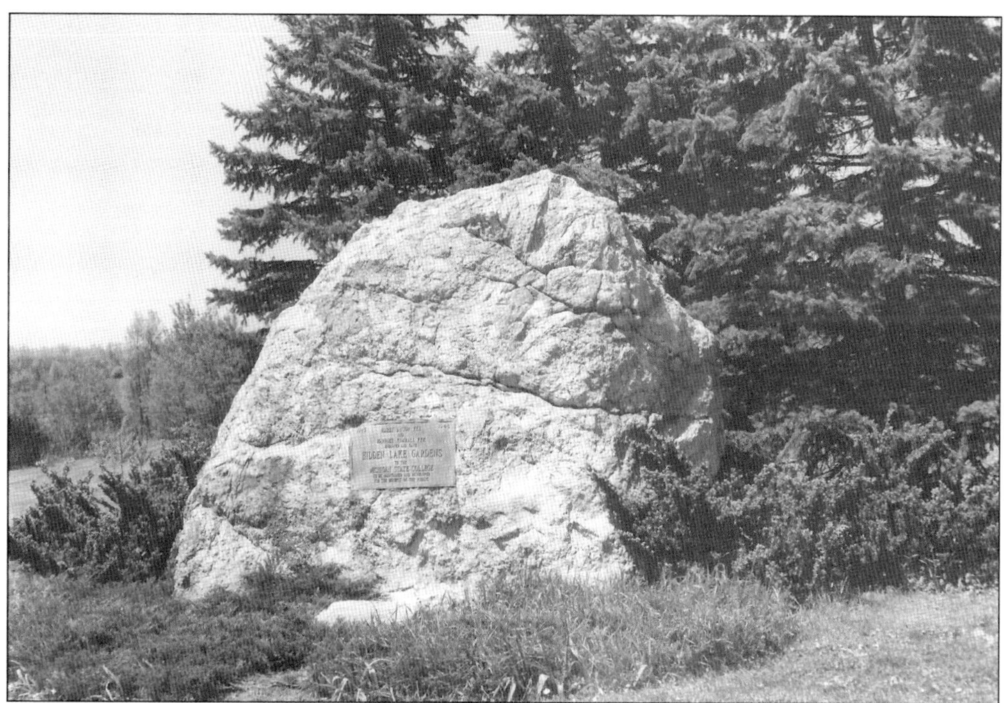

THE BIG ROCK. Representing the glory of nature, this boulder was chosen not just as a landmark but as a representation of geological history. A plaque explains the story behind the travels of this rock. A coarse granite pegmatite, it was brought down from its location on the north shore of Georgian Bay, Canada, by the glaciers thousands of years ago. It came to rest some 25 miles west of this site in Wheatland Township of Hillsdale County when the ice melted. (Courtesy of Hidden Lake Gardens.)

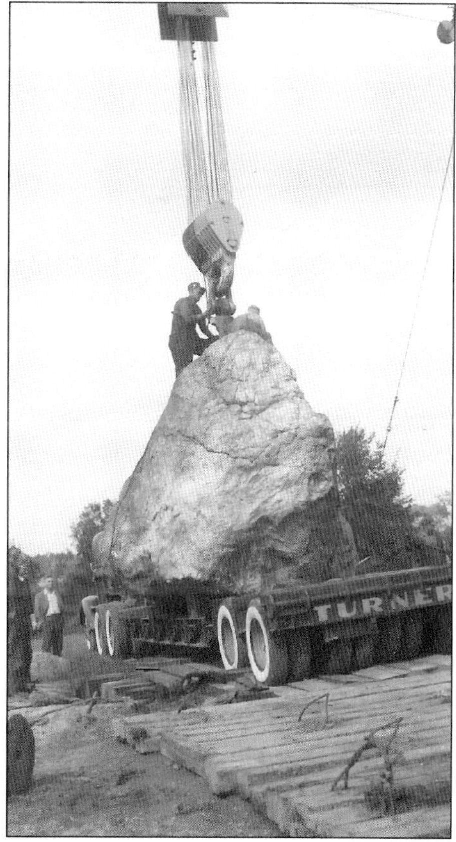

BOULDER LOWERED TO TRUCK. Carefully lowering the boulder was a tedious task requiring precision. Although a mighty rock, avoiding damage of any sort to this specimen of geology was important. What is considered the underside of the rock was smooth, being protected from the mighty forces of the shifting glacial ice for centuries. The crew seen here had every intention of keeping it that way. (Courtesy of Hidden Lake Gardens.)

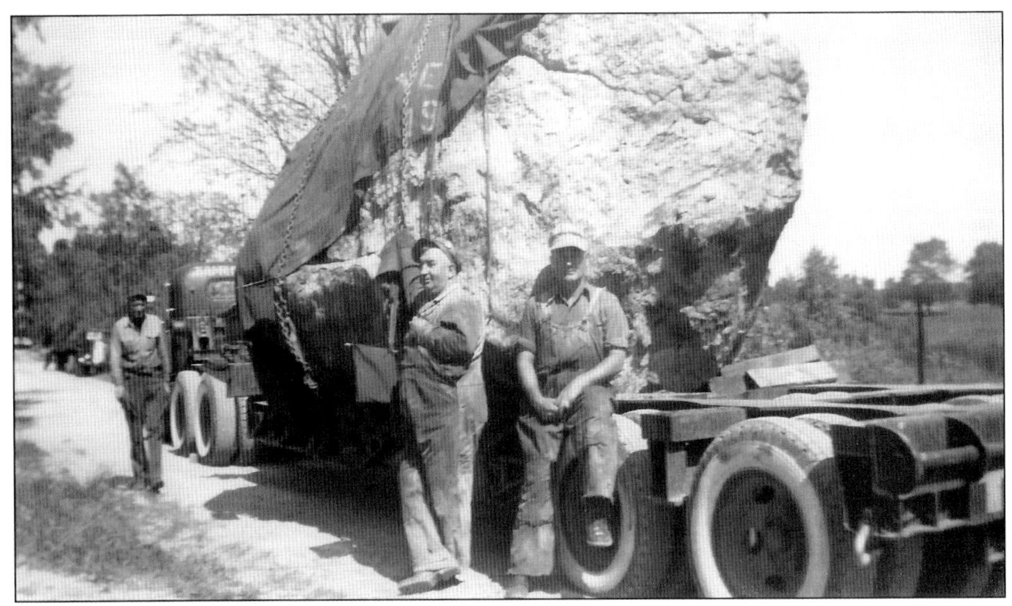

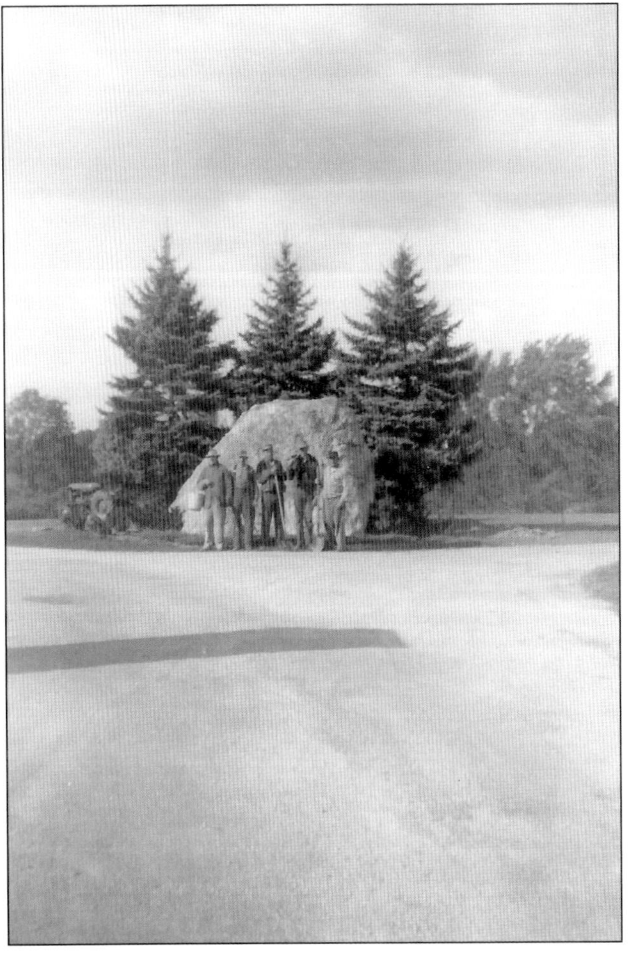

Waiting to Haul the Big Rock to Hidden Lake Gardens. The crew is posing as though it has just been an easy day after raising the boulder onto the platform and securing it to haul down the road. (Courtesy of Hidden Lake Gardens.)

The Big Rock in Place. This image shows the monumental boulder from the bed of Lake Erie in place at Hidden Lake Gardens with the men who brought it here. It is on display to intrigue and educate all who pass by. (Courtesy of Hidden Lake Gardens.)

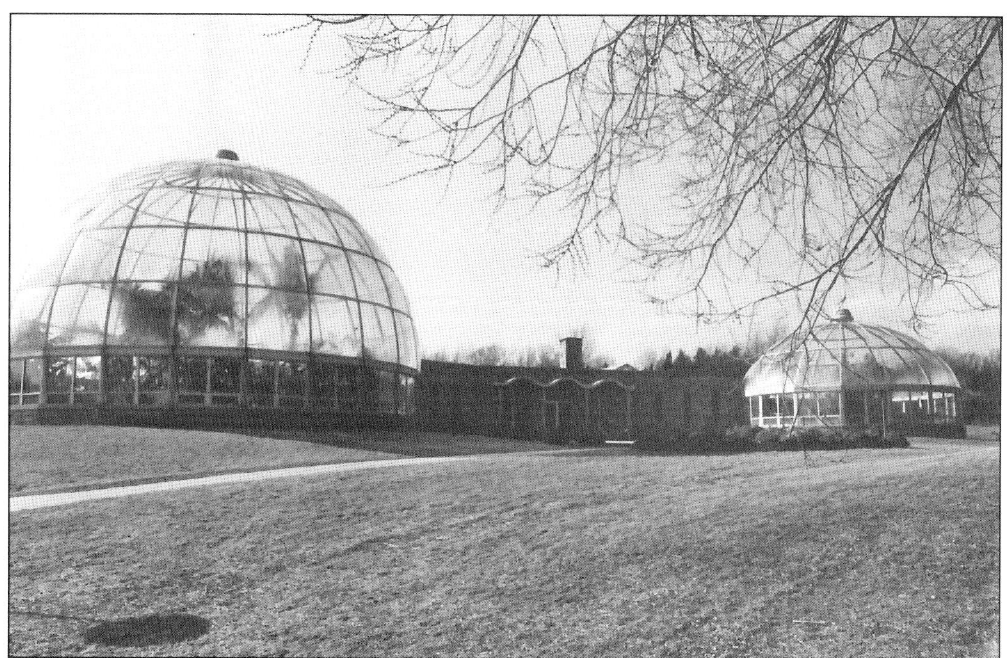

Tropical Dome, 1951. This is a view of the tropical dome (left) at Hidden Lake Gardens, where plants such as sugarcane, coffee, and vanilla grew in the enclosed dome. The arid dome is on the right; there, humidity is kept at a minimal level for cacti and other prickly plants to thrive in the sunlight. (Courtesy of Hidden Lake Gardens.)

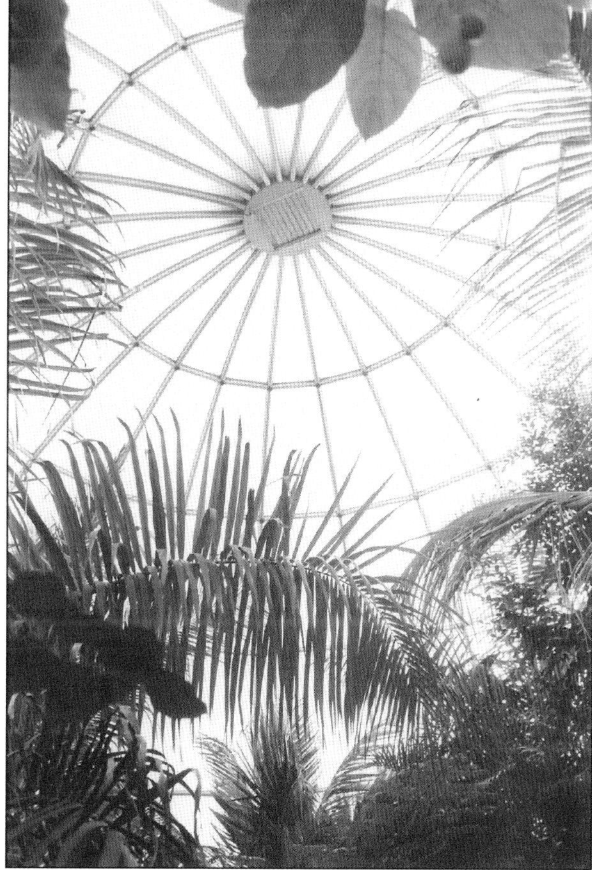

Interior of Tropical Dome. The design and construction of the tropical dome is as intriguing as the plants themselves. Eight thousand square feet of gardens under glass were built in 1968. (Courtesy of Hidden Lake Gardens.)

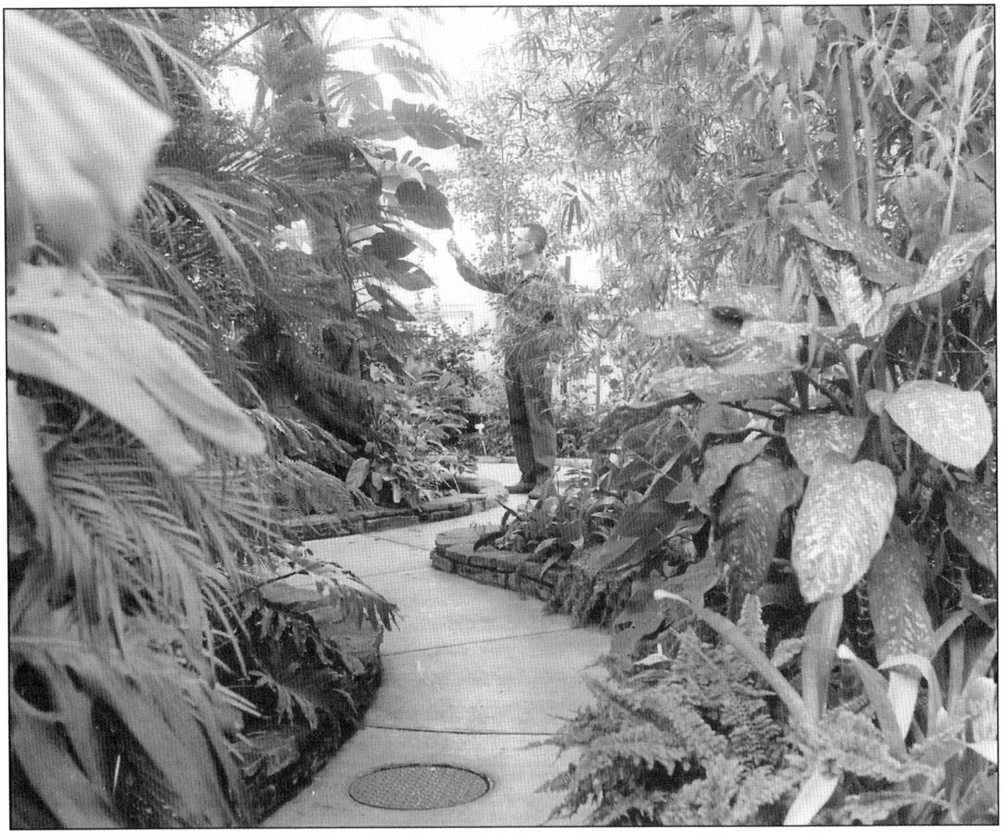

INSIDE THE TROPICAL DOME WITH JACK WILKE. Jack Wilke is inside the tropical dome in 1969, tending to the plants. The success of Hidden Lake is owed to the employees and volunteers who have helped create and maintain the gardens. Donations, in both monetary and plant form, have been a major factor in keeping the gardens alive. (Courtesy of Hidden Lake Gardens.)

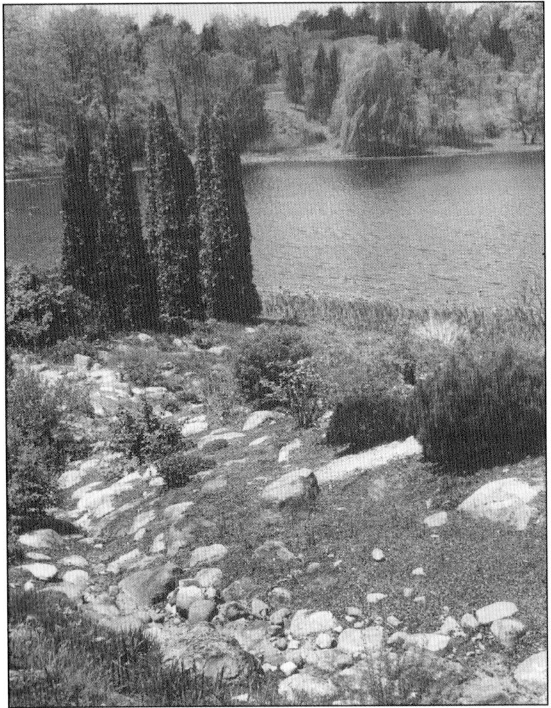

ROCKY LAKE PATH. It seems as though these rocks were carefully placed along the lakeshore instead of being laid to rest by the mighty glaciers. (Courtesy of Hidden Lake Gardens.)

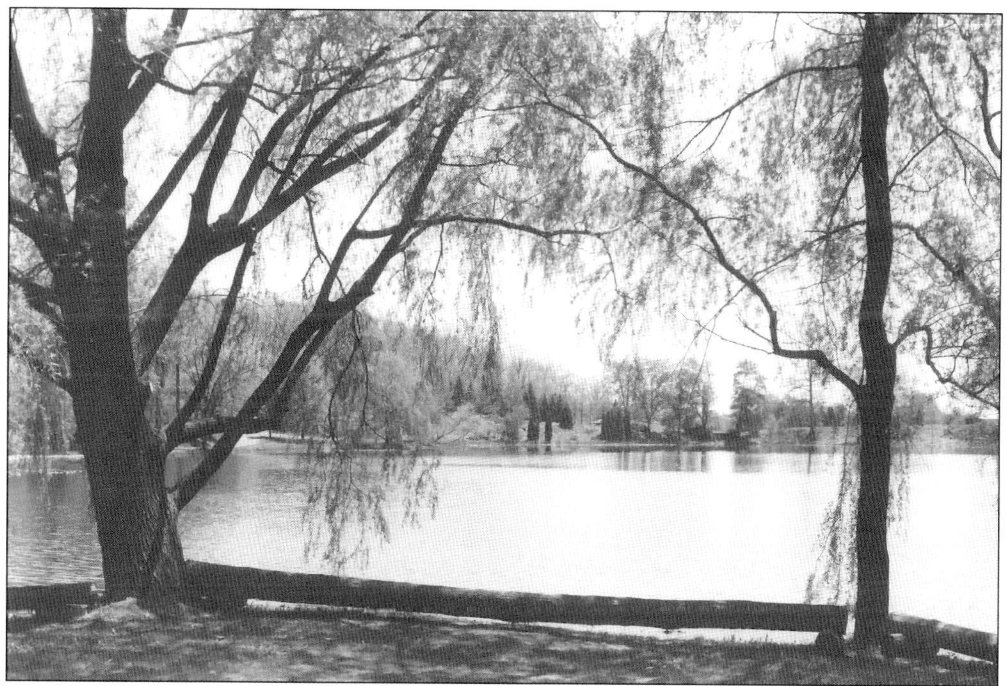

A Lake View. This is a peaceful view of Hidden Lake through the trees. (Courtesy of Hidden Lake Gardens.)

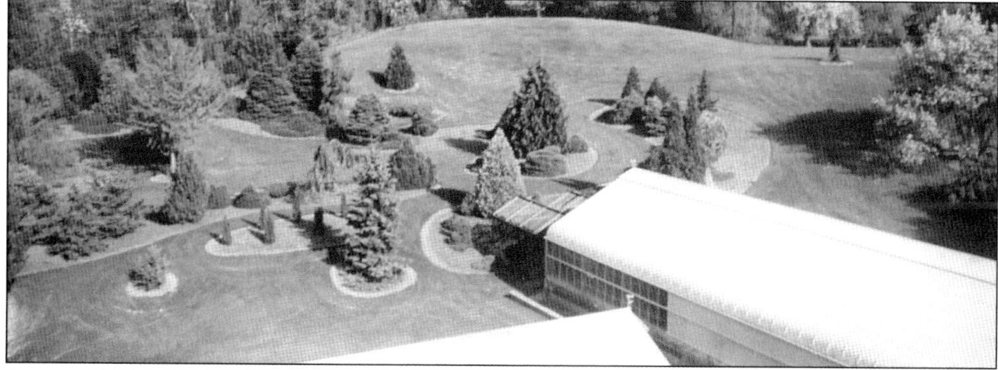

Aerial View of Temperate House. Taken in May 1999, this aerial view shows the temperate house and surrounding grounds. Here, visitors can see spring blooms during the winter. (Courtesy of Hidden Lake Gardens.)

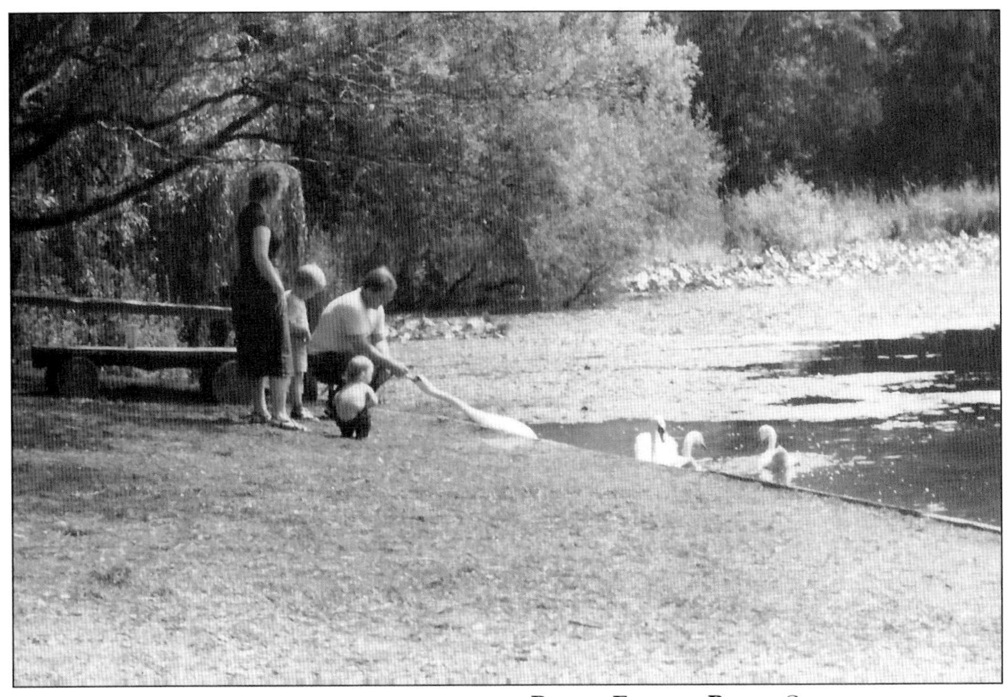

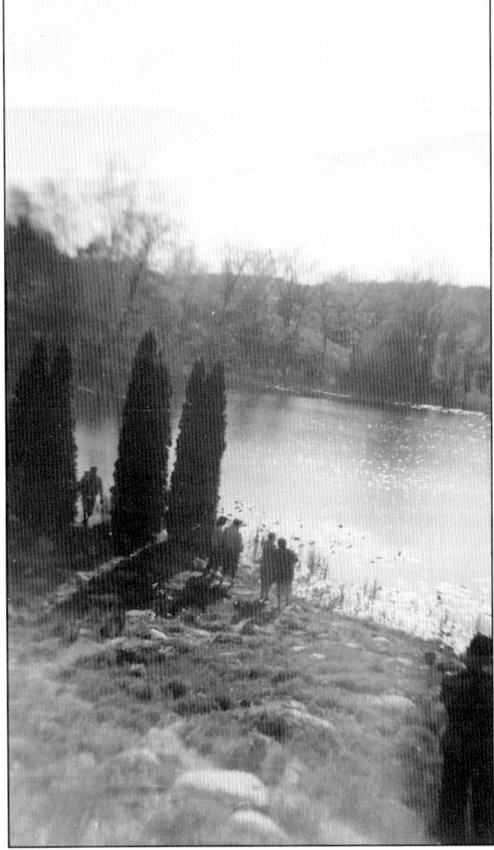

People Feeding Birds. Swans were introduced in the 1960s with the intention of providing patrons the opportunity to share peaceful moments with nature. Feeding the swans creates a gentle connection with nature's creatures. (Courtesy of Hidden Lake Gardens.)

People on Lakeshore. Fred Freeman, the curator of Hidden Lake Gardens, is shown on the shore with his family during the mid-1950s. In the words of Harry A. Fee, "I hope that you will carry on long after I have vanished into the infinite azure of the past and will always keep the idea that the Gardens are primarily for the Benefit and Education of the Public." This hope has been respected by those who have read these words. Others feel Fee's dream and admire what he created. (Courtesy of Hidden Lake Gardens.)

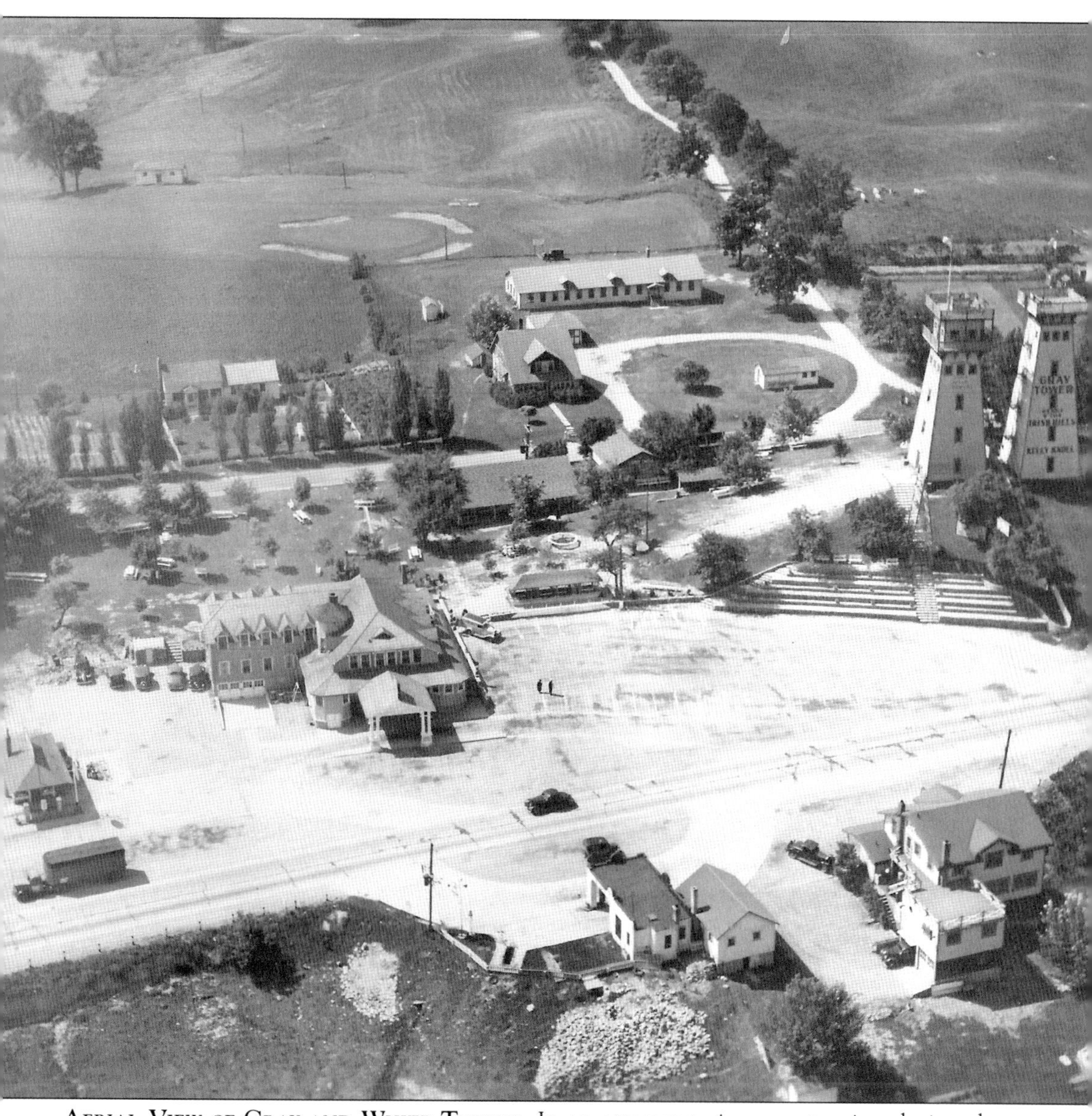

Aerial View of Gray and White Towers. In an attempt to increase tourism during the 1920s, the Michigan Observation Company located property on a knoll on US 12 in Cambridge Township with the intention of erecting a 50-foot wooden tower with a platform for viewing the surrounding land, water, and sky. On October 4, 1924, a celebration of the opening of the Irish Hills Observatory occurred. Riding an electric elevator over 100 feet takes visitors to 1,227 feet above sea level. The original White Tower and its neighboring Gray Tower, named because of their original paint, were listed in the National Register of Historic Places in 2007. Construction of the second tower began immediately. The adjoining property owner, who would not sell to Michigan Observation Company, completed construction of his own tower, just a little higher than that of his neighbors, in November 1924. A platform was then added to the first tower. A height competition continued until the towers were equal. The towers were owned and operated separately until the 1950s. Due to safety precautions, the towers were closed in 2000. Efforts to save and renovate the towers have been ongoing for several years.

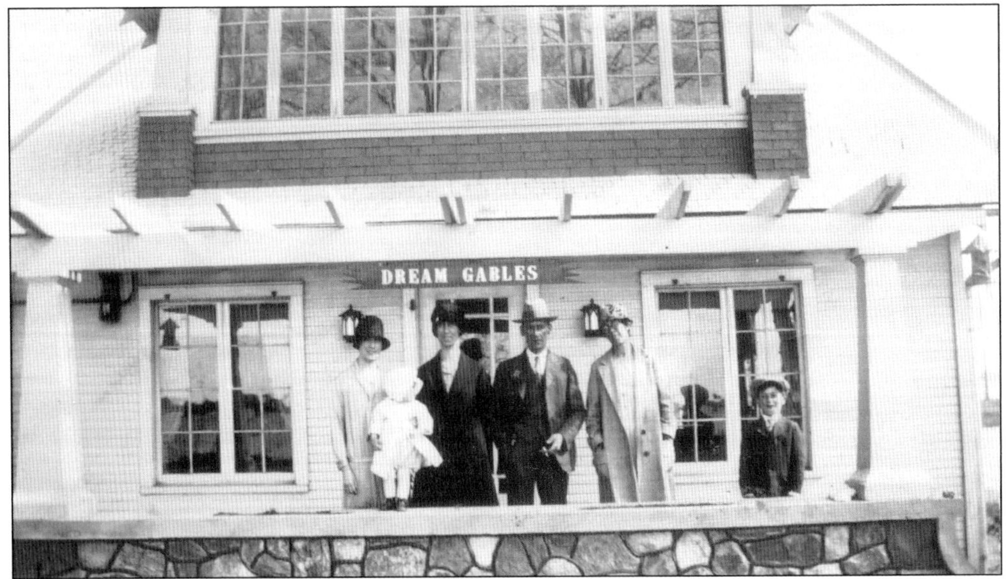

DEVIL'S LAKE DREAM GABLES. Bert and Ella Flatt Keller offered novelties and homespun candy from their gift shop. Located on the corner of the channel between the two lakes, it was a perfect location for visitors and cottage residents. Several women's clubs held their picnics here. Ella was also a poet for the *Log Cabin Weekly*. Dream Gables operated from the 1930s into the 1950s, with each stop made by visitors creating a memory of pleasant travels to the lake.

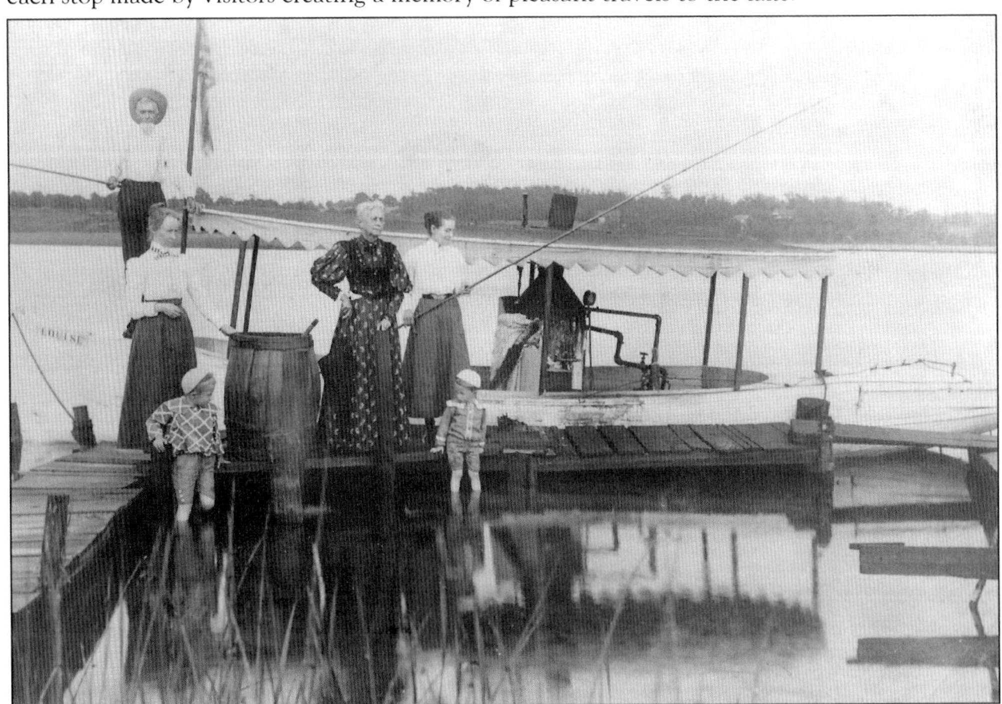

FISHING AT THE WELCH HOME. Standing on the dock in front of the Club House Hotel, owned by Hope Welch, the Welch family enjoys the simple pleasure of fishing at Devil's Lake. In this photograph are Hope Welch, Emma Todd Wesley, Lisle Todd Wesley, Julia Welch Todd, Jennie Burke, and Ken Wesley.

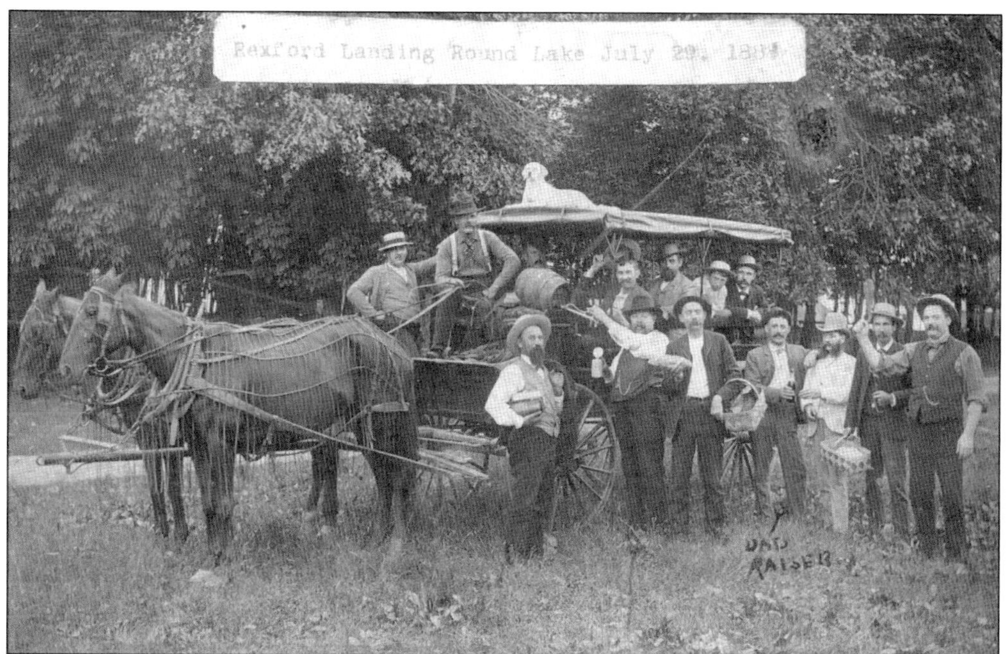

Rexford Landing. Next door to Devil's Lake, Round Lake is one of the smaller and quieter locations in the Irish Hills. These men arriving at Rexford Landing with their picnic baskets and a dog on the canvas roof of their wagon in July 1888, assuredly were prepared for a pleasant afternoon.

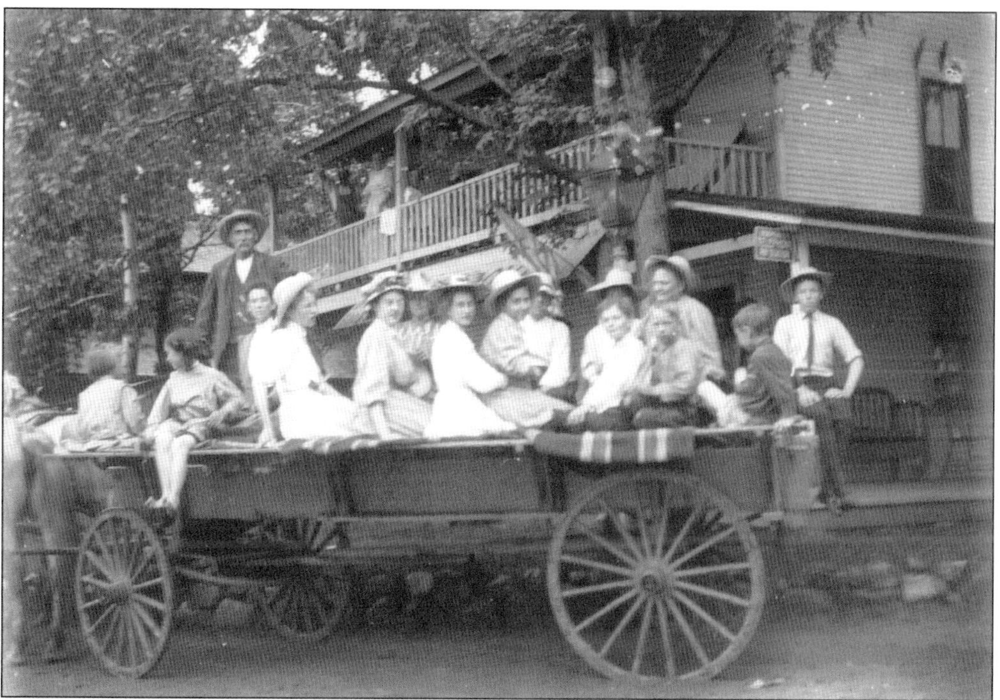

Wampler's Lake Wagon Ride. It was commonplace for vacationers to ride to Wampler's Lake for an afternoon picnic and a change in the air. Even riding together for an afternoon of shopping at the nearest town was a joyful group event while visiting the Irish Hills area.

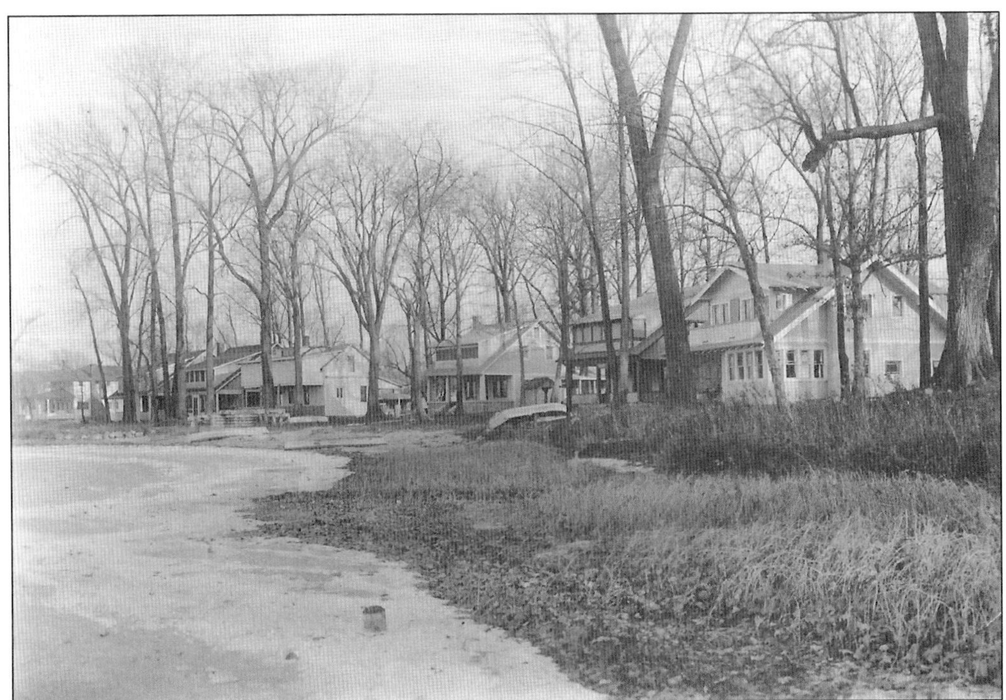

Devil's Lake Cottages. This row of lakeside cottages illustrates the modest retreats and aura of simplicity that so many sought here. As years have passed, some have chosen more elaborate designs, while others continue to stay with modest designs, whether for a year-round home or a cottage. Being inexpensive was the goal at one time. Lakefront property was typically reserved for hotels.

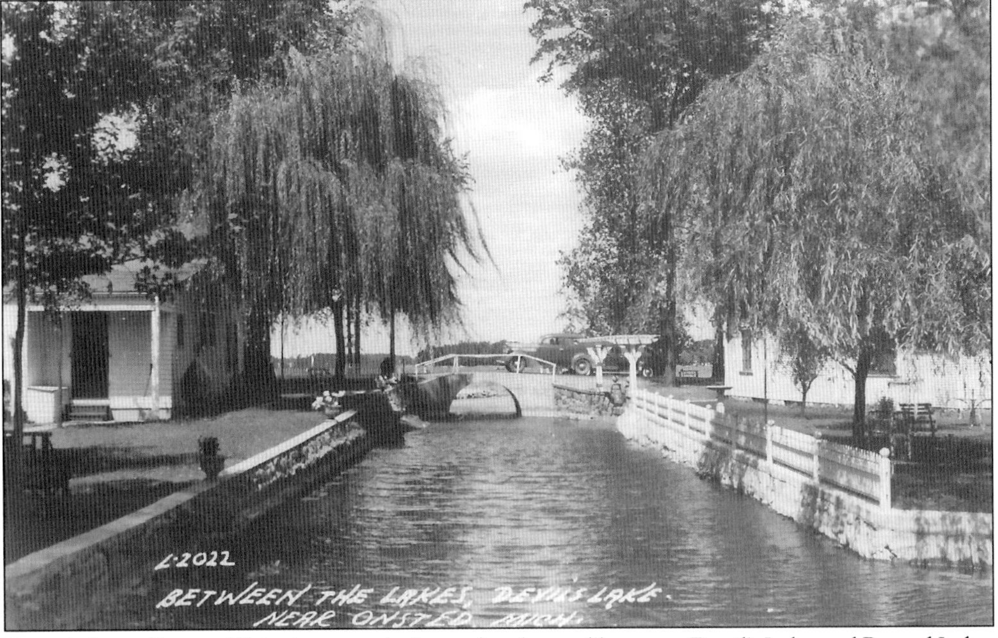

Devil's Lake Canal. This photograph shows the channel between Devil's Lake and Round Lake. A small bridge allowed people to walk across the channel.

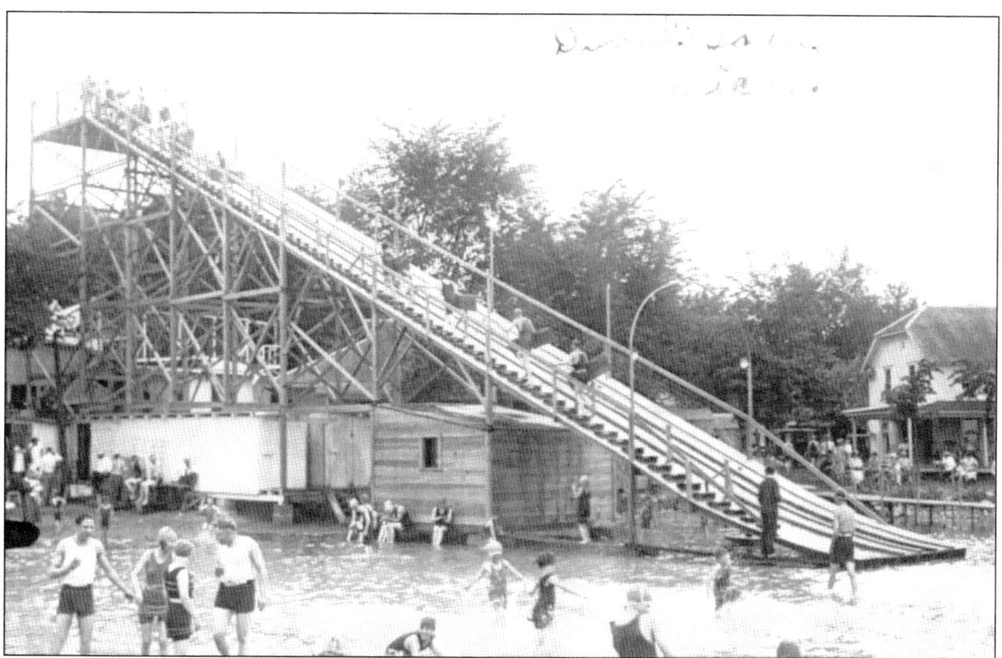

Manitou Beach Toboggan Slide. The first toboggan slide opened in the summer of 1892 and brought fun-filled days to many throughout the years. The three-story wooden slide allowed daredevils to slide down on a toboggan and splash into the water. On June 25, 1925, Captain Raymond, the owner of the property, opened a new slide that was 50 feet high, 150 long, and illuminated.

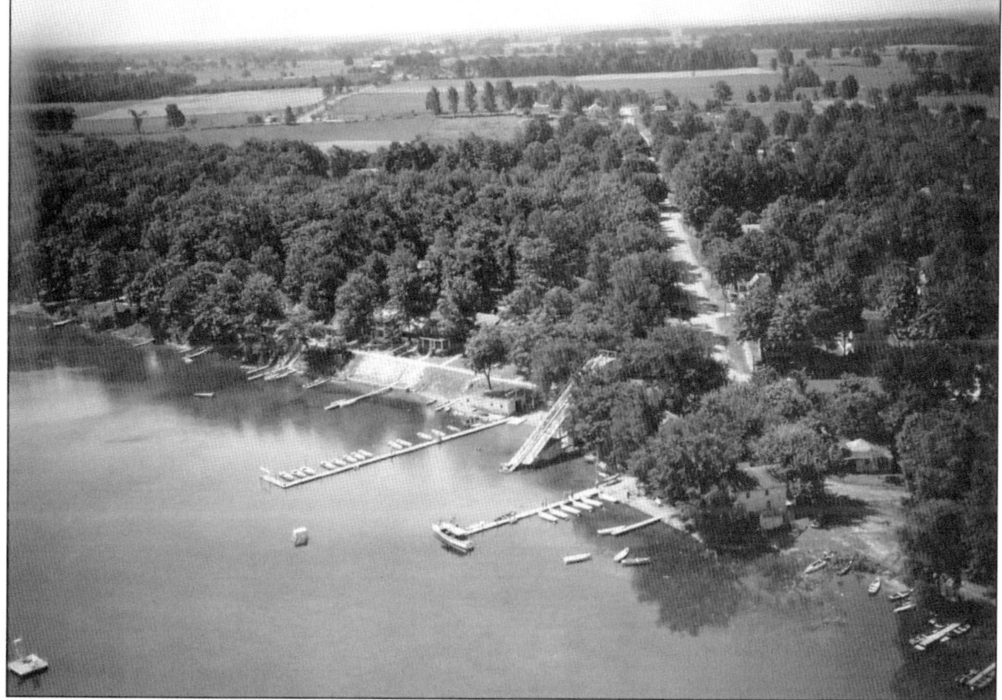

Aerial View of Manitou Beach. In this view showing plentiful trees interspersed with cottages with farmland in the distance, a sense of the serenity found at Devil's Lake is represented.

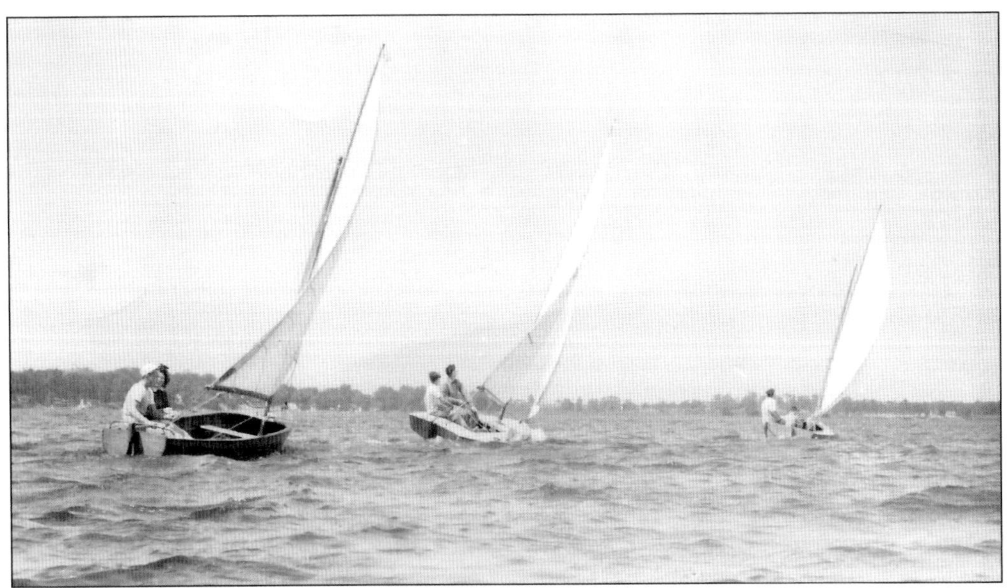

DEVIL'S LAKE NIPPER RACE. Weekly sailboat races were held at Devil's Lake. The Nipper (shown here) and Lightning were popular types of sailboats on the lake. Several boating associations existed, including the yacht club, which hosted many events.

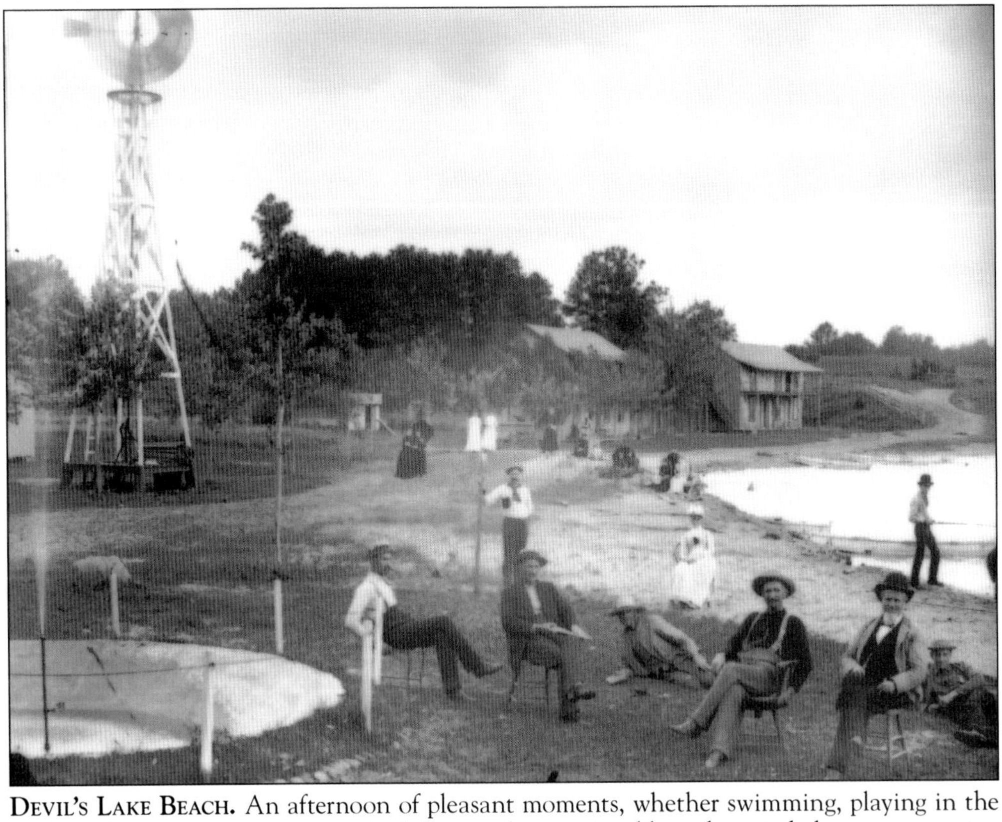

DEVIL'S LAKE BEACH. An afternoon of pleasant moments, whether swimming, playing in the sand, or sharing a conversation at the lake was always enjoyable and created pleasant memories. Several beaches were established around the lake.

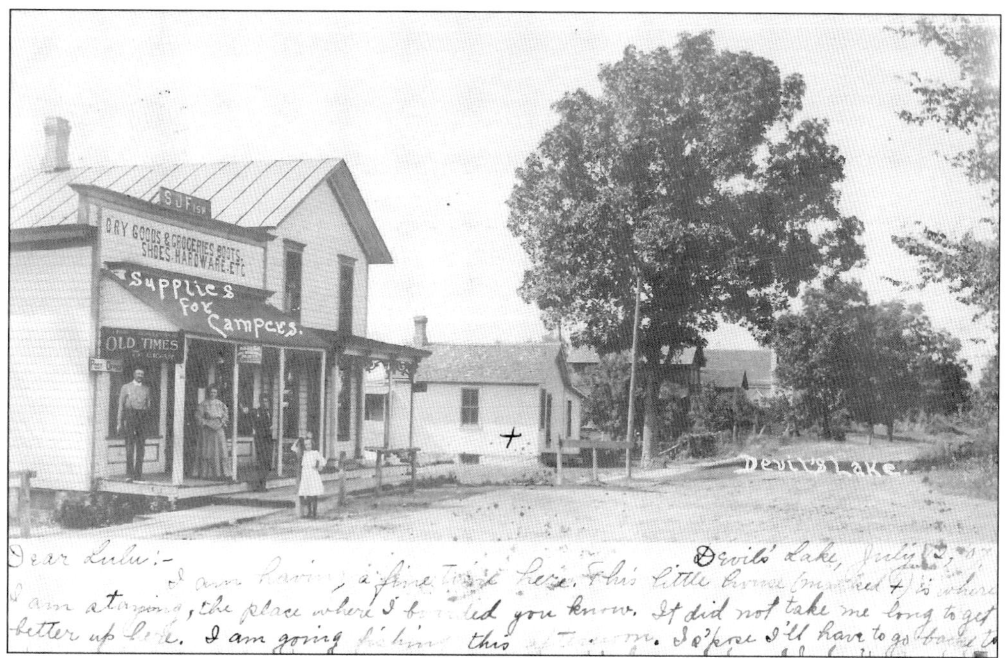

Devil's Lake Postcard of General Store. A postcard of the Squire J. Fish General Store, located on Devil's Lake Highway and Winter Street, has a note reading, "Dear Lulu, I am having a fine time here. This little house is where I am staying, where I boarded you know. It did not take me long to get better up here. I am going fishing this afternoon."

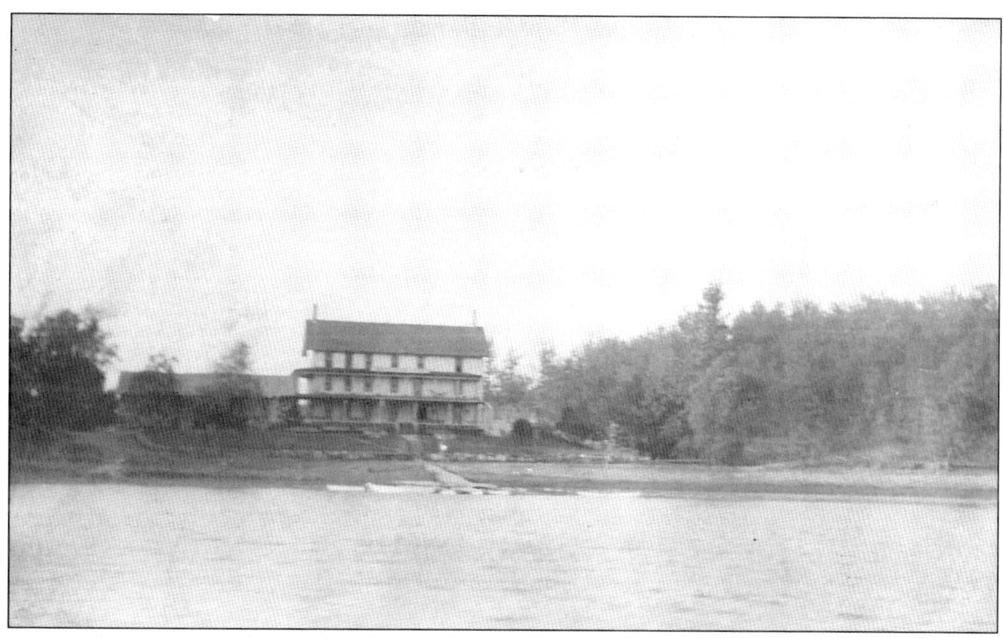

North Shore Hotel. Located on the north side of Sand Lake, those who visited this lake sought a quieter getaway than other lakes were known for. Built in the 1870s on the hillside, the hotel provided a place for entertainment in the evenings or on rainy days for those who were staying at the campgrounds nearby.

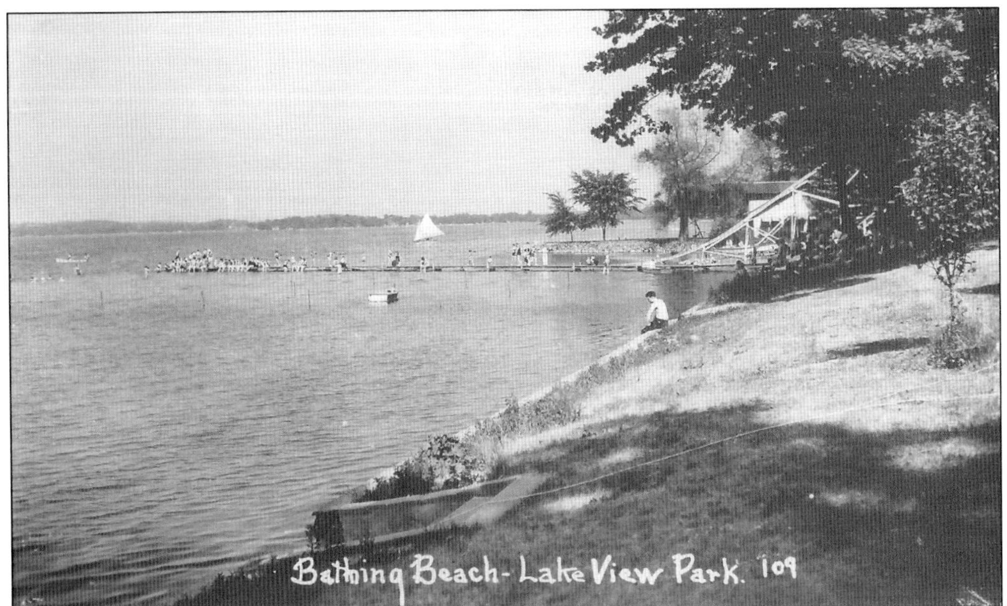

DEVIL'S LAKE BATHING BEACH. Lake View Park was next to the toboggan slide owned by Captain Raymond. Shallow portions of the lake were often designated as a bathing beach, creating some safety for the swimmers while allowing the boaters and fishermen to take advantage of the deeper waters elsewhere.

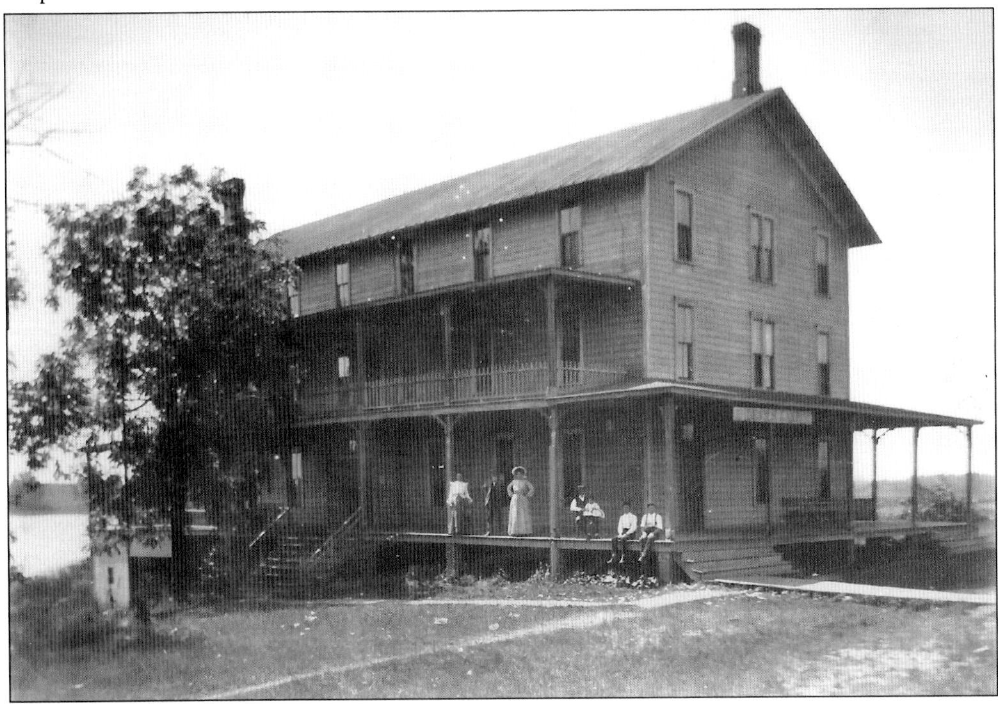

DEVIL'S LAKE CLUB HOUSE HOTEL. Built on the north side of Devil's Lake, the Club House Hotel offered a dance hall on the second floor and 20 guest rooms. Offering entertainment and relaxation along the lakeshore, this was more than many had to offer. A dock was also part of the amenities available to those staying at the hotel. A train stop was added to the hotel in 1884.

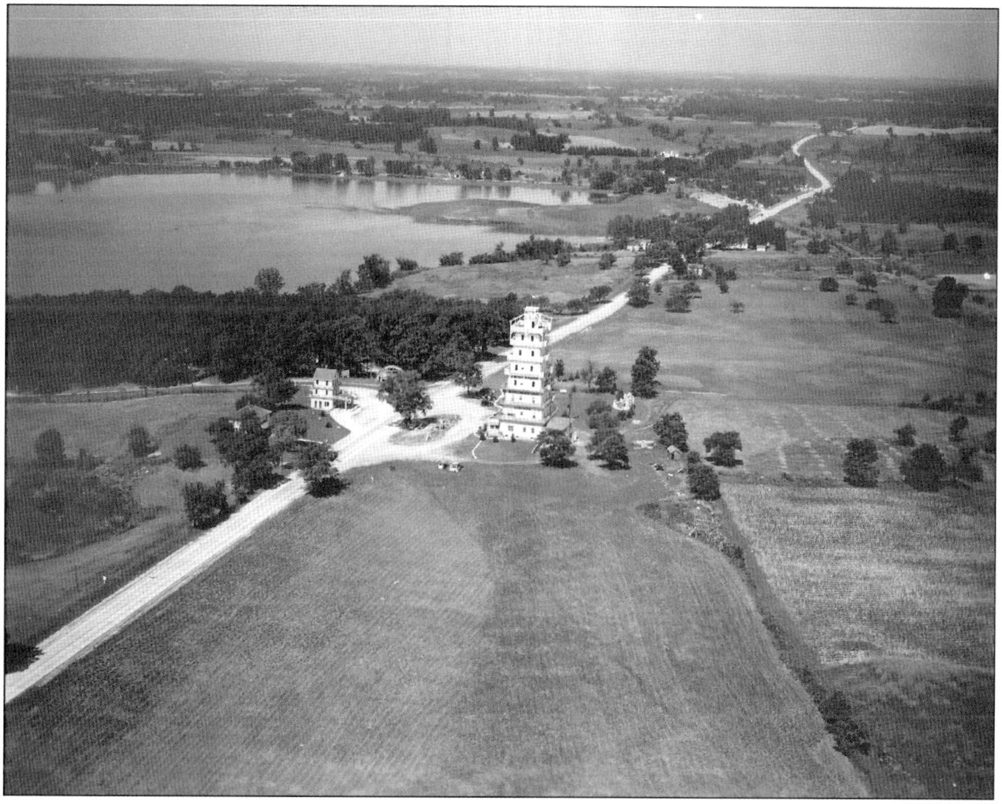

White Swan Electric Tower. This aerial view shows the White Swan Electric Tower on Highway 223 in Woodstock Township. An ice cream fountain, restaurant, and gift store were available to visitors. Taking the electric elevator to the top to enjoy the breathtaking view was a luxury. Standing opposite Clearwater Beach on Devils Lake, the tower became part of the Devils Lake Golf Course.

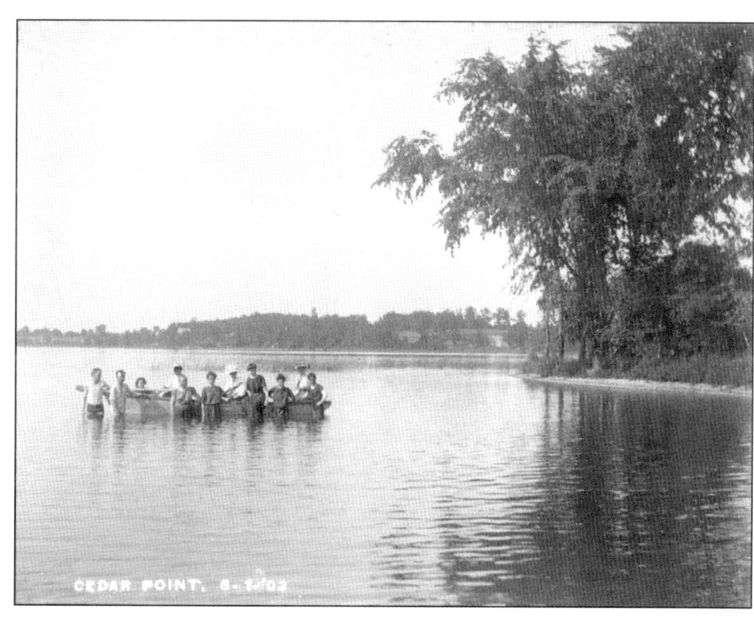

Boating and Swimming at Devil's Lake. Seen in this August 1903 image, this group shares a moment to pose at a part of Devil's Lake known as Cedar Point, named after the clusters of cedar trees that stood there years ago. Canoeing, swimming, or just wading and splashing in the water brought fun for all ages.

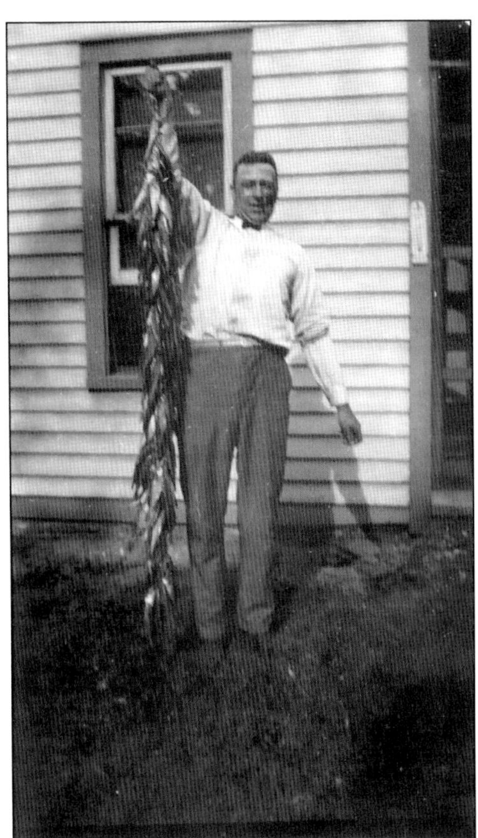

One Evening's Catch. This gentleman proudly displays his reward after a day of fishing.

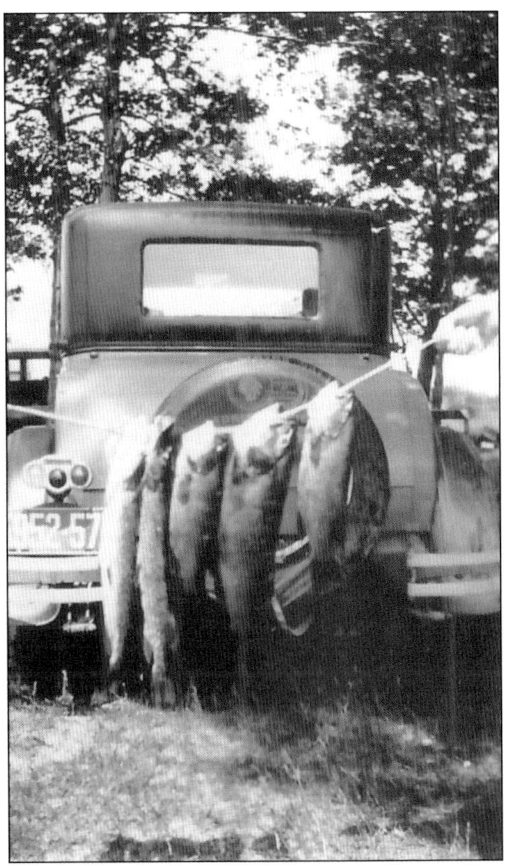

Hanging Fish, 1930s. Here is a display of the success so many had while fishing on the lakes of Lenawee.

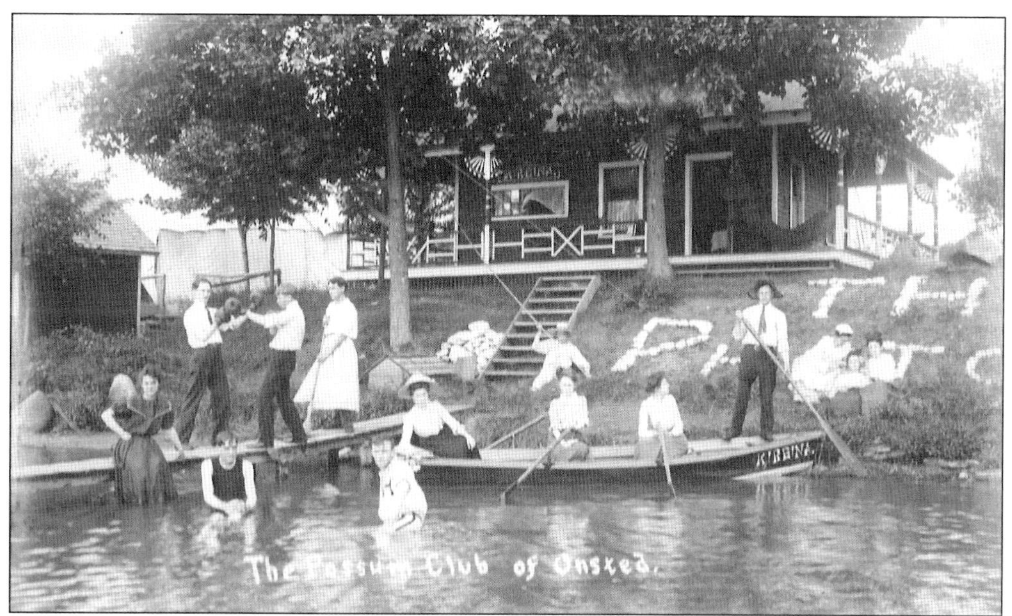

Onsted Possum Club at Clark Lake. One of many social organizations throughout the county, the Onsted Possum Club is shown enjoying a day at Clark Lake.

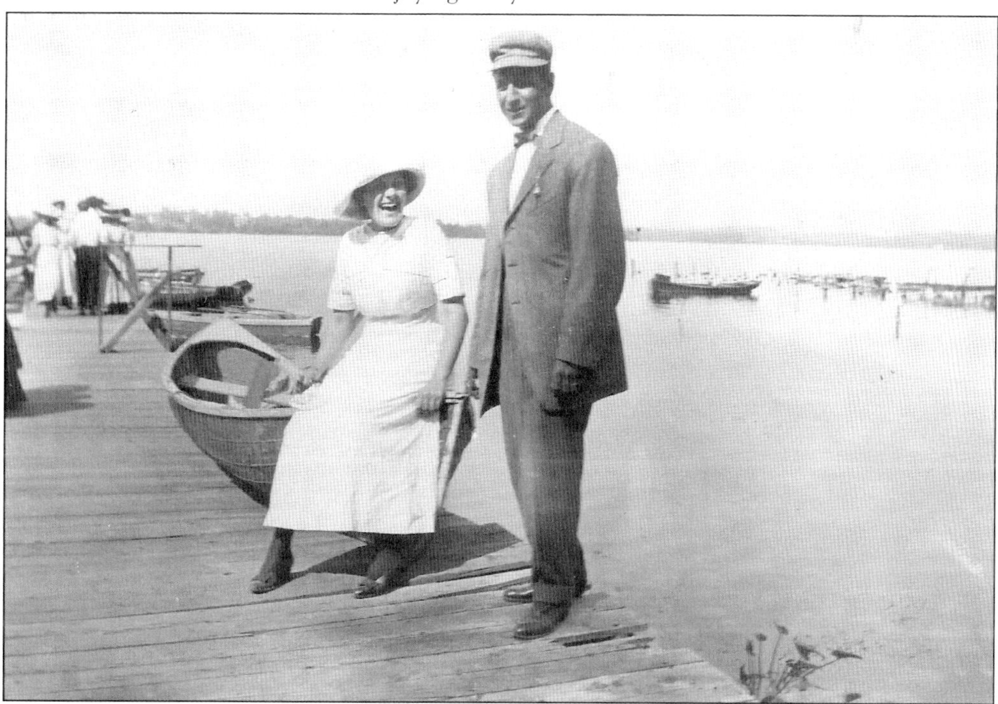

Devil's Lake Farmers' Picnic. The tradition of an annual farmers' picnic began around 1869 and continued into the early 1900s. The railroad transported guests from all around Lenawee and Hillsdale Counties for many years. The horse and buggy brought those fortunate enough to have one. It was a full day of fun-filled events, with bands, lots of good food, boating, swimming, and one time, even airplane rides. The picnic continued for over 60 years. After a lapse, it was revived in 1952.

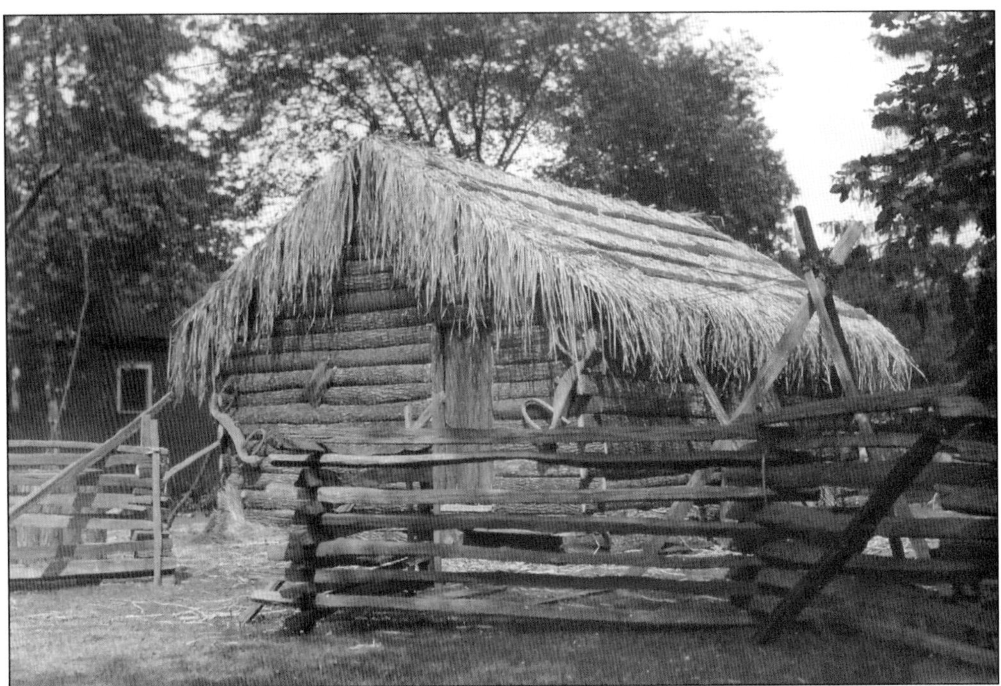

Exchange Club Tribute to Pioneers. In 1898, the Exchange Club created a tribute to the pioneers at the annual Lenawee County Fair. This log cabin measured 20 by 30 feet and was composed of logs donated by each city and town in the county. The club's goal was to build it with the same tools and techniques used by the first settlers. The cabin was located on the Lenawee County Fairgrounds, with primitive household articles on display to the public.

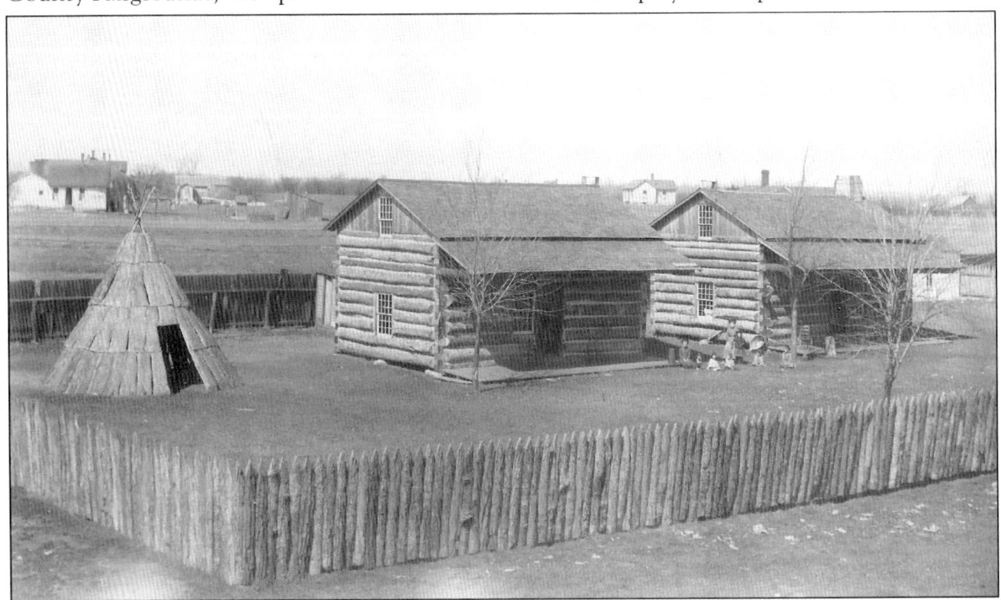

Fairground Tribute to Pioneers. As a tribute to the pioneers and the Native Americans who guided them, two cabins and a tepee were erected on the Lenawee County Fairgrounds. Logs from each township were paraded to the fairgrounds, led by Col. B.F. Graves on August 29, 1898. Many pioneers were still alive at the time and participated.

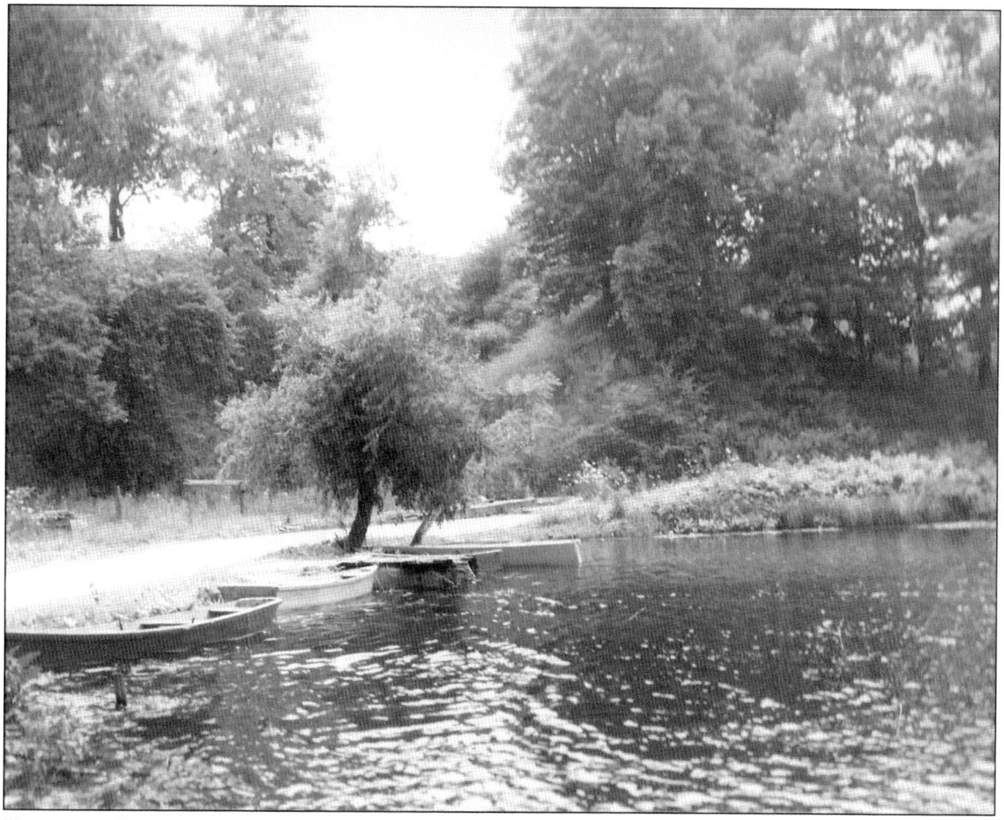

Tranquil Days before Prosperity. This view of the mill pond around 1937 led someone to write, "The Tranquil Days Before Prosperity" on the photograph. Tranquility still exists, perhaps not as much compared to the untouched ground that the pioneers walked upon; however, for many, compared to the highly developed and commercialized areas, tranquility is still in the air here.

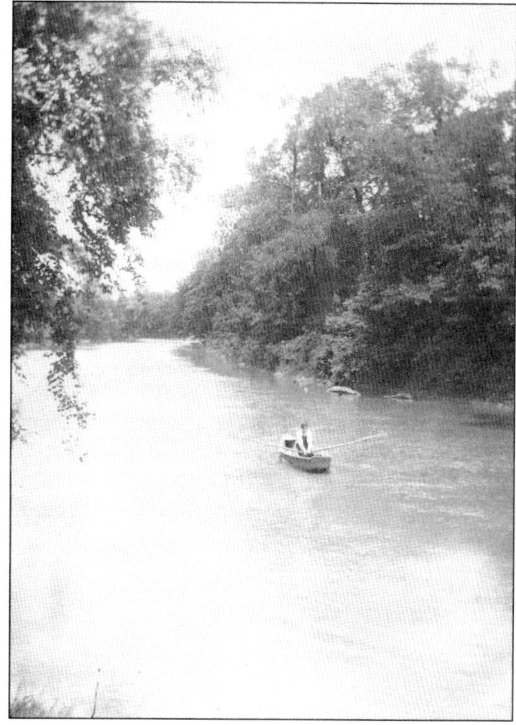

View of the River Raisin from Near Blissfield. No matter where one is in Lenawee, they can just say, "Let's go for a drive," or "Let's go for a walk," and be on the way to remote areas in minutes. Gazing at the open sky, the woods, or admiring the farmland can bring the same degree of separation from a busy life that the pioneers sought by leaving civilization in the eastern states and moving into untouched territory. Today, the boarded-up schoolhouses and dilapidated barns and farmhouses offer an opportunity to wonder or reminisce about just what it really was like back then.